CONTINUITY AND CHANGE IN COMMUNICATION SYSTEMS

An Asian Perspective

COMMUNICATION AND INFORMATION SCIENCE

A series of monographs, treatises, and texts
Edited by
MELVIN J. VOIGT
University of California, San Diego

William C. Adams • Television Coverage of the Middle East
William C. Adams • Television Coverage of International Affairs
William C. Adams • Television Coverage of the 1980 Presidential Campaign
Alan Baughcum and Gerald Faulhaber • Telecommunications Access and Public Policy
Mary B. Cassata and Thomas Skill • Life on Daytime Television
Hewitt D. Crane • The New Social Marketplace
Rhonda J. Crane • The Politics of International Standards
Herbert S. Dordick, Helen G. Bradley, and Burt Nanus • The Emerging Network Marketplace
Glen Fisher • American Communication in a Global Society
Oscar H. Gandy, Jr. • Beyond Agenda Setting
Oscar H. Gandy, Jr., Paul Espinosa, and Janusz A. Ordover • Proceedings from the Tenth
  Annual Telecommunications Policy Research Conference
Edmund Glenn • Man and Mankind: Conflict and Communication Between Cultures
Gerald Goldhaber, Harry S. Dennis III, Gary M. Richetto, and Osmo A. Wiio • Information
  Strategies
Bradley S. Greenberg • Life on Television: Content Analyses of U.S. TV Drama
Bradley S. Greenberg, Michael Burgoon, Judee K. Burgoon, and Felipe Korzenny • Mexican
  Americans and the Mass Media
Cees J. Hamelink • Finance and Information: A Study of Converging Interests
Heather Hudson • When Telephones Reach the Village
Robert M. Landau, James H. Bair, and Jean Siegman • Emerging Office Systems
James Larson • Television's Window on the World
John Lawrence • The Electronic Scholar
John S. Lawrence and Bernard M. Timberg • Fair Use and Free Inquiry
Robert G. Meadow • Politics as Communication
William H. Melody, Liora R. Salter, and Paul Heyer • Culture, Communication, and Dependency:
Vincent Mosco • Broadcasting in the United States
Vincent Mosco • Policy Research in Telecommunications: Proceedings from the Eleventh Annual
  Telecommunications Policy Research Conference
Vincent Mosco • Pushbutton Fantasies
Kaarle Nordenstreng • The Mass Media Declaration of UNESCO
Kaarle Nordenstreng and Herbert I. Schiller • National Sovereignty and International
  Communication
Harry J. Otway and Malcolm Peltu • New Office Technology
Ithiel de Sola Pool • Forecasting the Telephone
Dan Schiller • Telematics and Government
Herbert I. Schiller • Information and the Crisis Economy
Herbert I. Schiller • Who Knows: Information in the Age of the Fortune 500
Jorge A. Schnitman • Film Industries in Latin America
Indu B. Singh • Telecommunications in the Year 2000
Jennifer Daryl Slack • Communication Technologies and Society
Dallas W. Smythe • Dependency Road
Sari Thomas • Studies in Mass Media and Technology, Volumes 1–3
Barry Truax • Acoustic Communication
Georgette Wang and Wimal Dissanayake • Continuity and Change in Communication Systems
Janet Wasko • Movies and Money

In Preparation:

William Dutton and Kenneth Kraemer • Modeling as Negotiating
Fred Fejes • Imperialism, Media, and the Good Neighbor
Howard H. Fredericks • Cuban-American Radio Wars
Kenneth Mackenzie • Organizational Design
Armand Mattelart and Hector Schmucler • Communication and Information Technologies
Everett Rogers and Francis Balle • The Media Revolution in America and in Western Europe
Keith R. Stamm • Newspaper Use and Community Ties
Robert S. Taylor • Value-Added Processes in Information Systems
Tran Van Dinh • Independence, Liberation, Revolution

CONTINUITY AND CHANGE IN COMMUNICATION SYSTEMS:
An Asian Perspective

EDITORS

GEORGETTE WANG
National Chengchi University
Taipei, Taiwan

WIMAL DISSANAYAKE
East-West Communication Institute
Honolulu, Hawaii

Preface by
Emile G. McAnany

Ablex Publishing Corporation
Norwood, New Jersey 07648

Library of Congress Cataloging in Publication Data
Main entry under title:

Continuity and change in communication systems.

Includes bibliographies and index.
1. Communication—Cross-cultural studies. 2. Social
change—Cross-cultural studies. 3. Asia—Popular culture—
Case studies. 4. Communication—Social aspects—Asia—
Case studies. I. Wang, Georgette. II. Dissanayake,
Wimal. III. East-West Communication Institute.
HM258.C64 1984 302.2 84–2969
ISBN 0–89391–150–X

Ablex Publishing Corporation
355 Chestnut Street
Norwood, New Jersey 07648

CONTENTS

Contributors and Editors

TEVIA ABRAMS (Ph.D.) is at the United Nations Fund for Population Activities, New York.

BINOD AGRAWAL (Ph.D.) is at the Space Application Centre, India.

ISAO ARAKI teaches in the Department of Sociology, Bukkyo University at Kyoto, Japan.

CHIEN CHIAO teaches at the Chinese University, Hong Kong.

DEBRA VAN HOOSEN is at the East-West Center, Honolulu, Hawaii.

DEBRA HUGHES is a graduate student in the Department of Public Health, University of Hawaii, Honolulu, Hawaii.

MEHEROO JUSSAWALLA (Ph.D.) is a Research Associate at the East-West Communication Institute, Honolulu, Hawaii.

ROSS KIDD is at the International Council for Adult Education, Toronto, Canada.

KYUNG JA LEE (Ph.D.) teaches in the Department of Mass Communication, Kyung Hee University, Seoul, Korea.

REGINA ORDONEZ is at the Asian Institute of Management, Manila, Philippines.

KENNETH K. F. PANG teaches in the Journalism Department, Chu Hai College, Hong Kong.

MAJID TEHRANIAN (Ph.D.) teaches in the Deaprtment of Communication, University of Hawaii, Honolulu, Hawaii.

VICTOR VALBUENA (Ph.D.) is at the Population Center Foundation, Manilla, Philippines.

MICHAEL T. K. WEI (Ph.D.) teaches in the Department of Journalism and Mass Communication, Chinese University, Hong Kong.

GEORGETTE WANG is Professor at the Graduate School of Journalism, National Chengchi University in Taiwan. She received her Ph.D. in 1977 and has worked at the East-West Communication Institute as a Research Associate. She has taught at colleges in Hong Kong and worked on one of the largest daily newspapers in Taiwan. Her research interest and publications have centered on audience behavior, intercultural communication, and the role of culture in development communication.

WIMAL DISSANAYAKE is Assistant Director and Research Associate at the East-West Communication Institute. He received his Ph.D. degree from University of Cambridge in 1969 and was head of the Department of Mass Communication, Sri Lanka, before joining the East-West Center. He has been Visiting Fulbright Research Scholar at the University of Pennsylvania, an award-winning broadcaster, and a working newspaper journalist. His research interest includes communication theories and indigenous communication systems.

Acknowledgment

In 1979, a number of communication scholars from Asia met at the East-West Center in Honolulu. They came from different cultural backgrounds, with different types of training and interests, but there was a strongly felt consensus on the need to deepen an understanding of communication in non-Western societies. The idea for a book dealing with these cross-cultural perspectives was thus conceived.

In compiling this book, we have had valuable help and suggestions from many people, and would like to thank in particular our colleagues at the East-West Communication Institute for their stimulating comments and helpful advice.

The editors are indebted to all of the authors who spent much time and effort in preparing the case studies at their own expense, without any form of assistance or reward. We are also grateful to a great number of friends, too many to mention by name here, who broadened our views and helped us to refine our thinking.

TO OUR PARENTS

Preface

There are a number of important themes in this volume on the indigenous communication media. First, tradition and cultural value have reasserted their place in social change theory. Second, the coming information age with its new technologies will need to be integrated into distinct cultural settings and with indigenous communication systems if the cultural values are to be preserved and the benefits of the technology received by the society. Third, the indigenous media systems of different countries can be useful instruments for advancing local, developmental change to benefit local, especially rural, people.

The rich variety of detail from eleven country cases provides us with the breadth of coverage that is necessary to get a feel for Asian indigenous media. There are examples from industrially advanced countries like Japan, South Korea, Hong Kong, and Taiwan and examples from countries with large traditional rural populations where folk media would supposedly be stronger like India, the Philippines, Sri Lanka, and Papua New Guinea. But there is another dichotomy of cases that may be as important in the analysis of the indigenous media systems, the industrialized uses of indigenous themes in modern media and the uses of indigenous communication to promote sponsored social change. It is concerning this latter division of cases that we might take a moment to reflect on the nature of indigenous vs. modern systems and development.

The cases concerned with the industrialized uses of indigenous themes are those dealing with bag puppetry in Taiwan television by Georgette Wang, the Indian cinema by Binod Agrawal, and chivalric themes in Hong Kong media by Kenneth Pang. These cases all reflect non-instrumental uses of indigenous themes in communication as a form of entertainment for modern audiences; the cases of Philippine and Indian theater, the Korean village *Bang-Sang Hui* (community development organization), Peking opera and pilot study with traditional media in Papua New Guinea all view indigenous media as appropriate vehicles for carrying development (change) messages to traditional audiences.

Two observations help to underline some of the problems that indigenous media and indigenous themes in modern media face in the years ahead. First, the industrial–market-oriented nature of modern media systems, like television and film in many countries, may have a great deal to do with their entertainment content, even when indigenous themes are used. Second, the delicate balance between indigenous themes and local needs of audiences is difficult to maintain, even with the best of intentions.

As Wang and Dissanayake have pointed out in their reappraisal of indigenous communication and development, two factors made indigenous media more attractive during the 1970s. The first was the threat of cultural imperialism in the form of many imported cultural products like television programs and films; the second was the failure of the modern mass media to create desired change. As policy makers emphasize self-sufficiency in entertainment products for their people, they will be looking for indigenous themes and the cases of Hong Kong, Taiwan, and Indian film will be interesting guide-posts. But before we too quickly agree on the directions they suggest, we need to explore the assumption that indigenous material, in competition with foreign entertainment material, will be more popular. C. C. Lee in his recent book on the problem of media imperialism* refers to this commonsense assumption. The three cases in this book suggest this may be true, but the conditions vary and the solution for reducing foreign products may not be as simple as it seems. There are three conditions. First, the nature of the audience is important. As an audience becomes larger and more heterogenous, there may have to be more localization of the themes, as in the case of India where different regions have their own film production units. Otherwise, the themes may become so diluted and trivial that the traditional values may be washed out. Second, the nature of the values carried in indigenous forms like chivalric stories or bag puppetry may diverge so much from traditional values that the indigenous culture is violated and audience protests are provoked in much the same way as some offensive imported programs. Third, market-oriented media like commercial television or film may have certain internal imperatives that contradict the values of indigenous content. The Hong Kong and Taiwan cases suggest the problems of appealing to the largest possible audience because of competitive pressures. Although it may be true that indigenous themes will appeal more to the audiences (even educated audiences in all three cases), it is also true that the distortion of cultural values in these forms may defeat the very purpose of a more self-reliant media policy. The dilemma for cultural policy makers is how to protect indigenous, traditional, values and still provide widespread entertainment for masses of people.

The question of balance in pro-development messages carried in

*C. C. Lee. *Media Imperialism Reconsidered: The Homogenization of Television Culture.* Beverly Hills: Sage, 1980.

indigenous forms is recognized by the editors. In chapter two, they point out that "very often little consideration is given to the nature of the indigenous communication channels and their flexibility in incorporating development messages." The danger is similar to that noted for commercial mass media, but in this case, the media are indigenous ones employed by the government to promote change. The problems presented in the cases of the Philippines, Indian theater, Korea, Sri Lanka, Papua New Guinea, and China are varied, but two common links may be found in the notions of planned social change and local needs and the role of culture in continuity in change. Both notions, of course, demand and receive extensive discussion in this book. Kidd points out in the Indian theater case that the underlying assumptions about the nature of planned change usually represent the views of central authorities and not the local needs of audiences. The difficulties in the imposition of values from outside local communities may not have anything to do with whether or not indigenous media are used. Unless there is genuine two-way communication and a respect for local needs and values, indigenous media in the 1980s will fail just as surely as did the mass media in the 1960s and 1970s. On the other hand, there is a strong recognition among the authors in this book that culture is a substrate to the most profound social change and that old values reassert themselves in changing situations. Both Tehranian and Chiao and Wei point this out for revolutionary Iran and China.

The wisdom of this book is that it stresses continuity in change and suggests to readers that they think about the dilemma to be faced by nations that wish to promote both. The final chapter by Jussawalla and Hughes on the information economy and indigenous communication suggests that, at bottom, we need a return to an analysis of the basic values that operate in even the most advanced, technological, and seemingly culture-free systems. They quote Daniel Bell on the nature of the new information society; he says that in such a society the "information is a pattern or design that rearranges data for instrumental purposes, while knowledge is the set of reasoned judgments that evaluates the adequacy of the patterns for purposes for which the information is designed." The instrumentality of information and of communication itself, may be a deeply ingrained cultural value peculiar to the societies that have created the information economy and may not be integrated easily into other cultural systems that often see communication not as instrument but as integrating action. The challenge of the next decade is to examine the indigenous and the modern systems to see how each may contribute to the integration that is called for in a nation's development without sacrificing either basic cultural values or the advancement of human needs. This volume is the starting point for serious work in this area.

Emile G. McAnany
University of Texas at Austin

Introduction

Continuity and change are no longer novel to students in the social sciences. Although expressed in different terms by different authors (Weaver, 1964; Foster, 1962; Galtung, 1980), they are generally viewed as principles upon which our universe functions and operates. The way continuity and change take place in the evolutionary process is like the Ying and Yang forces in Taoist philosophy; when one prevails, the other recedes, and vice versa. But one never totally dominates the other. In other words, everything in our world can be regarded as being in a state of change, whether it be a piece of rock, human relations, or mountains and oceans; however, the degree of change varies a great deal. At times, changes are so minute that they are hardly observable until centuries later. There are also times when changes are so drastic and overwhelming that nothing seems to have persisted. However, in both instances, some degree of continuity is maintained through changes. The two, therefore, need not be viewed as competing forces, but rather as forces which complement and regulate each other.

Weaver (1964, p. 23) has an excellent example illustrating what he perceives to be the laws of "status" (permanence) and "function" (change) of the world: "It is an ancient observation that 'no man can step in the same water twice,' yet we continue to conceive it as a river and to call it by one name."

In this example, "change" is the water that is constantly flowing and never staying exactly the same from one moment to the next. But at the same time, we also discern "continuity" because people still conceive of it as a river and use the same name to refer to it.

The same principle can be applied to almost everything around us. An individual, for example, changes from an infant to an old man in a matter of sixty years, but we regard him as the same person, not a different one. The coastline of an island may have been eroded by tidal waves at a rate of two inches every ten years, but no one can discount the difference it makes to coastal habitat and landowners. Interplay of the two forces exists in natural objects; it also exists in complex human societies.

According to systems theorists, cultures and societies are open systems. By definition, an open system is never in a state of chemical or thermodynamic equilibrium, but rather in a "steady" or "quasi-steady" state. Interacting components and the continuous flow of energy and information to and from the environment bring entropy and change. However, cultures do not passively absorb change; on the contrary, they may actively and creatively respond to stimuli and seek to incorporate and assimilate change (Bertalanffy, 1975). The implication of such an approach is that the past has been productively used as a basis for reacting to the present (stimuli). If the answer to the previous question is that, if indeed changes can occur without continuity, then the past must be cut off from the present, which then naturally leads to disorientation and confusion. According to Weaver (1964, p. 41), "men's very reality depends upon his carrying the past into the present through the power of memory." And if the memory is lost, men "will travel light. But it will be a deprived kind of traveling, cut down to immediate responses to immediate challenges."

The notions of continuity and change may have been accepted by some social scientists in explaining human evolution, but they failed to receive due recognition from communication scholars, especially in their study of non-Western societies. Rapid growth and expansion of communication technologies in recent years have led to the glorification of change and have discounted and underplayed the continuity of the past into the present. The focal point of research is how modern media change or replace old ways of thinking, behaving, or communicating. However, some elements of the old system remain and continue to play a vital role in communication in many regions of the world today. The implications of this continuity to development is not fully explored. On the other hand, creative responses of cultures to technological stimuli reveal a continuous interactive process in which changes take place while maintaining a certain degree of continuity.

Television, for example, is a technology. It has a social and cultural background in Western societies (Williams, 1974). Once introduced to a non-Western society, the technical features may remain the same. However, the needs of the audience, the attitudes toward television viewing, the program content, and, subsequently, its role and influence as a social institution would not be exactly the same as those in a Western society. For example, when television is first introduced into Third World nations, viewing is not what one is likely to find in an American family; on the contrary, it is more like going to a local folk play, with the television set taking the place of the live performers. Villagers gather together around the set in the evening to watch programs selected for them by village chiefs. They exchange greetings, comments, and gossip about the shows and they relate the programs to their own daily lives.

An "indigenous communication" pattern thus evolves around a modern mass medium. Eventually, television sets may find their way into individual homes. However, studies of television viewing behavior in Japan, a developed non-Western nation, show a certain degree of continuity can be predicted. In other words, television as a piece of technology is hardly making its international audience a homogenous group. Underestimation of the cultural influence, and its interaction with the technology and the principle of continuity and change, often leads to false assumptions and incomplete understanding of the situation. The negative impact of these misunderstandings on development planning is apparent, and costly at times.

It is indeed against this background of thinking that we feel an urgent need for in-depth analyses of Asian communication systems. The purpose of this book is to examine continuity and change in communication systems from different angles and in different societies. The book is organized around two major components:

Part I: Theoretical framework

Part II: Country studies which illustrate the theme of the book.

The two chapters in the first part lay out the theoretical framework for the country studies. The chapter, "Culture, Development, and Change: Some Explorative Observations," critically reviews the literature on both the old and the new paradigm of development and examines the role of culture in the process of development and change. The second chapter, "Indigenous Communication Systems and Development: A Reappraisal," focuses on the continuity and change of communication systems. An effort is made to analyze communication systems and behavioral patterns in the context of culture.

The second part, consisting of two categories of country studies, demonstrates points made earlier. The first category includes studies which specifically examine the use of indigenous communication media, channels, or beliefs in planned changes. In other words, these studies show the experience of different societies in utilizing communication media and channels, which are clearly continuous with the past, to achieve change. The issues examined are:

- The incorporation of Buddhist beliefs in development campaign messages in Sri Lanka
- The use of theatre arts for development in the Philippines
- The potential of traditional communication in promoting development in Papua New Guinea
- Revolutionary drama in China
- Performing arts for development in India
- Successes and failures of using folk drama for development in Asia

Each of the above studies describes a unique experience, and such experience often has profound implications on theoretical issues discussed in the "newer concepts of development."

The second category of studies examines the cultural features of communication systems in various changing societies. The cases discussed are:

- Communication dualism in Iran before revolution
- The integration of bag puppetry and television in Taiwan
- The cultural features of Indian movies
- Introduction of interactive telecommunications into a Japanese community.
- Popularity of chivalric stories, a form of popular literature in Hong Kong media
- Continuity of the Korean village meeting
- Paternalism and organizational communication in ASEAN-based corporations
- Indigenous communication in an information society

The above studies do not necessarily have direct bearing on development in the narrow sense of the term. They do, however, illustrate continuity and change as two interacting forces in the evolution of a given society's communication system.

It is our belief that continuity and change are the underlying principles for the development of communication systems at any given level in any given society. For this reason, we have taken a cross-cultural approach and sought to cover a number of areas in communication research: mass communication, interpersonal communication, and organizational communication. But it is impossible to cover the whole spectrum of issues. This book, therefore, is designed to stimulate the interest of communication scholars and concerned citizens and to alert them to the imperative need of addressing the points raised in the subsequent pages.

Georgette Wang

References

Bertalanffy, Ludwig von. (1975) "Cultures as Systems: Spengler and Beyond." In Edgar Taschdjian (Ed.), *Perspectives on General System Theory*. New York: George Braziller.

Foster, George. (1962) *Traditional Cultures: And the Impact of Technological Change*. New York: Harper & Row.

Galtung, Johan. (1980) *The True Worlds*. New York: Free Press.

Weaver, Richard M. (1964) *Visions of Order*. Baton Rouge: Louisiana State University Press.

Williams, Raymond. (1974) *Television—Technology and Cultural Form*. Fontana: William Collins Sons and Company.

PART I

THEORETICAL FRAMEWORK

1

Culture, Development, and Change: Some Explorative Observations

Georgette Wang and Wimal Dissanayake

The study of "modernization" and "development" has been a crossdisciplinary subject, as well as an international concern since the Second World War. The reasons these two concepts attract so much academic attention are easy to identify; they involve changes in almost every society in the world and the scope of the changes touches on everything.

Seldom has the study of change taken a bird's eye view. Frequently, one or two of the major aspects of change have been singled out to formulate theories, and these theories have then been used to explain, predict, or prescribe overall changes. Of course, many prior theories have been important. However, their weaknesses became apparent as reality deviated from, or even ran counter to, what the theories stated.

The purpose of this paper is not to formulate another "universally applicable" theory, but to point out the importance of one major factor which has not been given due attention in the study of development and change: the role of culture. Because misconceptions regarding culture and development account for part of the failure of the "old paradigm of development," culture, as one variable in the process of change, certainly deserves attention in the search for a "new paradigm." We propose to look at development as a dynamic process in which culture actively accepts, rejects, and directs change, while at the same time retaining a certain degree of continuity. But before there can be meaningful discussions on this subject, definitions of key concepts are both helpful and necessary.

Intrinsically, culture is difficult to define. In 1952, two anthropologists undertook this seemingly simple task. Kroeber and Kluckhohn (1952) found 154 different definitions, and countless incomplete definitions of, or statements about, culture. Since then, more definitions have been generated in various social science fields. The number reflects the elusive nature of culture as a concept in scientific research. Feibleman has described the problem (1968, p. 170):

> They [cultures] do not always have abrupt beginnings and endings; when flourishing, they have indistinct peripheries; and they shade off into one another in a quite indefinite way. We do not always recognize a culture when we see one.

Culture can be defined as social heritage, customs, or traditions. It can also refer to the way of behaving and thinking with or without the function of providing problem-solving mechanisms. It can even include "all non-genetically produced means of adjustment" or "the sum total of all that is artificial" (Kroeber and Kluckhohn, 1952, pp. 139, 125). Each definition of culture has strengths and weaknesses because the concept is so complex. For the purpose of this discussion, we would like to point out three important features of culture. First, culture has a memory manifested in traditions, customs, and beliefs. This memory of the past often serves to direct reaction and responses to present stimuli. The result is a degree of cultural continuity in most aspects of life. Second, culture is an open system. Constant interaction of elements within the system and interaction with the outside environment brings stimuli to change, and the extent of change varies. Third, through values, norms, and sanctioned behavioral patterns, a culture manages to keep its integrity by exercising a certain degree of authority over its members. At the same time, it acts to accept, integrate, or reject stimuli for change. Therefore, culture changes, but the presence of one or two manipulated stimuli does not always bring the desired change.

Given the above, a working definition of culture might include manifestations of man's attempt to relate meaningfully to his environment. Hence it encompasses artifacts as well as values, beliefs, and behavioral patterns which all tend to change with a certain degree of continuity. Culture is, therefore, much more than a static entity of spirit and practice accumulated in the past.

"Development" is no less ambiguous a concept. The term has often been confused with "Westernization," "industrialization," and "modernization." Each of these concepts should be distinguished from the other.

"Westernization" refers to the process of becoming like Western nations, but does not specify either which Western nation is considered the model or at what point in time. "Industrialization" emphasizes the growth and expansion of industry and the related social changes. "Modernization" essentially carries a meaning which includes both of the above terms. It refers to a process of social change brought by a change in the economic structure. The eventual product is expected to be something close to what Western nations are.

Over the years, the definition of "development" has undergone some changes. In its earlier stage of conceptualization, it resembled "modernization." For example, Rogers and Shoemaker (1971, p. 4) thought of development as

> a type of social change in which new ideas are introduced into a social system in order to produce higher per capita income and levels of living through more modern production methods and improved social organization. Development is modernization at the social level.

In recent years, scholars and policy makers in many Third World nations began to challenge such an orientation and its meaning has taken a more humanistic flavor. In this paper, the concept of "development" is defined as, "a process of social change which has as its goal the improvement in the quality of life of all or the majority of the people without doing violence to the natural and cultural environment in which they exist, and which seeks to involve the majority of the people as closely as possible in this enterprise, making them the masters of their own destiny."

Over three decades have now gone by since what is commonly considered the initial phase of development. A look at the current world situation indicates that, in spite of the great outlay of capital, more is needed.

From 1968 to 1977, economic assistance to the Third World nations from major international financial institutions[1] totaled over 10 billion dollars (Kurian, 1978). The expenditure of United Nations Development Program, one of the major international development agencies, reached 839.5 million dollars in 1980. United States economic aid to other nations from 1946 to 1979 totaled 134,181 million dollars (Statistic Abstract of the United States, 1980). Even more impressive is the constant and steady increase in aid to developing nations. Within a span of nine years, for example, assistance from international banks increased fivefold. Due to structural weaknesses in the Third World economy, continued dependence on international finance institutions is forecasted (World Bank Annual Report, 1981).

Although some success has resulted from the investment of money and manpower, two striking gaps remain: the gap between the rich and the poor in developing nations, and the gap between the developed and the developing nations in the world. For example, the gross per capita national income in North America was over $8,510 in 1978. However, it was $600 in Africa, $800 in East and Southeast Asia (except for Japan), $2060 in the Middle East, and $1390 is Latin America (United Nations, 1980). Approximately three-fourths of the population in developing nations receive a little over one-fifth of the total world income (Starr and Ritterbush, 1980). Per capita energy use in various regions also differs a great deal, and there will probably be little change in the future. It has

---

[1]Including World Bank, International Development Association, International American Development Bank, Asian Development Bank, and others.

been predicted that per capita energy use in Africa in the year 2,000 will increase from 0.3 metric tons of coal equivalent in 1965 to 0.9; Asia, from 0.4 to 1.5; and the figure for North America will double from 10 to 20. The United States, with 6% of the world's population, uses 33% of the available energy (Galtung, 1980). The illiteracy rate has decreased from 44.3% in 1950 to 34.2% in 1970 (Galtung, 1980), but, in absolute numbers, illiterate adults are now more numerous because of steady population growth.

The gap between rich and poor in developing societies is equally problematic. Because the sociocultural structure in developing nations is not usually considered where new technology is introduced, technology transfer has often served the privileged. The urban centers attract a surplus of labor to big cities and the result is a new class of city poor.

The international one-way flow of information and technology has raised concern because of a prospective loss of cultural identity in developing nations. Statistics give a grim picture. For example, 80% of the television programs presented in Latin America are produced in the United States, leading commentators to predict that viewers will abandon their traditional values and absorb the telecasted foreign stereotypes and prejudices (Dagnino, 1973). Researchers such as Nordenstreng (Nordenstreng and Varis, 1974), Varis (1974), and Schiller (1969, 1973, 1976) have shown how this phenomenon is related to global patterns of domination and dependence. This fear of cultural imperialism undoubtedly hampers the development effort.

These facts and figures demonstrate that development programs have failed to bridge the gap between rich and poor. Poverty still exists in large parts of the world and it is complicated by other problems. The dismal outlook for the future has fostered a serious reconsideration of development strategies and policy directions on both practical and theoretical levels.

A Review of the Old Concepts of Development

It is helpful to review briefly the claims of theorists working with the old paradigm and to examine the criticisms they received. Social development was studied extensively and from various angles by the many social scientists who in the fifties and sixties formulated the standard modes of analysis. The approaches and their principal proponents can be categorized into five main groups:

APPROACH	ATTRIBUTES	ARTICULATORS
1. Historical	Emphasis on broad historical evolution and movement towards modernization	Black (1966)

Writers have argued that colonial structures still persist, only in other forms, i.e., economic aid, transnational corporations, and international monetary institutions. According to Galtung, there has recently been a trend in which peripheral nations control more activities in the economic cycle to "ensure that more of the surplus generated accrues to the Periphery" (Galtung, 1980, p. 153).

The "newer concepts of development," contain three major shifts in emphasis relevant to our discussion. First, more attention is focused on local scenes. The "target audiences" for change are no longer viewed as passive beings who can be transformed with a touch of the magic wand. Attempts are made to motivate people to actively participate, or take the initiative, in development programs. Local level decisionmaking and bottom-up communication are encouraged. Second, endogenous factors and conditions are no longer considered as the sole reasons for underdevelopment and indigenous beliefs, systems, and practices are not seen as primitive and backward. On the contrary, they are recognized by scholars and decision makers as essential to the achievement of development goals. Third, economic growth is still important, but the goal for development is the improvement of every aspect of life instead of mere material comfort. In addition, an "end state" of development is suggested, but instead each nation is expected to define for itself the goal of "development."

Although rarely stated, all of the above changes point to the important role of culture in development. It is therefore appropriate to give further consideration to the role of culture in development.

The Role of Culture in Development

The concept of development has undergone some modifications in the past, however, the central notion of change remained intact. Development advocates encourage change and discourage the maintenance of status quo, believing that only when changes takes place will there be progress and improvements.

Change does not take place in a vacuum. It always occurs within a certain sociocultural system, and each sociocultural system has its unique features and past history. Stimuli for change are generally brought forth through the interaction of the elements of the system, or through interaction of these elements with those of the outside environment.

Stimuli for change may take various forms. In the process of development, they often appear as technological innovations or new behavioral patterns. But stimuli for change are not changes themselves. They are often rejected and change never occurs. Sometimes stimuli are accepted, but the expected change fails to occur, or does so with unexpected side effects.

The cultural system, with its "center of authority" actively responds to stimulus for change. When the stimulus is found to be useful and compatible, elements in the system interact to form a favorable environment for its growth. However, if the stimulus is incompatible it will wither in a hostile or apathetic environment and be rejected.

Computer chips today and Galileo's discoveries in astronomy in the sixteenth and seventeenth century are illustrative examples. In today's computer age the discovery of chips was welcomed by industrialized societies. The chips enhanced the capacity, effectiveness, and efficiency of the highly valued computer system. The compatibility and utility of chips to the system were quickly recognized and thus immediately adopted. In a poverty-stricken, developing area, the same chips would have stood little chance of acceptance, since the desire for an efficient and effective computer system would have been subordinated to basic survival needs, if a computer system even existed in the society. Thus, computer chips would be incompatible with this environment.

Galileo made one of the first important discoveries in astronomy in the sixteenth and seventeenth century. His theory was received with a hostility which eventually affected him personally. Heliocentrism conflicted with claims made by the church and Italian culture at the time of Galileo was dominated by religion. This stimulus was considered too radical for immediate acceptance.

History is full of similar examples. Rejection of stimulus for change is a common feature of the process of change. However, one distinction between change and development is that development usually has predetermined goals. In order to achieve these goals, changes in the system are necessary so that rejection and ignorance of stimulus are not permissible at times. Three different approaches have been taken in the past to deal with the situation: the imposition of the stimulus on the system; alteration of elements which are not compatible with the stimulus; or modification of the stimulus so that it is better able to adapt to the system.

The Imposition of the Stimulus on the System

It is easy to find a cultural gap between the ruling elite and the masses in many developing nations. Policy decisions are made which enforce change. Little room is left for those who do not comply or conform. Such measures frequently violate the prevailing cultural norms and values not to mention customs and behavioral patterns.

In China, for example, the Confucian thinking which dominated the Chinese culture for thousands of years, was denounced during the Cultural Revolution, and a new culture was to be created using the Marxist-Maoist philosophy. Massive campaigns were staged and strict measures were taken to force acceptance of the new philosophy.

The Iranian Revolution is another example. The modernization policies of the Shah often conflicted with traditional cultural norms. As Mowlana (1979) observed:

The Iranian revolution of 1978–79 grew naturally from native soil. The impetus for revolution has been traced to many factors such as the political and economic conditions, foreign interests and the challenge to traditional social structures. Cumulatively, these factors contributed to what could be best described as a conflict between the official culture of the government and the ruling elite which represented and promoted Western influence and the traditional cultures of the masses rooted in Iranian national and religious traditions.

With the rapid exploitation of oil resources and the increasing accumulation of petro-dollars, Iranian society took the path to virtual disaster. The elite used new wealth to import not only modern technology, but also Western ways of life. However, the majority of the people still depended on agriculture and lived according to the time-honored traditions. In their eyes, the introduction of new technology was a direct threat to the culture they cherished. The potential dislocations which resulted from the introduction of technological innovations into the culture were ignored. The result was a great social outburst of mass anger which culminated in revolution.

Imposition of a stimulus for change also marked the failure of many earlier development programs in other Third World nations. Villagers and peasants were often instructed to change their behavior. The sociocultural background of the target audience was not considered.

Alteration of Elements in the System which are Incompatible with the Stimulus

Cultural values, norms, and behavioral patterns often date back a long time. They may still be cherished today, even though some are no longer beneficial to those who observe or practice them. In order to implement the desired change, elements may require alteration before any improvement can be made.

In ancient China, for example, a large family was considered necessary to prosperity. Due to a higher infant mortality rate, a need for the labor of family members, and the importance of carrying on the family name, and the desire for male offspring persisted through centuries. Industrialization and the population explosion of today call for family planning which conflicts with this traditional mentality. In order for family planning to be accepted, "prosperity" and "happiness" were redefined by social policy makers. In Singapore, the social welfare system was designed to promote two-child families and additional children became a burden both financially and socially to the parents. Use of contraceptive methods thus became more acceptable.

The success of family planning in Singapore is significant as an example here because it demonstrates that "changing elements in a system" are very seldom one-dimensional. In the past, development programs singled out one or two sociocultural elements which were considered impediments to change. Such elements may be obstacles to progress, but they are only parts of a system. If other interrelated areas and interacting variables remain the same, it could be futile to try to change just one or two elements in the system. More precisely, an environment favorable in its entirety should be created for a stimulus to grow.

Modification of the Stimulus so that It Can Better Adapt to the System

The idea of appropriate technology is based on this conviction. As mentioned earlier, a stimulus for change may come from interactions among elements within the system, or with the outside environment. Although stimuli coming from within the system may also prove to be unacceptable, the conflict is usually greater from the outside. Given underlying values and functions alien to the indigenous culture, it is often difficult to transplant a stimulus without modification. In order for a stimulus to take root and grow, local needs and the sociocultural background must be carefully considered.

Advocates of "appropriate technology" had found numerous cases where modification of the stimulus was necessary. A common example is the tractor. In many developing areas, land is precious to the peasants. Fertile or barren, it is viewed as the symbol of mother nature, and giving up land is one of the greatest sins in life. Small plots aren't suitable to the cost-effective use of modern, high-power, expensive tractors. Since peasants are unlikely to support a land reform program, an alternative way of increasing their yield is to develop smaller less expensive farming machinery to satisfy local needs.

In recent years, development planners have discovered the benefit of adapting a stimulus to the system by incorporating in the stimulus existing elements in the system. Rogers (1978), for example, called for the integration of indigenous communication channels with mass media. Similar trends are found in other aspects of development programs. This tendency is consistent with what happens after a stimulus is introduced into a sociocultural system.

When a stimulus is accepted by a cultural system, it is very seldom accepted passively. The system actively responds. While the new element interacts and affects other elements, they in turn affect, modify, and redefine it. Neither the stimuli nor the cultural system remains exactly the same. As Leed (1978) indicated, it is easier to find examples of a society integrating a new medium of communication into its culture than it is to find a new medium transforming a society. Leed cites examples from the Abut where writing is used to carry out religious rituals. The tribes people on Mindanao use writing to support the conventions of courtship (Leed, 1978). In these examples, changes were brought to the rituals and to the conventions of courtship because of the new element in them. But at the same time, the function of these new elements was also modified in the accepting cultures. The same principle holds true in countless other instances. Malaysia, for example, adopted the British judicial system, which brought changes to the way conflicts were settled among people. In fact, the conflicts were often still handled in the conventional way, and the court only formalized the results.

The introduction of one common set of stimuli never results in two identical cultural systems. Cultures and societies are all different to begin with, and they will remain different despite similarities in technological expansion, life style, and other features.

For comparison purposes, the older approach to development can be represented as follows:

Culture   Technology

In essence, culture is seen as sided with tradition which is diametrically opposed to modernity. With the proper role of culture taken into consideration, tradition and modernity are seen as two aspects of one entity—culture.

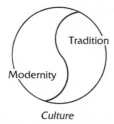

Culture

Through interaction of elements within culture, changes are brought forth while maintaining a certain degree of continuity.

Cultural considerations have been incorporated into strategies for social development. Consider the example of Gandhi in India. He sought to propagate new ideals, values, and thought patterns consonant with modern times, but in terms of traditional cultural symbolic systems. He endeavored to propagate such concepts among the Indian masses as egalitarianism, non-violence, and the emancipation of women, all in the cultural idiom of the people. His success can be attributed to this strategy. Indeed, the measure of his success in blending tradition and modernity is the difficulty in separating the traditional from the modern. One commentator even asked if Gandhi were a tranditionalist or modernizer. The question illustrates the immense difficulty in separating the various streams in reform and social change flowing through the Indian subcontinent. Certainly, his genius lay in uniting disparities, and in utilizing the traditional authority of the holy man for social reforms and for political union (Gusfield, 1967).

The Sarvodaya Movement of Sri Lanka is another example. Begun in 1958, it has development activities in over 2,500 villages. Over 250,000 people participate in work camps annually. In stressing the need for personal and community awakening, the architects of this movement have drawn upon Buddhist terminology as a vital element of traditional Sri Lankan culture. According to this Buddhist tradition, personal awakening rests on the cultivation of four main qualities: *Metta*, friendliness to all and respect for life; *Karuna*, compassionate action which results in the alleviation of suffering; *Muditha*, joy emanating from altruism; and *Upekkha*, or equanimity. These traditional values, familiar to everyone, are interpreted in terms of modern social developmental goals in the way that Gandhi interpreted some of the traditional Hindu concepts in India.

Conclusion

What we wish to do in this chapter, and in the entire book, is to register a plea. We urge an enlightened approach to social development in which culture might play a more crucial role. The old bifurcations of culture and technology, tradition and modernity, and traditionalism and technology should give way to a meaningful synthesis of these elements.

What we are really talking about is cultural authenticity as a necessary precondition to the development process. Cultural authenticity is the manifestation of the uniqueness of each society. No program or plan of social development can afford to ignore it. If it does, it does so at its own peril. Cultural authenticity is the real touchstone of the validity of both tradition and modernity.

Clifford Geertz (1973, p. 241), who has written so perceptively on the role of culture and communal life, employs two very useful terms: "epochalism" and "essentialism." By "epochalism" he refers to the cosmopolitan future-oriented spirit of the age. By "essentialism" he means the traditional aspects of life. According to Geertz, the crucial question facing development planners is to find the right balance between these two seemingly contradictory entities. The most productive agency through which this balance can be affected is, of course, culture.

REFERENCES

Alisjahbana, I. (1974). "Technology and Development." Paper presented at the International Broadcasting Institute General Meeting.

Bendix, Reinhard. (1967). "Tradition and Modernity Reconsidered." *Comparative Studies on Society and History 9*, pp. 292–348.

Black, Cyril E. (1966). *The Dynamics of Modernization: A Study in Comparative History.* New York: Harper and Row.

Bodenheimer, Suzanne T. (1970). "The Ideology of Developmentalism: American Political Science's Paradigm - Surrogate for Latin American Studies." *Berkeley Journal of Sociology 15*, pp. 95–137.

Bordenave, Juan Diaz. (1976). "Communication of Agricultural Innovations in Latin America." In Everett M. Rogers (Ed.), *Communication and Development*. Beverly Hills: Sage.

Cochrane, Clynn (1979). *The Cultural Appraisal of Development Projects*. New York: Praeger.

Dagnino, E. (1973). "Cultural and Ideological Dependence: Building a Theoretical Framework." In P. Bonilla and R. Girling (Eds.), *Struggle of Dependency*. Stanford: Stanford University Press.

Eisenstadt, Shmuel N. (1966). *Modernization: Protest and Change*. Englewood Cliffs: Prentice-Hall.

Eisenstadt, Shmuel N. (1973). *Tradition, Change, and Modernity*. New York: John Wiley & Sons.

Feibleman, James. (1968). *The Theory of Human Culture*. New York: Humanities Press.

Galtung, Johan. (1980). *The True Worlds*. New York: Free Press.

Geertz, Clifford. (1973). *The Interpretation of Cultures*, New York: Basic Books.

Goulet, Denis. (1971). *The Cruel Choice: A New Concept in the Theory of Development*. New York: Atheneum.

Gusfield, Joseph R. (1967). "Tradition and Modernity: Misplaced Polarities in the Study of Social Change." *American Journal of Sociology*. 72(4), pp. 351–362.

Hagen, Everett E. (1968). *The Economics of Development*. Homewood, IL: R. D. Irwin.

Hazard, Leland. (1969). "The Power of Technology." In Kurt Baier and Nicholas Rescher (Eds.), *Values and the Future*. New York: Free Press.

Kroeber, Alfred L., and Clyde Kluckhohn. (1952). *Culture*. New York: Vintage Books.

Kurian, George T. (1978). *Encyclopedia of the Third World*. New York: Facts on File.

Leed, Eric J. (1978). "Communications Revolutions and the Enactment of Culture." *Communication Research 5*, pp. 305–319.

Lerner, Daniel. (1958). *The Passing of Traditional Society: Modernizing the Middle East*. Glencoe: Free Press.

Lerner, Daniel. (1976). "Technology, Communication, and Change." *In* Wilbur Schramm and Daniel Lerner (Eds.), *Communication and Change*. Honolulu: University of Hawaii Press.

McClelland, David C. (1961). *The Achieving Society*. Princeton: Van Nostrand.

McCord, William and Abdulla Lutfiyya. (1971). "Urbanization and World View in the Middle East." In A. R. Desai (Ed.), *Essays on Modernization of Underdeveloped Societies*. Bombay: Thacker.

McLuhan, Marshall. (1965). *Understanding Media: The Extension of Man*. New York: McGraw-Hill.

Mead, Margaret. (1955). *Cultural Patterns and Technical Change*. New York: Mentor.

Mowlana, Hamid. (1979). "Technology versus Tradition: Communication in the Iranian Revolution." *Journal of Communication* 29(3), 107–112.

Nordenstreng, Kaarle and Tapio Varis. (1974). *Television Traffic—A One-Way Street*. (Reports and Papers on Mass Communication, No. 70) Paris: Unesco.

Parsons, Talcott. (1964). "Evolutionary Universals in Society." *American Sociological Review 29*, 339–357.

Pye, Lucian and Sidney Verba. (1965). *Political Culture and Political Development.* Princeton: Princeton University Press.

Rogers, Everett M. (1978). "The Rise and Fall of the Dominant Paradigm." *Journal of Communication* 28(1), 64–69.

Rogers, Everett M. and F. F. Shoemaker. (1971). *Communication of Innovations.* New York: Free Press.

Rostow, Walter W. (1960). *Stages of Economic Growth.* Cambridge: Cambridge University Press.

Schiller, Herbert I. (1969). *Mass Communications and American Empire.* New York: A. M. Kelley.

Schiller, Herbert I. (1973). *The Mind Managers.* Boston: Beacon Press.

Schiller, Herbert I. (1976). *Communication and Cultural Domination.* New York: International Arts & Sciences Press.

Schramm, Wilbur. (1976). "End of an Old Paradigm?" *In* Wilbur Schramm and Daniel Lerner (Eds.), *Communication and Change.* Honolulu: University of Hawaii Press.

Schumacher, Ernst F. (1973). *Small is Beautiful.* New York: Harper & Row.

Singer, Milton B. (1971). "Beyond Tradition and Modernity in Madras." *Comparative Studies in Society and History* 13(2), 160–195.

Starr, Chauncey and Philip C. Ritterbush (Eds.), (1980). *Science, Technology, and Human Prospect.* New York: Pergamon.

Statistic Abstract of the United States. (1980). Washington, D.C.: U.S. Department of Commerce.

United Nations. *Yearbook of National Accounts Statistics—1979.* New York: United Nations, 1980.

Williams, Raymond. (1974). *Television: Technology and Cultural Form.* London: Fontana.

World Bank Annual Report. (1981). Washington, D.C.: World Bank.

2

Indigenous Communication Systems and Development: A Reappraisal

Georgette Wang and Wimal Dissanayake

In the previous chapter, we advocated the need to consider culture as a crucial factor in development and change. Now we will enforce the theme of this book: culture as an essential element in two closely-related aspects in the study of communication, development communication, and the development of communication systems. There is an increasingly compelling need to better understand the so-called "indigenous communication system" ingrained in the culture and still functioning in most rural and, to some degree, in urban areas of developing nations. Further, cultural continuity and interaction between indigenous communication channels and mass media characterize communication systems in every society, a fact unfortunately ignored in the past. Our discussion begins with a look at the indigenous communication system and its place in the old paradigms.

An Examination of Indigenous Communication System

In the past few years, drastic changes have taken place in the field of development communication. With the fall of the old paradigm of development, efforts were made to reassess the situation in search for clues to new paradigms. New ideas reexamining the role of mass media in development and the appropriateness of old communication strategies were introduced. To aid in better research strategies, the terms "folk media" or "traditional media" were often suggested to assist in solving present problems in development. There was, however, little effort in defining or delineating the scope of traditional media or folk media, and even less frequently were they looked at as part of an indigenous communication system.

As presently used, the terms "folk media" and "traditional media" are often confused. If a distinction must be made, "folk media" should apply mainly to the performing arts which include, but are not limited to, puppetry, shadow plays, folk drama, folk dance, ballads, and story-telling. Folk media originate in different cultural activities and, there-fore, differ in nature. Ranganath (1979) delineated three categories of folk media: ritual, historical/traditional, and functional. Among the three, ritual folk media are the most rigid, both in terms of form and content. The other two are more adaptable to changes and modifica-tions, especially the functional folk media. But regardless of their na-ture, they are indigenous modes and have served society as tools of communication for ages, as Parmar (1975) suggested. They have been integrated over the years into patterns of behavior and institutions of the people.

"Traditional media" are also indigenous modes of communication, but they seem to focus on interpersonal channels and networks of com-munication, such as meeting places, including community tea houses, marketplaces, religious centers, and social-community institutions, such as the Indonesian *banjar*, the Korean mothers' club, and the Chinese *hui* (loaning club). Together with folk media, they form the indigenous com-munication system.

There is no formally accepted definition of "indigenous commu-nication system." For the purpose of the present analysis, we will opera-tionally define it as a "communication system embedded in the culture which existed before the arrival of mass media, and still exists as a vital mode of communication in many parts of the world, presenting a certain degree of continuity, despite changes." The media and channels within the system have their distinct roles and functions; together they interact with one another in the transmission of information and sociocultural messages.

The indigenous communication system differs from the mass com-munication system in at least three counts: size of audience, degree of content flexibility, and rootedness in local culture. While mass media typically aim at a large, undifferentiated audience, those who are in-volved in indigenous communication are often limited both in size of audience and geographical spread. Puppet shows, for example, cannot accommodate more than 100 people at one time. Community networks such as *banjar* involve only married males in a village. Therefore, people involved in indigenous communication are usually ethnolinguistically homogenous.

Small-size audiences result in intimacy between communicators and receivers, as well as among the participants in a network. The content of messages reflects this intimate relationship. While mass me-dia attend to the greatest common interest of people, indigenous media may appeal to the unique background and to the most delicate and subtle feelings of their audience. Although many of the folk arts do have plots and/or scripts, except, perhaps for ritual performances, messages transmitted by folk media are usually highly flexible in adapting to local taste, need, and experience. The clown in folk drama, for example, often plays the role of a social commentator and addresses contemporary issues.

Not only are indigenous communication systems close to people, but they are also woven into the community structure and are part of local social activities. As described by Nketia (1970), the indigenous communication system is often found operating within a community framework:

> It is in the community environment that folk media . . . can be greatly exploited, for they facilitate the dissemination of information in a very informal manner and in contexts in which the learning process is not separate from social experience or personal development.

Folk songs, usually regarded as purely an entertainment medium, can be both effective and efficient as communication media in a society which has a strong oral tradition. As observed in Botswana (Kidd and Byram, 1976), folk songs can "make social commentary, to express feelings or thoughts, to arouse people to action, or to insult those who misbehaved." They can be quickly learned, become popular, and are extremely important in the transmission of socially-useful messages. Traveling folk artists such as storytellers and puppeteers, the news carriers in the region, are often invited to become essential features of local festivities or other social occasions. On the other hand, the communication function of interpersonal networks is seldom separated from social, economical, or political functions. Although in recent years there has been marked development in community-oriented mass media such as cable television, there is, in general, a greater degree of integration of local community with indigenous communication systems rather than with mass communication systems.

Indigenous Communication Systems in the Old Paradigm

The importance of communication in development has long been recognized by social scientists. The focus of attention, however, has been on mass media, not on indigenous communication systems. As suggested by Lerner (1966, p. 558), a (mass) communication system is both an index and an agent of change in a total social system. His assertion is based on two general features that appear to be common to all societies. First, the direction of change in communication systems follows a linear path from oral tradition to technology-based media. Second, the degree of change in communication behavior appears to correlate significantly with other changes in the social system such as urbanization and the literacy rate.

Lerner's observation is consistent with two basic assumptions of the old paradigm of development—the tradition-modern dichotomy and the power of the media to change attitudes as well as to transmit information. According to these assumptions, the indigenous communication system and the mass communication system constitute another dichotomy. The indigenous communication system is embedded in the culture, closely associated with the traditional way of life, and the messages it conveys reinforce cultural values of the audience. The mass communication system is imported; it can efficiently and effectively transmit information necessary to motivate change and is regarded as an essential part of a modern society. According to the direction of change suggested by Lerner, the indigenous communication system, characterized by oral communication and direct participation by the audience, will eventually be replaced by the mass communication system. The end of the indigenous communication system was, therefore, inevitable. On the other hand, given their potential to reach a large audience, mass media and the development of mass communication systems became major concerns for planners and social scientists.

Great amount of financial as well as human resources were expended in setting up satellite communication networks, distributing radio sets to villages, and using close-circuit television for educational purposes in order to achieve the goals of inducing change. In the meantime, very little attention was given to the role and value of the indigenous communication system in development until early 1970s when some efforts were made to use folk media for family planning campaigns. It was generally regarded as outdated and irrelevant by theorists advocating the old paradigm.

The indigenous communication system seemed to be on the verge of being phased out during the heyday of the old paradigm. Puppeteers and storytellers were reported to have been made superfluous because their audiences were glued to television sets, and the marketplace was no longer a venue for information exchange since radio was capable of supplying news reports about virtually everything that was worthy of attention. The change seemed inevitable, but not necessarily laudable, as Lubis (1978, p. 2) observed:

> In most cases the new attitudes and appetites work to the detriment of traditional culture, and traditional products, and change social as well as cultural values, including ethics and esthetics. . . . TV, radio and film and cassettes compete against the old traditional dances, wayang, storytelling and other expressions. Lack of funds, skills, and experience with the new communication media in the third world allow for the invasion of commercials which whet consumers' appetites and create new needs which are not really needed, but also software which is not relevant to the real needs of the developing societies.

Lubis indicated some of the problems engendered by the rise of mass media, namely the erosion of indigenous culture and commericalism leading to a gap between people's desires and what they could reasonably expect to acquire. Whether indigenous cultures disintegrate under the dominance of television is debatable. Two other factors which re-versed this trend so that indigenous communication systems regained favor: the concern over what was dubiously termed cultural imperi-alism, and the limit of media power in promoting change.

Cultural imperialism can be viewed as a lack of coordination be-tween the hardware growth and the software growth of media. That is, the ability to provide media content. Dazzled by the miracles that a modern mass communication system promised to bring to a society, policymakers in many developing nations hurriedly set up television networks, preferably linked up with satellites. Their initial enthusiasm, however, was soon dampened by the problems in producing local pro-grams—in most of the developing nations, lack of resources and trained personnel made television production extremely difficult and expensive. Many broadcasters, therefore, were forced to rely on imported films to fill up the hours, with the result that imported television programs often became the major part of television program content. For example, 80% of the television programs broadcast in Latin America were produced in the United States. To many policy makers, direct communication via satellite evading government sanctions could only worsen the situation. Imported programs coupled with the long-existing imbalance of infor-mation flow among nations, were viewed not only as threats to the survival of indigenous culture, but were also shown to be related to the global patterns of domination and the dependency theory (Schiller, 1976; Varis, 1974).

Mass media precipitated some problems unforeseen by planners. The effectiveness of media in inducing change fell far short of expecta-tions. Social scientists working with the old paradigm of development adopted a view of the media as mighty tools in changing the mentality of villagers and peasants so that they could be readily mobilized for devel-opment. Later research findings, however, showed that mass media are best in providing information and materials for people to think about, but not in telling people what and how to think. It was found that attitude change can be achieved only when the media work with other social psychological variables. Centralized planning and top-down, one-way, communication were also found to be ineffective in promoting development because of their inherent insensitivity to local needs and culture. The view of the role of mass media thus changed considerably with the emerging new paradigm. As indicated by Rogers (1978, p. 68), the main role of mass communication and government development agencies at present is to provide technical information and to circulate news of self-help projects providing information or inspiration to others.

Although the role of mass media in development has changed, difficulties still exist in Third World nations. As indicated by Parmar (1975, p. 11), the uneven distribution of media is one of the major factors which obstruct mass communication within a country. A quick survey of the situation reveals that mass media in most of developing nations are urban-based and the primary audience is the elite. In remote villages, where illiteracy is still high and electricity lacking, mass media are rarely available. A survey in Sri Lanka (1979) showed that only 5.3% of the urban group did not listen to radio at all, but the percentage rose to 35.77% with the rural sample. This uneven distribution of media leads to inequality in the dissemination of information resulting, in turn, in a wider gap between the already-privileged and the masses.

This frustrating experience with the mass media can be attributed partly to a failure to recognize the role of culture in the introduction of technology. As pointed out in the previous chapter, for technology to grow properly, the culture must provide a supportive environment and resources. The compatibility of the technology with socio-cultural norms, values, and lifestyle of the people must be established before growth can take place. When the environment is hostile or indifferent the growth of technology will be limited, if not impossible. Television broadcasts, for example, are controlled in Indonesia because of so-ciocultural considerations. The Indonesian government abolished televi-sion commericals because of the social problems they seem to be creat-ing. The old paradigm of development, therefore, has been criticized for the assumption that technology can be adopted and utilized regardless of the sociocultural context.

Some Issues in Using Indigenous Communication Systems for Development

Concerned with cultural imperialism and the ineffectiveness of mass media in reaching those who need change most, decision makers and planners turned their attention to other alternatives. The new paradigm for development now focuses on the consumers. Local activities, con-sumer-initiated change, participation of the villagers in planning, and decision making are encouraged. "Little media" such as radio are now more desirable in promoting development (Rogers, 1978). Some atten-tion has also been given to the indigenous communication system. Efforts were made to preserve folk media as cultural treasures and to utilize them for development. The indigenous communication system began to be appreciated in development efforts not only because of its reach and credibility, but because it was consistent with new ideas in communication for development; it was low-cost, flexible, credible, lo-cally-oriented, and encouraged audience participation. As indicated in a UNESCO document on communication and cultural policies, "Whether new technology can solve social problems more effectively and effi-ciently than so-called traditional methods will determine if nations should leap into the new space age" (Yogyakarta, 1973, p. 20).

Recently, much discussion has centered on the significance of the space age to developing nations. The uses of "traditional" methods, however, did not receive much academic attention. According to Abrams (1980), programs which use indigenous social structures and traditional media in non-formal education and development can be seen in many developing nations today. Experimental projects and activities were reported in Egypt, Kenya, Nigeria, Bangladesh, Papua New Guinea, the Philippines, Haiti, Mexico, not to mention India, which made much progress in this area over the years. As widespread as the geographical area seems to indicate, efforts made are still at a initial stage of trial-and-error process. As McAnany (1980, p. 9) indicated, the full potential is yet to be explored:

> Although such (social) networks, as well as folk media, could be used to transmit . . . development information, no successful formula has yet been devised to tap into this potentially rich resource on a large scale.

A quick review of the literature shows that our knowledge about the effectiveness of such uses is also meager. The studies conducted so far on indigenous communication systems can be divided into three basic categories: indigenous communication channels as used in development programs, folk media as forms of entertainment, and the cultural characteristics of folk media. Of the three, apparently only the first is basically concerned with development. Many of these reviewed or proposed efforts of using indigenous channels or folk media for family planning campaigns in the early and mid-1970s (Kincaid and Yum, 1976; Rogers and Adhikarya, 1979; Parmar, 1975). Except for a few, the majority are descriptive in nature and the scope is often limited to one type of media in one geographical area. Concepts are inadequately formulated and many serious questions are left unanswered.

It seems that although indigenous communication systems have great potential in development campaigns, the absence of academic attention is associated with an apparent lack of enthusiasm on the part of development planners. Without proper understanding of the nature of the system, in-depth analyses of past experience and clarification of cloudy issues, no great breakthrough can be expected in the field. At least three issues are worthy of discussion here: the impact of using indigenous communication channels on their own growth, the evaluation of effects, and the problems associated with the integration of folk media and mass media.

In the past, people have argued that once an indigenous communication channel is used instrumentally, it can no longer be legitimately termed an indigenous medium. While it was maintained that the uniqueness was interfered with, this clearly is not the case.

In past development programs, development messages have been improperly inserted into the content of folk media, and interpersonal networks have also been "utilized" for specific purposes. Very often, little consideration was given to the nature of the indigenous communication channels and their flexibility in incorporating development messages. The Chinese Peking Opera, for example, is ritualistic and traditional by nature, with little flexibility in its content. During the

Cultural Revolution, drastic changes were effected in order to incorporate specific political messages. It was quite apparent that the "revolutionalized" version of the opera did not maintain its identity as a "folk medium." In addition, using channels often contradicts the very characteristics of folk media. While two-way communication is vital to indigenous communication channels, a one-way approach is often employed in their use. Scripts and plots are designed by top-level officials who are unfamiliar with local situations. Negative feedback, poor effectiveness, and, subsequently, suspicion on the potential of indigenous channels in transmitting development messages are therefore predictable results.

In fact, change is a built-in strength of indigenous communication systems allowing them to transfer development messages without the danger of self-destruction. History shows that development planners are not the first to utilize indigenous communication channels for propaganda and related purposes. One well-known example is the use of Indian folk media in advocating independence from British rule. In Indonesia, various forms of the traditional *wayang* were used for religious teachings and political purposes (Van Hoosen, 1979). Similar examples can be found in many other nations. In other words, politicians, missionaries, social reformers, and educators have long recognized the communication potential of indigenous communication channels. None of the past uses seems to have impaired the growth of the system. However, in order to bring genuine success to development efforts, the nature and the strength of the system must be recognized. According to Parmar (1975), the uses of indigenous forms of communication for development purposes may not do harm or restrict their growth if their nature is well understood. If well-designed, the use of an indigenous communication system for development purposes will not have a negative effect on the system as some have feared.

Evaluation of the effectiveness of indigenous communication channels also, at times, constitutes a problem. The indices of success employed by development planners are unclear—attendance, on-the-spot reaction, ideological change, attitude change, or behavioral change? They recognize that attendance and audience reaction can provide some clues to success. But some have argued that these indices may be good predictors of the quality of performance and its entertainment value. They do not, however, guarantee that the development messages got through to the audience, or that the messages have had an impact in any way. Apparent behavioral changes seem to be the best indicators. If, for example, following a thorough discussion among members of a mothers' club, there is a substantial increase in the number of members adopting contraceptive methods, the effort can claim success. However, there are also intervening variables such as the nature of change and changes in other social or economic conditions to be taken into consideration. A folk media campaign, for example, was reportedly successful in India. Later, it was found out that those who adopted contraceptive methods were way over their reproductive age. A systematic and scientific evaluation scheme is therefore highly necessary for people to learn from experiences.

The integrative use of indigenous communication channels and mass media for development is being advocated today by some scholars. Rogers (1978), for example, is one promoter of such communication strategy. There could be several forms of such integration. Ideally, folk performances, which are best in arousing emotional feelings of the audience, create an atmosphere for change. In the next stage, modern media such as slide shows and films can follow with detailed information and vivid illustrations. And after the audiovisual exposure, a discussion aiming at soliciting feedback and discovering questions and need for further information from the audience is held. However, not all the "integrative uses" so far have followed such a pattern. Folk plays were often recorded on video or audio tapes, saving the trouble and the expense of bringing whole groups of performers. However, discussion at the end is normally omitted. Such a strategy may have little effect. First, with the folk play on tape, interaction between communicator and audience is eliminated. Its potential for arousing emotion through close identification is weakened. Second, the absence of discussion continues to imply a one-way communication approach. The value of incorporating folk performances is, therefore, insignificant.

Thus far there are very few studies on the cost-benefit analyses of different integrative uses of folk and mass media. In the absence of such studies, little substantial progress can be made in the field.

Our review of the situation shows an urgent need for more and better research in the general uses of indigenous communication system for development purposes. In fact, not only has the study of indigenous communication systems largely been neglected in the past, but the evolution of communication systems which manifest interaction between indigenous channels and the mass media has also been overlooked. The communications literature, especially in non-Western nations, typically focuses on the expansion of mass media coverage, isolating them from any cultural context. An "end state" seems to be implied for communication systems as well as for other aspects of development. It must be recognized that a communication system is one sub-system within the cultural system. It too, constantly undergoes change while maintaining a certain degree of continuity. The rate of change may vary from country to country and within countries. In many developing nations, the indigenous communication system is left largely intact and still flourishes in rural areas where few technological changes have taken place and where people depend on agriculture to make their living. Mass media growth, especially for radio, is reported in recent years in these areas. But the indigenous communication system still functions as a self-contained system, serving to satisfy the needs of a given segment of society.

In the relatively developed nations, or urban areas of the lesser developed nations, changes in communication systems are more noticeable. The decreasing number of folk performing groups and the dwindling importance of meeting places have been interpreted as signs of the decay of indigenous communication systems. However, it should be recognized that an open system seldom dies. At a time when the number of folk performing groups is decreasing and meeting places are losing their importance, a new form of "indigenous communication" is forming. A UNESCO document made the following observation (UNESCO, 1973):

> The performing arts thus provide a particularly good meeting-point for traditional values and the requirements of progress. Their form is by no means set in rigid structures; the strict requirements of oral tradition and of handing down from memory necessitate social supervision of creation and rule out too personal and individual performance . . . Their traditional content is subject to constant change, as the experience of each generation is slowly passed onto the next, fulfilling a social purpose.

This new form of "indigenous communication," of course, is different from the traditional concept. Indigenous and mass communication are two distinctly different systems, each dominating one geographical area; i.e., rural and urban. The boundary between the two gradually becomes blurred as close interaction tends to amalgamate them into a single entity. The evolving system may manifest the outlook of a mass communication system. However, continuity of the indigenous system and its cultural features are clearly visible.

Statistics on television programs imported by Third World nations and on the unbalanced flow of information from developed to developing nations sound alarming; media dysfunction observed. Total Westernization, however, has not taken place, even in technologically developed nations such as Japan. Brandon (1972) observes that, while mass media are Western-inspired and technology-based, they have the potential to express people's culture as well as any other media. Mass media can accelerate change in cultural forms and media forms in some nations, but they may inhibit change in others by using programming to reinforce traditional cultural values. They are, according to Goulet (1977), two–edged swords.

In reaction to fears of cultural imperialism, broadcasters in many developing nations are seriously looking into the possibility of drawing upon folk resources for mass media content. Examples of success are easy to find. Storytelling and shadow plays have become popular radio programs in Iran and Indonesia, bag puppet shows were once the highest-rated television programs in Taiwan, and All India Radio has explored the Indian heritage in music. This development is not free from side-effects and nagging problems. As Lee (1980) pointed out, commercialism and the overall sociopolitical situation often dampen the efforts to revive folk media on television.

In addition to the integration of folk media and mass media, unique cultural features have become manifest in other aspects of the development process of a communication system. For example, technological dimensions added to the folk drama in Indian cinema. They provide an excellent example of the interface between a folk medium and a mass medium. The popularity of chivalric stories, one form of folk literature, in mass media in Hong Kong is another such example. On the other hand, marriage advertisements in Indian newspapers are a cultural feature inherited from the continuing traditional practice of arranged marriages. Many other examples can be found in communication systems in any society.

Cultural features also exist at the conceptual level. The definition of news may serve as one example. We tend to think of the concept of news as universal. but it too may be culture-specific. The same is true for the concept of communication. Kato (1979) found that such key terms in communication research as "communication," "network," "feedback," are either not translatable or are hard to translate into languages such as Japanese, Hindi, Bahasa Indonesia, and Tagalog (Filipino). In order to thoroughly understand the role of culture in the development of communication systems, several aspects of social science research must be covered and coordinated: philosophy, semantics, rhetorics, and communication-from past to present.

There is apparently an information "black box" at two related aspects of communication studies: uses of indigenous communication style for development purposes, and the role of culture in the development of communication system. As pointed out by McAnany (1978), very little is known about the information environment of the rural poor in Third World nations. In fact, we know little about the general nature and structure of communication systems within specific cultural contexts in most non-Western societies. Awa (1979) attributed this lack of research on indigenous communication system to the Western bias at both the theoretical and methodological level in diffusion research and to the mentality of the Western-trained intelligensia in Third World nations. The lack of funding has further constrained people interested in this area.

Another reason for the relative neglect of indigenous communication systems and cultural features of any communication system is that attention has been concentrated solely on the informational and educational aspects. As a result, very heavy emphasis has been placed on cosmopolitan mass media. However, a communication system is also a mechanism for cultural expression. The values, norms, ideas, and life-styles of a people are reflected in various forms of entertainment and information transmission. The influence of communication systems cannot be isolated from the people and their sociocultural environment. It is only logical to study them within such a context. The chapters which follow explore this idea in a narrow compass. Hopefully, these pages will constitute the first step in a continuous effort in this direction.

REFERENCES

Abrams, Tevia. (1980). "The Use of Indigenous Social Structures and Traditional Media in Non-Formal Education and Development." Paper presented at International Seminar, Berlin.

Awa, Njoku E. (1979). "Ethnocentric Bias in Developmental Research." In Molefi Ki Asante et al. (Eds.), *Handbook of Intercultural Communication Research.* Beverly Hills: Sage.

Brandon, James. (1972). *Traditional Asian Plays.* New York: Hill & Wang.

Goulet, Denis. (1977). *The Uncertain Promise: Value Conflicts in Technology Transfer.* New York: IDOC/North America.

Kato, Hidetoshi. (1979). "Translatability of Key Concepts on Communication Research." Unpublished paper.

Kidd, Ross and Martin Byram. (1976). "Folk Media and Development: A Botswana Case Study." Paper printed by the Botswana Extension College.

Kincaid, D. Lawrence and June Ock Yum. (1976). "The Needle and the Ax: Communication and Development in a Korean Village." In Wilbur Schramm and Daniel Lerner (Eds.), *Communication and Change, The Last Ten Years—and the Next.* Honolulu: The University of Hawaii Press.

Lerner, Daniel. (1966). "Communication Systems and Social Systems: A Statistical Exploration in History and Policy." In Alfred G. Smith (Ed.), *Communication and Culture.* New York: Holt, Rinehart and Winston.

Lubis, Mochtar. (1978). "Interaction between Culture and Communication." Paper prepared for the International Commission for the Study of Communication Problems.

McAnany, Emile G. (1978). "Does Information Really Work?" *Journal of Communication 28* (1), 84–90.

McAnany, Emile G. (1980). "The Role of Information in Communication with the Rural Poor: Some Reflections." In Emile G. McAnany (Ed.), *Communication in the Rural Third World.* New York: Praeger.

Nketia, J. H. K. (1970). "The Use of Traditional Media in Social and Health Education." Paper presented at Family Planning Education in Africa Workshop, Ghana.

Parmar, Shyam. (1975). *Traditional Folk Media in India.* New Delhi: Geka Books.

Ranganath, H. K. (1979). *Folk Media and Communication.* Bangalore: W. Q. Judge Press.

Rogers, Everett M., and Ronny Adhikarya. (1979). "A Proposal: A Case Study of the *Banjar* Approach to Family Planning in Bali, Indonesia: The Communication Strategy in Utilizing Local, Indigenous Community Groups." Submitted to the Pathfinder Fund, Boston, Massachusetts.

Schiller, Herbert I. (1976). *Communication and Culture Domination.* New York: International Arts & Sciences Press.

Sri Lanka University. (1979). "Report of Survey." Colombo: Dept. of Mass Communication, University of Sri Lanka.

UNESCO (1973). "Communication and Cultural Action: a) The Performing Arts, b) The Mass Media." Paper presented at the Intergovernmental Conference on Cultural Policies in Asia, Yogyakarta, Indonesia, December 10–20.

Van Hoosen, Debra. (1979). "The Barefoot Actor: An Examination of Asian Folk

Drama in the Contemporary Role on Development." Master Thesis, University of Hawaii.

Varis, T. (1974). *International Inventory of Television Programme, Structure and the Flow of TV Programs Between Nations.* Tampere, Finland: Research Institute of Journalism and Mass Communication, University of Tampere.

PART II

THE USE OF INDIGENOUS COMMUNICA- TIONS SYSTEMS FOR PLANNED CHANGE

Overview—Part II

Wimal Dissanayake

Indigenous communication systems are usually noted for their evolutionary history and close association with cultural traditions and customs. They are, therefore, representations of continuity from the past. This characteristic, however, does not put indigenous communication media and channels in an adversary relationship with change. As pointed out in Chapter Two, they are often adaptable in meeting sociocultural change, and, in recent years, they were found to be more efficient and effective in introducing change in many areas of the Third World. The first category of country studies specifically looks at the use of indigenous messages, media, or channels for planned change; how the indigenous communication system has been pressed into service to meet contemporary social goals, and other related issues. This section consists of six studies, each describing the unique experience of using indigenous communication for development purposes.

The first chapter of this section (Chapter 3), "Buddhist Approach to Development: A Sri Lankan Endeavor," discusses the *Sarvodaya* Movement of Sri Lanka—a voluntary self-help movement concerned with social change and development. What is distinctive about the Sri Lankan Sarvodaya Movement is the purposeful way it has sought to draw on traditional Buddhist attitudes, values, and patterns of communication to mobilize popular support for planned social change. As discussed in the chapter, the achievement of the movement is, thus far, attributable in large measure to the imaginative use of indigenous norms and styles of communication for the promotion of social change.

The second chapter in this section (Chapter 4) deals with the manner in which the theatre arts of the Philippines could be used as a powerful instrument of development communication. This paper maps out the uses of theatre arts by various institutions—both private and public—and argues against the view that traditional theatre arts are inappropriate and inadequate for conveying development messages to the people. On the contrary, drawing on contemporary experiences of the Philippines, the author points out how important an ally they can be, if used wisely and creatively in the development effort.

The use of indigenous media for development has not been totally successful in the past. One of the reasons was a lack of understanding of the nature of the media—their strengths and weaknesses in transmitting development messages. The chapter on the potential use of traditional communication systems in Papua New Guinea (Chapter 5) describes a project sponsored by the United Nations Fund For Population Activities and the local government in an effort to plan the use of traditional systems for change carefully. The author seeks to make the point that various factors must be taken into consideration in order to achieve the desired objectives.

The chapter on the revolutionary opera in China (Chapter 6) is an illuminating study, which points out the danger to which one must be alert when employing indigenous media to meet contemporary needs. At one point, revolutionary opera was the most widely deployed art form in China. It was harnessed for the purpose of achieving various political goals under the direction of the "Gang of Four." This type of opera, as pointed out by the author, differs considerably from the traditional form of Peking Opera especially in terms of theme.

Different approaches to the folk media for development reflect a diversity of thinking. The chapter on folk media and campaigns in India (Chapter 7) examines the Indian experiences in social animation theatre. The author makes the observation that theatre can be used, on the one hand, as a medium for propagating the world view and values of the dominant class, and, on the other hand, as an instrument which facilitates the expression of the problems of the people, the deepening of their understanding and, thereby, as a medium which hastens social transformation.

The final chapter in this section (Chapter 8) focuses attention on the advantages and disadvantages in the use of folk drama for development purposes. The author's observations and analyses are made within the framework of the "new paradigm" of development and communication emphasizing the role of two-way communication, popular participation in the planning and decision-making processes, and the integration of indigenous and cosmopolitan media of communication.

This section, then, emphasizes the need to pay more attention to the purposive and imaginative use of indigenous media of communication in the task of social change and development. It also calls attention to some of the dangers to which we should be alert. The indigenous communication systems of the Third World countries, which have evolved with time, and the expansion of the consciousness of the people reflect in a particularly compelling manner the elements of continuity and change in dynamic communication systems. The way these systems can be harnessed for development purposes calls attention to the constructive use of that dynamism.

3

A Buddhist Approach to Development: A Sri Lankan Endeavor

Wimal Dissanayake

The objective of this chapter is to examine a social experiment in Sri Lanka concerned with the development of a Buddhist approach to social development. This experiment—the Sarvodaya Shramadana Movement—bears directly on the purposeful deployment of traditional forms and philosophies of communication to meet contemporary needs. The experiment is now over twenty years old, and one can point out certain defects and shortcomings which need to be rectified. However, by and large, the achievements of the Sarvodaya Movement in Sri Lanka are substantial, and the movement certainly invites closer study.

Sarvodaya literally means the welfare of everyone. The Sri Lanka Sarvodaya Movement was started in 1958. It was aimed at the individual and the social betterment of the people, drawing as much as possible on the moral consciousness of society. The movement is a self-help organization, currently with development programs in over 2,500 villages scattered throughout the island. The Sarvodaya Movement conducts camps regularly with over 250,000 people participating every year. Its objective is community awakening through self-help and the formulation of development programs which bear the unmistakable imprint of the indigenous culture. Rather than blindly following the developmental scenarios that have been written in the West—no doubt, of Western interests—the architects of the Sri Lanka Sarvodaya Movement are engaged in a timely and arduous endeavor to formulate and put into practice a development strategy springing from the deepest currents of the culture that permeates society.

I use the term "deepest currents of culture" advisedly. Sri Lanka has essentially a Buddhist culture. From ancient times it has been the most powerful force in shaping the culture and outlook of the people. Buddhism was introduced to Sri Lanka in the third century B.C., and has played a predominant role in the life of society ever since. Today, nearly 70% of the people on the island are Buddhists. The arts, architecture, literature, values, ideals, lifestyles, norms of conduct, etc., bear the unmistakable imprint of Buddhism. It has penetrated the collective consciousness of the people as no other force. Hence, it is natural for the leaders of the Sarvodaya Shramadana Movement to draw on the Buddhist *weltanschauung*. However, Sri Lanka is a multi-religious society where, in addition to the Buddhist, about 18% are Hindus, 8% Muslims, and the rest Christians. Hence, one can question whether adoption of a Buddhist approach might not alienate the sympathies of other religious groups. Fortunately, this is not happening because the architects of the movement emphasized universal virtues like compassion, kindness, and charity, as advocated by Buddhism which are shared by other denominations. The more parochial ritualistic aspects have been ignored.

During the last 20 years or so, the Sarvodaya Movement of Sri Lanka has made tremendous progress and a very real contribution to the welfare of the people. The following table of the peoples' participation in the Shramadana campaigns reflects the enthusiasm that the movement has generated (Progress Report of the Sarvodaya Movement, 1978).

YEAR	NO. OF CAMPS	NO. OF PARTICIPANTS
1958	3	97
1959	12	318
1960	22	620
1961	13	3,052
1962	6	1,318
1963	6	4,057
1964	33	22,895
1965	23	4,414
1966	61	11,516
1967	56	9,310
1968	72	9,726
1969	43	8,453
1970	38	3,008
1971	18	1,102
1972	65	2,613
1973	171	14,320
1974	137	13,486
1975	169	18,683
1976	342	73,543
1977	454	138,580

The camps are the kernel of this voluntary movement. From a practical point of view, the objectives of the Sarvodaya Shramadana Movement have been to:

1. Create an awareness of the problems confronted by the villagers and to devise ways and means of solving them.

2. Develop community leadership skills.
3. Inculcate economically profitable skills and organizational aptitudes.
4. Encourage planning of development programs and find resources for their execution.

Some of the main social activities performed by the Sarvodaya Shramadana Movement at the village level are testimony to these objectives.

1. Agricultural training (theoretical and practical), imparted in various educational centers and farms.
2. Training in batik making, printing, carpentry, blacksmithing, masonry, mat-weaving, etc., carried out in educational centers and villages.
3. Informal training in skills, carried out in the villages under village masters and craftsmen, the youth serving as apprentices.
4. Training Buddhist monks in community development, by equipping them with practical knowledge related to the regeneration of the villages.
5. Preschool teacher training programs (carried out together with community kitchen programs), in which young women and school dropouts are trained to become preschool teachers and helped to set up preschools in villages where such schools are lacking. The teachers are equipped with a "know how" that helps them to promote profitable socialization of children and health care programs in the villages, with emphasis on nutrition and the health of the aged and infants.
6. The training of health workers, at times with the assistance of the Department of Health (Ratnapala, p. 30, n.d.).

The Sarvodaya Movement of Sri Lanka is fundamentally concerned with the total development of the human being. It envisions development not merely in terms of GNP and per capita income, but also in relation to the flowering of the total human personality. A. T. Ariyaratne (n.d.), the "live wire" behind this movement, says that development goals need to point to balance growth with material and spiritual dimensions. He believes that the individual, the family, and the village, should be regarded as the basic units of development. Technology is indeed vital for social development. However, it should be introduced and function in a manner that does no violence to the spirit of the individual, family, or village.

According to the leaders of the Sarvodaya Movement, the norms associated with political life should strengthen participatory democracy and lessen the stranglehold of bureaucracy. Personal human relationships and small scale economic pursuits should be the foundation of the national economy. Every effort must be made to minimize the dominant role played by the institutionalized economies. Clearly, given the imperatives of modern life, these ideals, laudable as they are, cannot be realized without great imagination.

The Sarvodaya Movement is built around important Buddhistic notions of interpersonal and group communications. These notions have penetrated deeply into the consciousness of the people and form a deep substratum of culture. In the latter half of this chapter, I shall explain these Buddhistic notions of communication and how they can facilitate social developmental processes. First, I should like to present the four main approaches to development communication and to point out how the philosophy of the Sarvodaya Movement conforms to the final one. I will demonstrate how this movement exemplifies the use of indigenous forms and philosophies of communication to meet contemporary needs and, thereby, ensure continuity.

The term development is of crucial importance to those working in development communications. It is an elusive term and admits of a plurality of definitions. However, for our present purposes, I will define development as the process of social change having the goal of improvement in the quality of life of all, or the majority, of the people without doing violence to the natural and cultural environment in which they exist. Development, by this definition, seeks to involve the people as closely as possible in the enterprise putting them in charge of their own destiny. This departs markedly from the standard definitions current among development communication scholars in the 1950s and 1960s. Rogers and Shoemaker (1971) defined development as:

> Development is a type of social change in which new ideas are introduced into a social system in order to produce higher per capita income and levels of living through more modern production methods and improved social organization. Development is modernization at the social systems level (p. 11).

In the past, development was measured by quantifiable indices such as GNP and per capita income. However, more and more, development communication scholars emphasize the fact that these indices are inadequate and misleading. A large number of countries chalked up a rapid rate of GNP growth while, at the same time, creating very high rates of unemployment and underemployment. Furthermore, in several instances, the rapid growth in GNP went hand in hand with a widening of the gap between privileged and underprivileged in respective societies. Therefore, to pay attention to the GNP and per capita income without adequately taking into consideration income distribution and other forms of social justice only serves to create a misleading picture. Therefore, the traditional criteria of economic growth are being supplanted by the new criteria of social growth.

In this regard, the following comment of Dudley Seers (1969) is illuminating:

> The questions to ask about a country's development are therefore: What has been happening to poverty? What has been happening to inequality? What has been happening to employment? If all three of

these have declined from high levels, then beyond a doubt, this has been a period of development for the country concerned. If one or two of these central problems have been growing worse, especially if all three have, it would be strange to call the result "development" even if the per capita income doubled (p. 2).

Seers' remarks exemplify the newer perception of development. It is in this sense that I use the term "development" in this paper—not as a synonym for economic growth, but as a term which also encompasses distributive justice and general human fulfillment.

Let me turn now to the term communication. Communication is the veritable lifeblood of human society—no society can possibly function without it. Therefore, we must pay very close attention to the role of communication in any development effort. One of the major weaknesses of early development plans of developing countries was the insignificant role assigned to communication. *Lucien W. Pye's observation (1963) is relevant in this regard:*

Communication is the web of human society. The structure of a communication system with its more or less well-defined channels is in a sense the skeleton of the social body which envelopes it. The content of communication is of course the very substance of human intercourse. The flow of communication determines the direction and the pace of dynamic social development (p. 4).

I will now outline the four main approaches to development. The first approach was popular in the 1950s and 1960s. It emphasized industrialization, capital-intensive technology, and centralized planning. Advocates claimed that developing countries could progress only by following the lead given by industrially advanced countries. Rostow's (1960) book, *The Stages of Economic Growth: A Non–Communist Manifesto,* had a profound impact on this mode of thinking.

Communication scholars like Schramm (1964), Lerner (1964), and Pye (1963) endorsed this approach to development. They expressed the view that mass media can play a highly significant role in creating the climate for development. This approach stressed the need for increased productivity through speedy industrialization. It was said that productivity is the key to development and that the most productive sector of modern society is the industrial sector. Communication efforts inclined in this direction.

This approach to development generated a great deal of optimism. However, by the 1970s, it was clear that the strategy advocated in this approach to development had failed to deliver the goods. Although the GNP had increased and exports were up, many existing problems such as the increase in unemployment and underemployment and urban congestion were aggravated in the process. Proponents maintained that the benefits accruing through this approach would have a "trickle-down"effect. This, too, failed to materialize. Actually, the gap between rich and poor in the developing countries widened appreciably.

By the 1970s, many development communication scholars began to find fault with this approach. Four counterarguments are particularly relevant. First, it was ethnocentric and held up the Western experience as a model to be imitated by the developing countries, without paying adequate attention to questions of historical background, uniqueness of cultural context, etc. Second, it posited a unilinear view of history. Critics argued that there was not one, but several paths to development, and that the historical route taken by the developed countries was not the only one available to developing nations. Third, it concentrated on exogenous factors of development to the exclusion of endogenous factors. Fourth, it placed too much emphasis on the individual and laid the blame at his door without taking into sufficient consideration effects of the social structure. Adherents of the first approach often accused the peasants in the less developed countries of being too traditional, superstitious, fatalistic, etc. and of not being motivated by the "protestant work ethic." Counter-critics argued that these claims totally ignored the effect of the social structure, which would otherwise explain more cogently some of these features (Rogers, 1976, pp. 121–148).

The second approach to development is a reaction to the first. Rogers (1976), closely associated with the first approach, has pointed out the central concerns of the second approach very lucidly. He designates one as the "old" paradigm and the other as the "new" paradigm.

The first approach emphasized economic growth, industrialization, centralized planning, and exogenous factors of development. On the contrary, the second approach underlined income distribution, decentralized planning, labor-intensive technology, and endogenous as well as exogenous factors in development. This shift in emphasis was accompanied by a related effort calling attention to the quality of life, the need to blend modern and traditional media of communication, appropriate technology, and popular participation in the decision-making process.

The proponents of the second approach focused their attention on such questions as: How can distributive justice be achieved? How can the ideals of self-reliance and self-management be realized? How can the old and the new media of communication be integrated productively? How can culture best be employed as a mediator and facilitator of development? How can one construct more history-conscious and society-specific models of development communication? How can one bring social-structural factors impeding development into the equation?

This shift in the meaning of development was accompanied by a parallel shift of regarding the meaning of communication. The old mechanistic, linear, one-way communicator-based model of communication gave way to a more organic, interactive, two-way model. Communication scholars like Berlo (1977) pointed out the processual and interactive nature of communication.

This new approach to development communication represents a potentially more rewarding perception of development and communication. Many of its strengths can be seen as efforts to remedy the defects of the older approach. However, several contradictions remain. It does not emerge from a consistent social philosophy, as does the first, and it seems to incorporate many conflicting trends of thought. Indeed this new paradigm or approach manifests not one, but many, paradigms. On the one hand, it talks of the interdependence of the developed and the developing countries and how they form a world system. On the other hand, much is made of the notions of self-management and self-reliance. But these ideas are not developed in a sufficiently comprehensive manner enabling us to comprehend their full implications and to take cognizance of their conflicting demands.

This leads to what I term the third approach to development. It is characterized by insistence on the interdependence of the developed and the developing countries and the need to make this relationship a central concern. However, one has to bear in mind that when the spokesmen for this approach employ the term "interdependence," they are talking of a viciously asymmetrical relationship in which the developed countries thrive at the expense of the developing countries. Therefore, they believe that a basic precondition for development is the elimination of this asymmetrical relationship.

The advocates of the third approach to development stress the futility of discussing communication and development in a national setting without examining the historical evolution of each society and the way in which the world economic system conditions and regulates its development. Nordenstreng and Schiller (1979), while complimenting the spokesmen for the second approach, observe that the old paradigm has not been entirely abandoned. They maintain that the notion of a relatively isolated nation, developing according to conditions determined mainly within that society, remains largely unexamined and that this is a fundamental issue which should not be ignored. Nordenstreng and Schiller argue that, while advocates of the second approach to development and communication talk of external courses of development and dependence theory, such notions do not appear to significantly influence their conceptualization.

The colonial experience of the less developed countries is crucial to this mode of argument. The factors which brought about the growth of industrially advanced countries also brought about the conditions of poverty existing in Third World countries. Obtaining political independence from foreign domination does not appear to have appreciably altered the picture. Scholars like Galtung (1980) express the view that the colonial structures still persist, but with the systems of control exercised in a subtler fashion. Economic aid, transnational corporations, and the international monetary institutions are cited as examples of newer and subtler modes of imperialism. Scholars argue that this imperialism is found not only in economics but also in the political, military, communications, and cultural domains. According to this approach, then, unless there is a structural rearrangement in the international relationships, less developed countries are unlikely to make much progress.

Finally, the fourth approach to development and communication is currently gaining wide recognition. It is characterized by a strong emphasis on self-reliance. This approach to development brings together a number of ideas that have surfaced in recent times including integrated village development, popular participation in the decision-making processes, grassroots development, productive use of local resources, fulfillment of basic needs, maintenance of the ecological balance, popular definition of development problems and culture as a mediating force in development.

Galtung (1980) lucidly presents the essence of the strategy of self-reliance in the development process:

> Self-reliance is a dynamic movement from the periphery, at all levels—individual, local, national, regional. It is not something done for the periphery. Thus, control over the economic machinery of a country by national and even by local, state or private capitalists in order to produce for the satisfaction of basic needs is not self-reliance. It may be to "serve the people," but it is not to "trust the people"—to use the Chinese jargon. Self-reliance ultimately means that the society is organized in such a way that the masses arrive at self-fulfillment through self-reliance—in participation with others in the same situation (p. 401).

This, undoubtedly, is an idealistic proposition. Galtung himself has pointed out that there is as much economics as there is psychopolitics involved. This fourth approach to development discourages the widespread tendency in developing countries to imitate the goals and strategies of Western countries and to engage in the impossible task of catching up. Instead, it urges a radical rethinking of the issues and implications of development.

We can now examine the Sarvodaya Movement of Sri Lanka against this background. Clearly, its philosophy of development conforms to the fourth approach to development. It is based on self-reliance, self-development, grassroots development, popular participation, maintenance of the ecological balance, and the importance of culture in social development—ideals espoused by those who advocate the fourth approach to development.

The concept of development promoted by the Sarvodaya Movement centers on the individual. He should have a precise notion as to how best to liberate himself, his community, and his nation, and for what reasons. The philosophy of Sarvodaya seeks to achieve this liberation at two levels. As Ariyaratne (n.d.) the leader of this movement says:

> First, wither one's own mind or thinking processes there are certain defilements one has to recognize and strive to cleanse. Second, one has to recognize that there are unjust and immoral socioeconomic chairs which keep the vast majority of people enslaved. Thus, a dual revolution pertaining to an individual's mental make-up and to the social environment in which he lives is kept formost in the Sarvodaya Shramadana worker's mind and behavior (p. 47).

In other words, the aim of Sarvodaya is in keeping with the message of the Buddha to cleanse one's mind of the impurities of greed, anger, ignorance, etc. that act as obstacles to the achievement of one's own liberation as well as that of others.

According to Ariyaratne, the Sarvodaya Movement of Sri Lanka operates at three levels: education, development, and participation. Through the process of *shramadana* (voluntary donation of labor) and the acts of working together and sharing it entails, a new educational re-awakening process is set in motion. This process leads to the Sarvodaya village reawakening and development program, resulting in the people's participation in the decision-making process of the development program. Popular participation in the process helps to engender a path of liberation that is essentially non-violent in character.

In the various activities of the Sarvodaya, four principles pertaining to the development of the personality are brought to the participants. These four principles, taken from the teachings of the Buddha, are *metta* (having kindness), *karuna* (compassion), *mudita* (sympathetic joy) and *upekkha* (equanimity). The development of these principles or habits of mind are essential for purposeful and harmonious living. Metta is seen as the frame of mind that instigates one to work with love and kindness to everyone. Karuna is the frame of mind that promotes the welfare of others and helps them to overcome suffering. Mudita is the sense of joy experienced when working with others and making them happy. Upekkha is the feeling of equanimity born of a well-integrated personality which enables people to encounter joy and sorrow, triumph and defeat with composure.

Sarvodaya is concerned not only with the individual; it is equally interested in the group or the community. Here again, there are four important Buddhist principles that should guide group behavior: *dana* (sharing), *priyavacana* (pleasant language), *artha charya* (wholesome activity), and *samanathmatah* (non-partisanship).

How these principles adhered to by the Sarvodaya Movement in Sri Lanka are actually put into practice can best be seen in *shramadana* or labor-donating camps. These camps promote such diverse village welfare activities as cutting roads, repairing and constructing irrigation canals and waterways, clearing land for agriculture, construction of schools and community centers, and rural housing schemes. The leaders maintain that these camps constitute a very important educational experience for the participants, with three significant benefits. First, they provide a wonderful opportunity for rural and urban people to encounter each other in a mutually useful way. This strengthens reciprocity of understanding and the pursuit of common goals. Second, these camps have the salutary effect of giving the peasants a new sense of purpose, and of the importance of self-reliance and self-development. For generations these people have led lives of total subservience and dependence. Third, the shramadana camps create new village leadership transcending caste, religious, and political barriers, and ready to address questions of social development.

How these shramadana camps help to achieve the objectives of personality awakening and group awakening promoted by the Sarvodaya Movement can be seen from the following chart (Kantowsky, 1980):

Personality and Group Awakening Through Shramadana

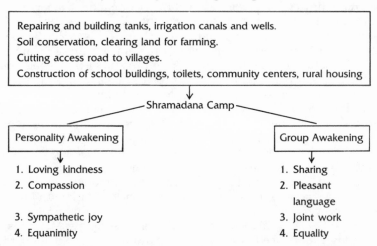

The architects of the Sarvodaya Movement of Sri Lanka envision a new social order based on Buddhist values. It is an attempt to go forward by drawing on the essence of the past. The present social order consists of an odd mixture of pre-colonial and post-colonial values, with only scant attention being paid to coherence and relevance. Hence, there is a need to create a new social order based on essential features of traditional culture. The essence of this new social order can be represented as follows (Kantowsky, 1980, p. 49):

PRESENT SOCIAL ORDER	THE NEW SOCIAL ORDER
1. Lack of emphasis on self-knowledge and self-reliance	1. Emphasis on self-knowledge and self-reliance
2. Respect for wealth, power status	2. Respect for wisdom, virtue and moral consciousness
3. Emphasis on greed and competition	3. Emphasis on sharing and cooperation
4. Capitalist economy, bureaucracy and party politics determining social forces	4. Social trusteeship economy, people's participation and party-free politics determining social forces
5. Encourages fragmentation of society along race, caste, religious and party lines	5. Encourages a unity that transcends race, caste, religious, political parties, etc.

6. Import-export economy based on production of commodities. Legacy of colonial experience
7. Dependence on capital-intensive large-scale organizations. Wastage of human labor. Environmental pollution.
8. Village subservient to city. Migration to urban areas. Social unrest.
9. Laws of punishment, instruments of law enforcement state power increase. Righteous living and power of people diminish.

6. Self-sufficient economy based on primary needs of the people
7. Dependence on small scale organizations. Utilization of human labor. Environmental pollution minimized.
8. Balanced rural and urban growth.

9. Laws of righteousness prevail. People powerful.

Quite obviously, there is a certain simple-minded optimism about this new social order. However, it does capture the idealism and sense of moral purpose that characterize the Sarvodaya Movement.

This concept of development and the new ensuing social order is closely allied to a concept of communication. It is, what I would call, the Buddhist concept of communication. The essence of this can best be understood when we place it against the typical Western or Aristotelian model. In the Aristotelian notion of communication the idea of manipulation is central. In the Buddhist model, however, the notions of sharing and mutuality are important. The differences between the two models can be schematically represented as follows:

ARISTOTELIAN MODEL	BUDDHIST MODEL
1. Emphasis on communicator	1. Emphasis on receiver
2. Influence a key notion	2. Understanding a key notion
3. Focus on control	3. Focus on choice
4. Emphasis on outward process	4. Emphasis on both outward and inward processes
5. Relationship between communicator and receiver asymmetrical	5. Relationship between communication and receiver symmetrical
6. Stress on intellect	6. Stress on empathy

This vision of society projected by the Sarvodaya Movement seems a logical extension of the Buddhist concept of communication.

Despite its remarkable success, the forward march of the Sarvodaya Movement was not easy. It encountered numerous obstacles—economic, social, and political. Today it is a vital force in the country. Development scholars who are showing a greater and greater interest in alternative paradigms are paying very close attention to the Sarvodaya

Movement. As pointed out by Kantowsky, the most distinctive aspect of this movement is that it provides rural youth with section-oriented programs securely based on indigenous cultural values, attitudes, and lifestyles.

The Sarvodaya Movement of Sri Lanka, then, can be taken as a very innovative approach to social development. Its real strength lies in the way it has deployed traditional Buddhist values and philosophy of communication to meet contemporary individual and societal needs. At the same time, this voluntary movement, which places so much emphasis on the notion of self-sufficiency and self-reliance, also calls attention to some structural constraints with which such a movement must contend. I wish to point out three main constraints.

First, the question of self-reliance and the maximum use of local resources, indeed one of the main objectives of the Sarvodaya Movement, is important. The achievement of this objective clearly requires a high degree of decentralized planning and management. However, in the case of the Sri Lanka Sarvodaya Movement, the important policy and program decisions are still made at the central headquarters near Colombo, and regional centers are usually guided by the central program coordinators. This has the adverse effect of discouraging grassroots initiative.

Second, the Sarvodaya Movement is a voluntary organization. It has to work out a meaningful policy of action with the national government which, while helping to lighten logistical burdens, will not in any way compromise its avowed principles. As one commentator points out, the Sarvodaya Movement is subject to obious limitations of resources, authority, and responsibility in pursuing an integrated development strategy (Ahmed, 1980). The role that it can most usefully play is to help build the institutional structures for participation of local people and mobilization of local resources. Local government institutions supported by appropriate national policies and agencies must bear the burden of carrying out the development programs. This calls for a carefully formulated plan of cooperative action with the government without getting involved in national politics.

Third, before embarking on an ambitious program of expansion, the Sarvodaya Movement would be well-advised to consolidate its current gains. The leadership should embark on a consolidation program to bring the present 300 or more villages with the Sarvodaya organizational structure to a minimum level of performance before new village organizations are set up. After all, people will judge the success of the Movement and agree to cooperate with it only on the basis of achieved success, rather than expressed hopes (Ahmed, 1980).

These limitations are associated primarily with the logistical and operational sphere and in no way spring from the movement's central philosophy.

The Sarvodaya Shramadana Movement of Sri Lanka presents a very exciting approach to Third World development. Instead of blindly imitating Western–constructed scenarios the architects of this movement have sought to envision an alternative path to development drawing on the deepest currents of the culture of Sri Lanka.

REFERENCES

Ahmed, M. (1980). "Introduction in the Sarvodaya Movement: Self-help Rural Development in Sri Landa." In M. H. Coombs (ed.), *Meeting the Basic Needs of the Rural Poor*. New York: Pergamon.

Aristotle. (1954). *Rhetoric*, trans. R. W. Roberts, New York: Random House Inc.

Ariyaratne, A. T. (n.d.). *Collected Works* (Vol. 1). Colombo: Sarvodaya Research Centre.

Berlo, David K. (1977). "Communication as Process: Review and Commentary." *Communication Yearbook*, 1, 11–27.

Galtung, J. (1980). *The True Worlds: A Transnational Perspective*. New York: Free Press.

Kantowsky, D. (1980). *Sarvodaya: The Other Development*. New Delhi: Vikas Publishing House.

Lerner, David. (1964). *The Passing of Traditional Society*. New York: Free Press.

Nordenstreng, Kaarle, and Schiller, Herbert I. (1979). *National Sovereignty and International Communication*. Norwood: Ablex.

The Progress Report of the Sarvodaya Movement, 1978.

Pye, Lucian W. (1963). *Communication and Political Development*. Princeton: Princeton University Press.

Ratnapala, N. (n.d.) *Study Service in Sarvodaya*. Colombo: Sarvodaya Research Centre.

Rogers, Everett M. (1976). *Communication and Development*. Beverly Hills: Sage.

Rogers, Everett M., and F. F. Shoemaker (1971). *Communication of Innovations: A Cross-Cultural Approach*. New York: Free Press.

Rostow, W. W. (1960). *The Stages of Economic Growth: A Non-Communist Manifesto*. New York: Cambridge University Press.

Schramm, Wilbur. (1964). *Mass Media and National Development*. Stanford: Stanford University Press.

Seers, D. (1969). "The Meaning of Development." *International Development Review*, 11(4), 2–6.

4

Philippine Theatre Arts as Development Communication

Victor Valbuena

"One of the main functions of the arts as communication is to transmit and reinforce beliefs, custom and values. In some art traditions this function may be extended to instruction or propaganda."

Ralph L. Beals

With the change in the political structure of the Philippines in 1972 came a change in the communication system, particularly in the operation and utilization of the various communication media. An ideology was imposed on the communication system, leading to a redirection of the media from predominantly entertainment to information, education, and propaganda as well. This ideology demanded the effective marshalling of all available resources and services in support of the country's development plans. Local development planners recognized that communication, as an intensified and organized activity, is a resource with great potential to rally popular support and positive action toward national development goals. Therefore, a policy of communication for national development must be the main thrust of the country's communication network if it is to be relevant in shaping the Philippine future.

The *theatre arts,* as a medium and as part of the total communication system, must assume a larger dimension and play a more challenging role, directed towards a more meaningful realization of its potential.

Conceptual Framework

The concept of using theatre arts as a channel for development-oriented communications derives from a synthesis of the basic philosophy of development communication as stated by Quebral (1972), Jamias (1973,

1975), Mercado (1976), and Braid (1979). Quebral defines development communication as the "art and sciences of human communication applied to the speedy transformation of a country and the mass of its people from poverty to a dynamic state of economic growth that makes possible equality and the larger fulfillment of the human potential." Jamias categorically states the major ideas that characterize development communication: it is purposive, value-laden, and pragmatic. Thus, the results of development communication should be judged by criteria determined by the communicator according to specific behavioral objectives.

Mercado defines development communication as an "incremental process which starts with the diffusion of new information and technology which stimulate people to bring about conditions in the environment favorable to maximum productivity and the improvement of the general well being." Braid says that development communication requires communication personnel to go beyond their traditional roles: "The communicator's role will be that of enabling people to express their aspirations through available media and to assist them in attaining greater productivity."

Common to all of these definitions is the purposive nature of communication—its intent to influence knowledge, attitude, and behavior with the goal of improving the quality of human life. It is assumed that information, instruction, and persuasive or motivational communication are carefully planned inputs of development. Invariably, a multi-channel approach is employed with the various forms of theatre arts fitting into the whole scheme of communication strategy. Theatre can be utilized as a medium for transmitting and reinforcing messages to specific groups of audiences, so that they learn to consciously and actively participate in the attainment of national development objectives which contribute to their general well-being and the improvement of their environment.

Theatre Arts as Development Communication

In 1979, the present author conducted a study (Valbuena, 1980), demonstrating that during the period between 1972 and 1979 the various forms of theatre arts were used extensively as a development communication channel in the Philippines.

Specifically, the study sought to answer the following questions:

1. What forms of theatre arts have been utilized as channels for development communication in the Philippines?
2. What has been the extent of utilization? Have these forms been integrated with and/or extended through other communication media to support national development programs?

3. What has been the impact on the achievement of national development goals?
4. What are the prospects for further development of these theatre art forms to fully maximize their value in national development?

The study was based on surveys, case studies, document analysis, and participant observation. It led to the conclusion that, indeed, over the past eight years, there has been extensive utilization of various forms of theatre arts in the Philippines as a channel for development communication. The effectiveness of individual agencies varied but the overall influence was extensive.

Between 1972 and 1979 at least seven existing forms of theatre arts in the Philippines were demonstrated as viable channels for development communication: drama, the *zarzuela*, the *cancionan*, the *balagtasan*, the *balitao*, the *bantayonon*, and the puppet theatre.

Drama. Performances of one-act plays, usually of the soap opera type, are standard offerings in many Philippine town fiestas. Plays with moral lessons are favorites of Filipino audiences, especially in the rural areas. Drama has a more serious function than mere entertainment in the Philippines. Watching a drama presentation is an opportunity for gaining new insights into life, for learning lessons about man's relationships, and their implications for personal as well as communal welfare. Thus, standard plots of many Philippine dramas revolve around a wayward youth who returns to his family; a philandering husband who returns to his wife and family; a rich landlord and the poor, exploited tenant. There is conflict between the young and the old, between new, emerging values and age-old, traditional behavior patterns.

A performance provides an opportunity for the audience to hear the message of the playwright, who assumes the important social role of critic and teacher (Bonifacio, 1976).

Zarzuela. The zarzuela is a musical play similar to light opera. The Filipino zarzuela has its roots in the Spanish zarzuelas—simple, comic operas dealing with the manners, customs, and foibles of different segments of Spanish society. The zarzuela is always accompanied by dances and songs, making the play a type of musical.

The main appeal of the zarzuela lies in the satire and the biting social criticism underlying the sharp, witty, humorous, and often earthy language of the dialogue. "The musical score and the lyrics give flavor to the zarzuela, so much so, that the songwriter or composer is as imporant as the playwright, if he is not himself both; and a script is often built around a musical score" (Coseteng and Nemenzo, 1975).

The home-spun wisdom, common problems, catchy tunes, lively dances, and attractive sets immediately involve the audience in the zarzuela. There is instant rapport, something not as possible with more sophisticated dramas and audiences.

The *zarzuela* has built-in originality and versatility. It is a flexible and dynamic dramatic form with local situations and issues, ordinary characters, familiar problems, and native songs and dances. The acceptability and versatility of the zarzuela as propaganda in drama form were apparent during the Revolution against Spain in 1896, against the United States in 1898, and in the struggle against the American occupation at the turn of the century (Bonifacio, 1972). The zarzuela is easily updated and the form can just as easily clothe the theme.

Although retaining the basic elements of the Spanish model, the Filipino zarzuela has developed into a full-blown, three-act melodrama. It may border on sentimentality, but it is complex in theme, plot, and characterization.

The play centers mainly on the family, and the conflict is usually due to familial and social relationships, romantic love, or economic difficulties. The values, morals, and social traditions of the middle class prevail in spite of all the action. The Filipino zarzuela has a variety of topics: dowry, capital and labor, cockfighting, the trade monopoly of the Chinese, the corruption of native politicians, and native customs (Edades, 1956). Its themes include: relationships between husband and wife and between in-laws; the love between young master and servant girl; between rich boy and poor girl, and vice versa; and, the conflict between young and old. All these are favorite topics of the zarzuela.

Cancionan. Very popular in the Ilocoa Region, the cancionan is a form of argumentation in song and verse. It is a usual feature in town fiestas, a contest that pits male against female in argument on any topic. In many instances, it appears as a double bill or an intermission number in zarzuela presentations. The cancionan uses wit, humor, irony, and satire as natural components preventing it from becoming a dull musical contest. It has remained a popular medium because it lends itself to any topic and provokes the audience to take sides.

Balagtasan. This is a poetic debate between two protagonists using rhythmic colorful language, with humor, satire, and irony. It is a popular form in the Tagalog Region. The balagtasan can provoke, not only arguments, but it also generates thinking and influence for the audience has to make a choice. The emotion that the *balagtasan* arouses is very much a part of the reaction of the audience.

Balagtasan can lend itself to any topic, issue, idea or sentiment, provided an opposing view (or several opposing views) exists, as it invariably does. Romantic, domestic, religious, ethical, political, or economic matters can be taken up in a balagtasan. Subjects range from ordinary, everyday problems to leftist sentiments and most controversial topics. In fact, the strength of the balagtasan is in argument and thought, giving it a directness which the zarzuela or the conventional drama could not approach.

Although the balagtasan is essentially a debate, it is invested with a sense of drama because of the fast and sharp exchange in the arguments between the protagonists which gives it an impression of a dialogue, perhaps planned, but certainly well-structured, compact, and rich. It is the kind of dialogue which demands the full concentration of the audience, broken only when the audience responds by applauding a protagonist who has won a point during the course of the argument or who has parried a counter-argument with a quick turn of wit and speech (Coseteng and Nemenzo, 1975).

Balitao. The balitao is a courtship-debate in song and dance, almost always extemporaneously performed by a man and a woman. The man presses his suit, and the woman, out of modesty, declines his advances and offers resistance to his sweet songs by singing and dancing her objections. In times past, at the end of a hard day's work in the fields, especially during the planting or harvest season, the young men and women would gather and perform the balitao to entertain themselves. They would either divide into two groups, male and female, and sing the debate in chorus; or select a boy and a girl who would play the balitao to the cheers and clapping of hands and laughter of the audience whenever one contestant had made a verbal thrust or a sharp retort.

According to Coseteng and Nemenzo (1975), although the subject matter of the balitao is mainly about love and courtship, it may have variations which are interspersed with other topics. The elaborations and digressions of the debate involve the ability, intelligence, and wit of the performers, and how well and fast they can construct short verses for repartee. Tradition, history, religion, customs, and sociocultural values can all be used in advancing an argument, pressing a point, or in challenging or warding off an opponent's argument. At the end, resolution may come when the girl accepts the suitor's proposal, but with the promises she has exacted. Because of the girl's ability and wit, she may succeed at other times in warding off the suitor and win the argument. The audience and the occasion may decide the subject matter of a balitao.

Fortunately, the balitao has retained its abundance of wit, quick repartee, and humor reflecting traditional beliefs and practices. It also contains the omnipresent moral lessons. Allusions, suggestions, comparisons, and other figures of speech are used often in appeals to both the emotion and the intellect. Strong sexual connotations bordering on the lewd and obscene are usually present, depending on the audience (Gutierrez, 1961).

Bantayonon. Another poetic debate form found in the Christian areas of Mindanao, the bantayonon usually focuses on love, courtship, and marriage. Today, however, public affairs and other popular current issues are integrated into the bantayonon.

Puppet Theatre. Puppetry is a prevalent art form in Asia. At one time there was a type of shadow puppet play in the Philippines called *carillos,* akin to the Indonesian *wayang.* Over the years, however, the tradition of the carillos was lost. In its place came the more colorful and popular hand or rod puppets now used in the development communication activities of at least four nationwide institutions in the country.

Forms of Theatre Arts Used. Organizations seem to prefer the use of drama and musical plays in their communication campaigns. For example, the Commission on Population and the University of the Philippines are noted for their pioneering efforts in using the Ilocano *cancionan,* the Tagalog *balagtasan,* and the Visayan *balitao* to support popular education and promote family planning. The Mindanao State University Sining Kambayoka use the Maranao *bayok* in its theatrical productions. The Ministry of Public Information encourages the use of the *bantayonon* as part of its theatre activities in Mindanao. The National Media Production Center and Catholic Relief Services are proponents of puppet theatre in development.

Much more can be done to promote greater utilization and popularization of these media forms. For example, they could be integrated with the more technologically-oriented media of radio, television, and the like thus expanding their audience. But efforts have been limited in this aspect of theatre arts utilization.

Very few institutions have made either quantitative or qualitative measures of the impact of theatre arts as development communication. Available findings, nevertheless, support the assumption that theater presentations have an impact, not only in terms of drawing crowds, but, more important, on educational attitudes, and on target audiences.

The lack of impact measurement is due to the inadequate recording and documentation by development agencies of data relevant to the presentation of theatre arts materials. There is a need for orienting the development agencies, in both the government and private sector, on the importance of maintaining an accurate record of significant events. The value of this material in planning and enriching the communication programs of other agencies, is obvious.

Nineteen of twenty-four respondent organizations in the survey have used theatre arts as a means of promoting their particular programs. These include four colleges, three foundations, one educational theater group, one private family planning agency, one religious agency, one government commission, and one government media office. In addition, seven government ministries have theatrical fare at one time or another used to carry their messages to target audiences: the Ministries of Agrarian Reform, Education and Culture, Human Settlements, Labor,

Natural Resources, Public Information, and Tourism. These ministries do not implement these theatre activities directly, but through affiliated or contracted agencies, a number of which belong to the group of other respondents in this survey.

For example, the Ministry of Agrarian Reform has contracted with the University of the East, a private university in Manila, for the presentation of "Ang Bagong Pilipina," a contemporary zarzuela on land reform by Ruben Vega, a local writer. The Ministry of Education and Culture has linked up with the Dangerous Drugs Board and the schools through the Ministry's Youth Civic Action Program (YCAP) Coordinating Center to promote its campaign against drug abuse. The Ministry of Labor has, from time to time, used the resources of La Tondena Incorporada Workers Theatre group to present plays on family planning. The Ministry of Natural Resources has contracted with the Mindanao State University (MSU), Sining Kambayoka to present "Ambon, Ulan, Baha," a contemporary zarzuela on the ills of forest denudation. The Ministry of Public Information has launched its "Movement for Cultural Revival," and, through its regional offices and other affiliate groups, has presented plays with development themes.

Of the other respondent organizations, the Commission on Population, the Population Center Foundation, the Family Planning Organization of the Philippines, the University of the Philippines Institute of Mass Communication, and the Capiz Institute of Technology have utilized theatre arts to promote family planning; as have the National Nutrition Council and Catholic Relief Services in the area of nutrition education.

The Ministries of Human Settlements and Tourism do not deliberately attempt, however, to clarify for the local people the significance of certain priority development programs. At best, their theatre presentations may be classified as cultural fare intended to enrich but not necessarily to enlighten.

The Zarzuela Foundation of the Philippines and the Philippine Educational Theatre Association (PETA) use theatre for carrying out their objectives. The Zarzuela Foundation has presented a series of contemporary musical dramas on family planning, nutrition, and land reform. PETA has also presented a family planning drama and has been used by the National Media Production Center (NMPC) and the Population Center Foundation/Development Theatre Program (PCF/DTP) to conduct theatre workshops which call for the integration of development-oriented messages in their script writing classes.

The NMPC, through a number of its offices, uses theatre activities to support the government's population, nutrition, and agrarian reform programs. The Communication Foundation for Asia cooperates with the NMPC in conducting workshops on the use of theatre arts for development. Mindanao State University implements development theatre activities through its Sining Kambayoka theatre group.

Rational for the Use of Theater Arts

Organizations that have tried theater arts for communication purposes agree that they are effective in disseminating concepts and information geared towards development, particularly because they have wide popular appeal and encourage mass participation. The general opinion is that the use of theatre for disseminating information, particularly at the grassroots level, is very effective.

For agencies like the Commission on Population, theater and drama are perceived to have certain advantages over more modern media. For them, theater is relevant and timely and audiences identify more closely with it than they do with film.

Communication Purposes. Many respondent organizations maintain that their utilization of theatre arts is aimed at dissemination of information and motivation. Theatre is used to create awareness of certain development programs and their implementation, as well as to persuade people to pursue the course of action recommended by these programs.

Extent of Utilization. Nationwide, the utilization of theatre arts for development communication has, to an appreciable extent, been institutionalized.

This is evidenced by the system-wide Development Theater Program for Drug Abuse Prevention and Family Planning of the Ministry of Education and Culture (MEC). The MEC reported at least one development theater project under this program, plus the individual theater projects of particular schools.

The National Media Production Center (NMPC)[1] covers the entire country, except Mindanao, through its *Teatro Obrero* and *Puppet Theatre.* The Teatro has a network of community theatre groups where members are laborers, factory workers (*obreros*), and students. The Puppet Theater is based in the Metro Manila Area, but trains pupeteers—teachers and students—to perform outside the metropolitan area. Both groups present plays and musicals on land reform, nutrition, family planning, and health and environmental sanitation.

Similarly, the Ministry of Public Information covers the country with its own network of communicy theatre associations whose presentations focus on such subjects as youth development, national identity, nutrition, and family planning.

There are strong indications that this institutionalization will grow. For instance, the impact of theatre arts in development communication made by the Commission on Population includes rural theatre and folk media in the POPCOM Five–Year Information–Education–Commu-

---

[1]Since 1981 the National Media Production Center and the Ministry of Public Information have been merged into what is now known as the Office of Media Affairs.

nication Plan. Similarly, the National Economic and Development Authority's Five–Year Plan for 1983–1987 will adopt both traditional and contemporary media in educational development programs to suit the cultural requirements of the community.

Source of Content Materials. The content of the theatrical projects of these organizations comes from their staff writers, commissioned non-staff writers, or students.

Seven government offices have opted for commissioned non-staff writers to develop dramas or scripts for folk media presentations. POP-COM, for instance, commissioned existing theatre groups to develop materials for its sponsored projects. The Ministry of Agrarian Reform commissioned Ruben Vega, a local writer, for its zarzuela production on land reform, "Ang Bagong Pilipina;" while the Ministry of Natural Resources asked the MSU Sining Kambayoka to produce its "Ambon, Ulan, Baha." The NMPC requested PETA to develop its family planning play, "Itay, Kain na Tayo;" while the Zarzuela Foundation of the Philippines commissioned two noted Filipino musical artists to write a series of family planning zarzuelas at Luneta Park.

While the NMPC resorted to outside assistance for its family planning play, it currently relies on resident talent to develop materials for other productions. Materials for the puppet theatre are developed by its Nutrition Communication Office as well as by the production staff of the puppet theatre group. Materials for other theater productions are developed by NMPC's Teatro Obrero and its resident theater director, Mag Cruz Hatol, as well as other theater members. Similarly, the Catholic Relief Services relies on its own staff writers to develop materials for its puppet theatre.

Three organizations, the Ministry of Education and Culture, the Population Center Foundation, and the Philippine Maritime Institute Development Theatre, regularly use student-writers to create materials for their theatre presentations. The Capiz Institute of Technology uses students and local community members as sources of materials for its theater activities.

The other organizations use the combined services of staff writers and outside consultants in developing their materials.

Category and Sources of Support

Lack of funds has been a major problem for development planners in the use of folk media. The agencies in this survey provide varying forms of support, total or partial towards the support for the continued use of theatre arts for development communication. Support includes: funds for production, travel costs, board, and lodging for cast and crew; and, in some instances, free use of costumes and props, as well as the auditorium or performance halls.

The Ministry of Public Information provides support in the form of funds for production. Its regional offices also extend assistance in making arrangements for the use of rehearsal and performance halls which are either free or available at low rental rates. Similarly, the Ministry of Agrarian Reform provided funds for the production of its zarzuela, "Ang Bagong Pilipina," and for the rental of halls during its subsequent run after its premiere at the University of the East. When the Ministry of Natural Resources commissioned the MSU Sining Kambayoka to do its "Ambon, Ulan, Baha," it paid production expenses, travel, rental of performance halls, and took care of the cost of costumes and props.

Other agencies may obtain outside funding from international sources, or depend on affiliate agencies to support theatre outreach activities. They might also provide assistance in identifying performance outlets or the certification of accreditation for development theatre work as well as occasional technical assistance and guidance.

Category of Performers Employed

Employment of performers and production staff is often directly related to funding. The respondent organizations reported using a variety of strategies. Some hired professional actors; some employed amateurs; others used volunteers and local talent.

The Commission on Population has employed professional as well as amateur talent in their theatre projects. POPCOM has also relied on paid performers, who were not necessarily professional, as well as local talent available in the communities where theatre presentations are given. The Ministries of Agrarian Reform employed professional singers, teachers, and students for its "Dulaang Maharlika sa BLISS" project; the Ministry of Public Information utilized professional actors and students in its regional presentation.

The University of the Philippines used professionals for its IMC project on the balagtasan, paid local talent for the balitao project, and YCAP students for its rural theatre activity. The National Media Production Center tried professional actors for its "Itay, Kain na Tayo" production. It continues to utilize its staff artists and paid semi–professionals for its puppet theatre shows and students and indigenous talents for its Teatro Obrero activities. The Philippine Educational Theatre Association continues to employ professional actors and students in its theatre repertoire.

The Family Planning Organization of the Philippines used three categories of performers for its folk media project: paid staff who participated in the production, volunteers, and indigenous talents. The Catholic Relief Services uses only its own staff to manipulate the puppets for its nutrition puppet shows.

The same pattern is true for the production staff. For example, the Commission on Population used four types of production workers; professionals, amateurs, and aides who were not necessarily professional production workers as well as local talent from the towns in which the productions were mounted. Others also use students.

In some instances, production is carried out entirely by amateurs. The Ministry of Education and Culture, the Population Center Foundation, and the Philippine Maritime Institute use a corps of amateurs consisting mostly of students to handle production. The Capiz Institute of Technology uses volunteers for the production staff of its Kabalaka theatre group. La Tondena Incorporada theatre group of the Ministry of Labor also uses amateurs; the clerks and factory workers of La Tondena form the cast and crew of their theatre troupe.

Media Integration/Extension

Six organizations have made arrangements for the integration of development theater projects with other communication media. Most of the work involved taping folk shows.

The University of the Philippines/Institute of Mass Communication videotaped the balagtasan and balitao performances held in connection with its folk media project for possible television broadcasting. The Capiz Institute of Technology experimented with a radio broadcast of one of its Kabalaka Mobile Theatre presentations in Capiz. Similarly, the Family Planning Organization of the Philippines, folk media project in Bulacán taped one of its family planning skits and broadcast it over a regional station. One theatre performance in its Surigao project was recorded on slides and tape, but mainly for documentation purposes.

The Ministry of Natural Resources videotaped the performance of "Ambon, Ulan, Baha" and arranged a television broadcast of the zarzeula. NMPC has also videotaped some performances of its puppet theatre and has documented others via comprehensive photo coverage. In addition, it has telecast one puppet presentation. Very recently it telecast "Pamilya Dimasupil, Walang Makapipigil," a family planning comedy in the repertoire of NMPC's Teatro Obrero.

The Zarzuela Foundation of the Philippines videotaped some of its Luneta Park presentations. One particular family planning zarzuela, "Ang Binhi," was telecast twice over Armida Siguion Reyna's "Aawitan Kita," an award–winning cultural program.

Conclusion

Most of the above-mentioned programs were carried out in the mid-to-late 1970s. Overall, the study's results indicate a positive attitude on the part of the agencies and organizations regarding the use of theatre arts for development purposes. The use of theatre arts is particularly advantageous because of the lively context in which messages are transmitted and the flexibility allowed in reaching villages where electricity is lacking and the audience is minimally educated. This is where the theatre arts are particularly effective and efficient.

However, there are also problems. There is often a lack of funding, and, as a result, the quality of script and performances may be below standards. For example, the incorporation of development messages in plots is often unsophisticated. "Hard–sell" slogans and interference with the main plot are not unusual. Local needs and background are not always considered.

The study suggests that the organization and planning phases of theatre arts for development should be at the local level with support from the local government and institutions such as schools. Adequate research is also needed to ensure that the theatre art forms adopted are suited to the audience, locality, and region. An efficient audience feedback system is essential.

Despite these problems, the agencies that have used the theatre for development purposes are united in saying that prospects are very bright for further development of, and innovation in, the use of theatre arts.

REFERENCES

Bonifacio, Amelia L. (1972). *The Seditious Tagalog Playwrights: Early American Occupation.* Manila: Zarzuela Foundation of the Philippines.

Bonifacio, Amelia L. (1976). "The Social Role of Theatre in Asia." In *Literature and Society: Cross Cultural Perspectives* (The Proceedings of the Eleventh American Studies Seminar, October, Los Baños, Philippines).

Braid, Florangel Rosario. (1979). *Communication Strategies for Productivity Improvement.* Tokyo: Asian Productivity Organization.

Coseteng, Alicia M. L. and Gemma A. Nemenzo. (1975). *Folk Media in the Philippines: Their Extension and Integration with the Mass Media for Family Planning.* Quezon City: University of the Philippines Institute of Mass Communication.

Edades, Jean. (1956). "The Zarzuela and Propaganda," *Sunday Times Magazine* (Manila), *11*, (May 20) 30–31.

Gutierrez, Maria Colina. (1961). "The Cebuano Balitao and How It Mirrors Culture and Folklife." Cebu City: University of San Carlos.

Jamias, Juan. (1973). "The Philosophy of Development Communication," *Solidarity* (Manila), *8*(5), 29–34.

Jamias, Juan. (1975). "Development Communication." Concept Paper. (mimeographed.) University of Philippines, Los Baños, Philippines.

Mercado, Cesar M. (1976). "Communication for Human Development; Theory and Practice," Concept Paper. (typescript.) Quezon City, Institute of Mass Communication, University of the Philippines, Diliman, Philippines.

Quebral, Nora. (1972). "Development Communication." Concept Paper. (mimeographed.) University of the Philippines, Los Baños.

Valbuena, Victor T. (1980). "Philippine Theater Arts as Development Communication: Perspectives and Prospects." Ph.D. Dissertation. Centro Escolar University, Manila.

5

Using Traditional Communication for Development
Report of a Papua New Guinea Study and Pilot Project Outline

Tevia Abrams

Introduction

Traditional communication modes possess great potential for reaching and involving rural communities in social and economic development activities. The realization of this potential may, however, be hampered by planners or users misunderstanding both the real needs of the communities concerned and the sensitivities and cultural taboos associated with entertainment or performance elements of the traditional communication systems.

The Government of Papua New Guinea (PNG), aware of the possible dangers, and sensitive to the development needs of its own rural communities, initiated a brief field study in 1980 to explore the potential use of traditional or folk media and to develop a plan for a pilot project on the basis of the findings. While the findings are uniquely culture-specific, and the conclusions and observations not necessarily applicable to situations in other developing nations, the approach as outlined in this chapter may serve as an example of design and planning where rural communities are at the center of concern.

The objective of this chapter, therefore, is to report on the study of possible uses of traditional communication systems for development purposes in PNG.

Background

Papua New Guinea's population in mid-1981 was estimated at 3.3 million with a growth rate of 2.8%, calculated on the basis of a crude birth rate of 44 per thousand and a crude death rate of 16 per thousand (Population Reference Bureau, 1981). The growth rate is thus very high, and there are severe consequences for government planners attempting to cope with social welfare needs, with rural-to-urban population shifts, and with provision of adequate health services for dealing with malnutrition, family planning, maternal and child health care, and family health in general. Of special concern to health authorities is the extremely high infant mortality rate of 128 per thousand. Socially and economically (the annual gross national product is calculated at $780 per person per year), PNG ranks among the poorer nations of the Third World.

On the positive side, the economy is buoyed by some large-scale mining and cash-crop operations; however, most of the rural population relies on subsistence-level farming, fishing, or hunting. To a great extent, PNG is just beginning to emerge from its primitive state.

The indicators of demographic and economic trends provide strong justification for the government's well-intentioned and ambitious development programs. If these efforts are to succeed, severe impediments need to be surmounted. First and foremost is the cruel geographical factor: the mainland is cut through its mid-section by a heavily forested, mountain spine that divides the northern and southern regions and that has slowed and considerably extended every attempt to develop normal surface transportation. Costly air services have been established as a major physical linking system. The rough terrain throughout the mainland and in the far-flung islands has further complicated local-level action programs in the agricultural and industrial sectors.

While primary education is now available to most children, few who enter the school system go on to secondary schools. Often frustrated, those who leave school tend increasingly to break out of traditional, clan-centered relationships and to develop disruptive behavior patterns that are as much a source of concern to village elders as they are to social planners.

PNG's cultural fragmentation, however, represents the greatest obstacle to development and modernization. There are estimated to be in excess of 720 languages and more than 1,000 tribes. The nearest thing to a common or linking language is Pidgin, but its coverage does not reach across the country—a fact which has plagued mass-media communication activities supporting the development effort. Since literacy rates are very low, print media have little impact upon the population, and the profusion of languages makes the electronic media appear unequal to the task.

The government views the impediments to effective communication with its people with growing concern, and it is actively seeking alternative approaches. One promising area of exploration is the use of traditional communication systems. The country is richly endowed with such systems. It is known, for example, that many tribes in the rural areas still hold beliefs in the spirit world—in ghosts and ancestral spirits—and that elaborate ceremonies and rituals are performed to placate evil spirits or praise good ones. Attention, however, has focused upon the more secular and entertaining traditions, including costumed performances in story, song, dance, and drama as well as in group *singsings.*

Government interest in the potential uses of traditional communication systems was kindled, in part, by the experimental work of some of the existing theatre companies—The National Theatre Company, the Raun Traveling Theatre, and the Raun Isi Traveling Theatre, among others—that have dedicated themselves to building cultural identity through preservation of PNG performance traditions and the development of new forms. In large measures, however, the government was especially impressed by the highly articulated perceptions about the communication needs in the country appearing in *Report of the Review of Information Services* (PNG Information Review Committee, 1979, pp. 74–77, 100). In particular, the report called attention to the heretofore "disproportionate concern with technology-oriented media" aimed at literate, urbanized audiences while rural populations were virtually ignored. The report developed a set of principles of communication, several of which refer to the rights of citizens for access to information and to shared communication processes and systems, including traditional face-to-face forms in their indigenous languages.

In 1980, at the invitation of UNESCO and the government of PNG, I undertook a month-long survey of selected villages in five provinces to identify those forms of performance which could be used as channels for development-oriented communication. Among the conclusions was a suggestion that elements of ceremonies and singsings, along with other traditional forms of village-level communication, might be used to tap their potential roles as message-carriers to and from the grass roots of the country (Abrams, 1981). This decentralized approach was seen as one way of intensifying the development dialogue between villages and local government extension workers and, therefore, of helping to overcome the linguistic barriers to communication. It was also seen as a restorative activity through which renewed life would be infused into certain dying performance traditions. Highlights of the study, including notes on methodology and the project outline, form the substance of this chapter.

TRADITIONAL COMMUNICATION SYSTEMS

Selected Forms

Performance-based communication forms in five provinces of Papua New Guinea were selected by villagers themselves. This approach to the selection process had advantages in that it eliminated taboo-laden forms which could not, obviously, be considered useful for secular, development-oriented work.

Storytelling as a communication medium or channel is an important form. Villagers expressed a preference for its use. The teller is an elderly person with much authority and to whom much respect is paid. Methods and traditions of presentation may vary according to custom in each village and within each language grouping, but in all cases, the storyteller colors the presentation with his personal style of interpretation, giving life to the form. Some performers are so persuasive that listeners have been known to take up the tale in song themselves.

Audiences for storytelling may be small groups within a village, an entire village of hundreds, or even several visiting village populations numbering over a thousand persons.

Traditionally, the storyteller is the person who passes on the knowledge and lore of his people. The form has enormous potential for development-oriented work; it is certainly seen within the country as a tool more powerful than the group singsing, which appears to be losing its impact in some areas, notably in East Sepik Province.

Storytelling, it appeared, might easily be combined with other elements of the traditional singsing in a government-sponsored effort to generate awareness and development consciousness among the people. The combination of performance elements could help strengthen and preserve those forms which appear to be dying out.

Singing is another important medium. Songs are produced in profusion all over the country. There are special songs for the dead and others for feasts and celebrations. There are secret compositions for recalling the genealogy of particular clans, and not-so-secret ones for everyday use or for extolling the virtues of love. Spirit worship may often be enshrined by song, and menial occupations such as gardening or fishing may be lifted to exalted planes by different songs with different rhythms.

Many of these song forms, their melodies and special rhythms, represent potentially useful traditional media channels to the rural development communicator. The *peroveta* song form in some villages of Central Province and the distinctive *geve* and *kasamba* forms found in areas of Northern Province were considered to be good material for such work, according to villagers interviewed. A rich field of research could be pursued if identification is made of such useful forms throughout the country. A sense of urgency might be added to this task, since a good many of the forms are dying out. Elders in a number of villages said that they would welcome experimental work as a means of restoring the forms and of acquainting the younger generation—the disaffected young school dropouts—with the elements of their own forgotten culture and with the life styles of their elders.

Dance is used to express some event, story, or state of feeling and it is almost always accompanied by singing. Dance is generally performed in groups and dancers are attired in traditional dress and decoration according to the region. Decoration is colorful and includes body paint, plumes, feathers, pigs' teeth, shells, and long leaves. Drums may provide the rhythm and pace for the dance. Dance-drama, the combination of many performing arts elements (singing, dancing, instrumental accompaniment, and mime), may be the highest achievement of PNG's traditional culture.

Traditional musical instruments in PNG include the *kundu* drum, the *garamut* slit drum, bamboo flute, Jew's harp, seedrattle, guitar (made traditionally), and conch shell. Use of these instruments, singly or in combination, varies from one region of the country to another. Instruments may accompany singing or dancing or both, providing distinctive traditional rhythms or melodies. The *garamut* not only produces the vigorous dance rhythms in Manus Island singsings but, for the dwindling numbers who remember, it can also be used in a telegraphic way to convey important messages over great distances.

The string band occupies a special place among the youth almost everywhere in the country. String bands are formed spontaneously in cities, towns, and even the remotest villages. Radio encourages this development and the National Broadcasting Commission devotes a good deal of air-time to promote the string band in different provinces and in different languages.

A band may be composed of a small group of, say, five guitarists who develop their own repertoire of borrowed, adapted, or new songs. Some competitions have resulted in new compositions of rare quality on selected themes, such as independence and love, but, for the large part, the string band is derivative of music from Western countries. With encouragement, however, the string band could become a potent form of expression, and it is worthy of being encouraged at the village-level, in such a way as to reduce the growing alienation between elders and youth. At present, the string band is seen by the village elders as the symbol of the breaking away from tradition by the young. Conceivably, village-level development efforts that involve traditional communication would need to ensure that the elders and the youth are associated with the task through the media which are closest to them.

The selected inventory of traditional media in the villages covered in the study also includes comical or satirical dramatic sketches and mime. Interestingly, most villages elders remember their parents and grandparents participating in short dramatic plays. But that tradition has largely disappeared and dramatic expression is now relegated to schoolchildren. (This was not, however, true of villages in Enga Province.) Most villagers expressed some interest in trying to revive this dramatic form. As for mime, it quickly appeared that it could not be separated from dance and dance-drama, or singsings, although it remains a distinctive element.

Methodology

In order to identify and analyze the most "useful-for-development" forms of performance, it was necessary to devise a reliable method of study. As it had been predetermined that over a month-long period I would visit some 20 villages in five provinces—Central, Enga, East Sepik, Manus, and Northern—a suitable questionnaire was needed. This was done with a view to the development of a reliable, if partial, inventory of forms. (From the start, however, it was evident that a complete inventory would require intensive field and library research over a period of years; my aim was, more modestly, to chart the direction such research might follow.)

The questions probed the villagers' views of the most *useful* forms of cultural expression, from varying perspectives: audience reach, popularity, flexibility in content-carrying capacity, availability of performers, and adaptability to integration with the mass media. The questionnaire also attempted to gauge interest in possible experimental activity, involving interaction between village performing artists and rural extension workers, to prepare informed presentations for wider groups of villagers in conjunction with demonstration programs on a variety of health, social welfare, and economic improvement topics.

Attention focused on the action-oriented potentials of the findings. It was evident that in the limited time available for the assignment, I could not pursue in depth the rich and complex fabric of cultural, linguistic, and spiritual traditions of the people in the villages to be visited. It was therefore left to the questionnaire to provide, in a two-hour session in each village, (it was impossible to allow more time than this) a result-oriented, if somewhat abstracted, profile of folk forms embedded in the active cultural life of the people.

Observations, on the manner and substance of the responses of villagers to question (as presented through interpreters) about the various folk forms served to qualify the validity of replies as finally translated into English. These observations were helpful in giving numerical weights to some of the findings.

The questionnaire was pretested in two villages in Central Province and the design was verified in follow-up discussions with government authorities, independent scholars, and the director of the PNG National Theatre Company. Minor modifications and additions were made as a result of the pretesting. With the assistance of national and provincial-level information officers, the questions were then posed to elders, village councillors, church leaders, women's club members, and other leaders in 17 villages of the other four selected provinces. (Often, sessions in villages occurred where whole populations became involved in a most democratic consensus-gathering process which provided truly collective responses.) Upon my return to Central Province toward the end of the assignment, a final questionnaire session was held in a village in the Port Moresby area, making a total of three villages sampled in Central Province and a total of 20 villages covered in the study.

The data from the completed questionnaire were then cross-checked and implications discussed with a variety of political, development-oriented, and academic authorities at both provincial and national levels. Results of the questionnaires were then charted and otherwise described and analyzed in a manner best calculated to interpret their usefulness.

The outcome of the study resulted in (a) the preparation of an inventory, with a profile of the characteristics of traditional forms of communication which might be used for development; (b) an outline of a two-year pilot project to generate information on folk media on a national scale and to develop pilot communication activities utilizing the most suitable forms, and (c) the identification of existing sources and documentation facilities relating to folk media in Papua New Guinea.

SELECTED FINDINGS

The following is a sampling of the substance and the form of presentation of the results of the inquiry from the findings in four villages of Enga Province. It should be noted that the findings were related to a follow-up action project which I had been asked by the government to design for the concluding section of my report.

Background Note (Enga Province)

Enga is a highland province with a population of 180,000. Enga language and its dialectal variations are spoken, or at least understood, by most people. Community life is so organized that a central area may serve as a base for group activities—schools, churches, clubs—while the majority of the population live in scattered hamlets.

Unifying links in Engan society have historical roots. Trade networks between the various clans or tribes fostered much contact and mobility, and the prevailing systems of exogamy and defense alliances (with periods of hostility followed inevitably by placating ceremonies) served as important cultural links. Periodic gift-giving cycles were also helpful in the development of reciprocal ties.

Wabag, the capital, is a fast developing town with a cultural center and a historical museum. The National Broadcasting Company has recently begun regular radio broadcasting in both Enga and Pidgin languages.

Many children who attend community schools continue on to high school. There are also vocational centers and adult education courses on a variety of subjects, ranging from literacy to cattle raising.

A strong nutrition program—a combined effort by the Departments of Health and Education—is designed to combat severe malnutrition through direct information campaigns. Community schools participate actively in this program.

The government believes that development is being hampered by the natural constraints posed by geography, notably the wet and mountainous terrain, and by the poor road network. Geography, among other factors, is hindering the government's efforts to deal with pressing problems such as high population growth, unfulfilled needs in health and education services, and lack of communication and transport facilities. Several airports serve the province as landing fields for the most urgently needed transportation links.

A strong traditional subsistence economy, based on growing vegetables and pig-raising, continues to sustain the Engas in their rural habitats; but the cultivation of coffee and pyrethuem flowers as cash crops is a new development in many villages. The introduction of the cash economy has also brought problems of social dislocation.

Questionnaire Findings (Enga Province)

The visit to Enga included discussions with provincial-level authorities and the administration of the folk media questionnaires in four villages.

Storytelling. This form should have great potential if illustrated with drawings or photos. Content would depend on the type of audience and age-group. For example, a poetic presentation could be made to adults only. Some singing may be involved at the conclusion of a session to reinforce an argument. The length of performance varies. The *tindi pii* variety, which is used for legends, may last from one to two hours; the *atome pii* variety, on historical events, might last an entire day. Stories can be told at any time; however, the time for the telling of legends is evening. The form is popoular throughout Enga.

Short, Amusing Skits or Dramas. Generally, those 21 and younger might volunteer to perform; however, if extension officers would assist in such activities, many adults would participate. Performance traditions and conventions are observed strictly—the artists take up positions in a line at a distance from their audience of about eight to twelve feet. There is no tradition of verbal interaction among characters; if action is called for, it is executed in mime. A performance might last for an hour. No musical instruments would be used and, in front of a mixed audience, men would assume all female roles. (Women are permitted to act only before audiences of their own sex.) Some taboos are observed. For example, girls would not be permitted to watch a demonstration of fighting. The form has a broad audience reach, and a tour of performances would be popular all over Enga; however, artists of one clan with enemies in other districts would have to be very selective about where to perform.

Mime. This is also popular, mainly among children. The central performer is a pretend deaf-mute. During interviews with villagers, however, it was impossible to verify the separate existence of such a form except as part of skits or dance-drama or of any general *singsing.*

Singing. Many song forms exist and some have been used to carry messages to the people about the importance of census activity in the province. Two song forms are the *tomo wee* and the *pasindia wee.* The first contains drawn-out notes with even melodic lines. It is performed on happy occasions, during rainy seasons, and in the evenings. The second form is sung at very high pitch and may be performed at any time. There is no instrumental accompaniment for these types of songs. Another form of singing is chanting, often dealing with lascivious subject-matter which is forbidden to children.

Dance-Drama or Singing and Dancing. There does not appear to be a formal kind of dance-drama; rather, there are song-and-dance types of performances, such as the *mali wee,* which is reserved for celebrations and other happy occasions. *Kundu* drumming provides distinctive rhythms for the male and female dancers standing in rows or circles.

String Bands. As explained earlier, the string band is the invention of the young. Good potential exists for developing special compositions relevant to contemporary issues.

Elders, church leaders, and others in Enga Province identified storytelling with illustrations as popular and useful performance-oriented folk media in development communication work. However, certain elements of these broadly-defined forms might not be suitable for a variety of reasons, including taboos; but sufficient scope exists for work within each of the categories described above. It should also be noted that a variety of folk forms are not included in this profile since they are not performance-oriented. Different strategies would be needed to codify their characteristics and usefulness for development communication activity. Examples of such forms are: the plastic arts (painting and wood sculpture); string configurations and the stories accompanying them; and the non-musical use of instruments (such as the *garamut* slit drum) for sending telegraphic-type messages over long distances.

In the four Engan villages radio was found to be practically non-existent as an information medium. A project involving live folk media would, therefore, be a valuable means of opening communication channels between government information personnel and the people. It could also be extended into, and integrated with, radio and with the portable videotape systems that are available in limited quantity for group discussion work at the village level.

PILOT PROJECT

From the findings of the five province village inquiries and other research undertaken as part of the 1980 study, I was able to draw up a detailed pilot project. Certain features of the project' outlines are described here to illustrate its evolution from the analysis of the data generated.

The long-range objective of the project is to strengthen traditional communication systems in rural Papua New Guinea in support of overall national development efforts. The more immediate objective was to combine research and pilot communication activities, especially those involving traditional media in rural Papua New Guinea. Specific project component objectives are listed below, more or less in chronological sequence:

1. To select a Project Steering Committee of three persons and a larger body to be known as a Project Advisory Committee.
2. To select and train (with the help of a short-term international consultant) a Project Director, whose duties would continue for an initial two-year period. Selection of the Project Director would be made by the government through the Advisory Committee.
3. To develop a *national* inventory of traditional media in rural areas by means of selection, training, and utilization of a full-time researcher for a two-year period. (This work would involve library research as well as extensive fieldwork.)
4. To launch action-oriented communication activities in pilot areas selected by the government, as well as to study their effectiveness.
5. To provide workshop training (with assistance of a short-term consultant) for provincial-level information liaison officers from the pilot areas, and to prepare them for working directly with village folk artists and extension personnel; and to provide training, as necessary, for extension personnel.
6. To provide, with assistance of the newly trained information liaison officers, workshop training in the selected villages for folk artists, and to involve development extension personnel in these workshops, as required.
7. To conduct baseline knowledge/attitude/practice surveys related to a number of development-related issues set by the government, to review the project at mid-term, and to carry out end-line evaluations of the activities in each pilot village to measure their relative effectiveness.
8. To integrate and extend the folk media activity into the mass media, where possible, for broadest possible outreach and, generally, to try to promote an integrated communication approach among ongoing vertical media programs at the local level.
9. To develop operating manuals for effective extension of the pilot program to other areas of the country.
10. To prepare a final report to the government, incorporating results of evaluations, and to make appropriate recommendations

about desirability and usefulness of continuing the activity for a
further period.

11. To make the findings known, at the close of the initial two-year
project period, to interested national and international organizations.

Institutional Framework

The project would be headed by a Project Director—a PNG national—
who would be administratively responsible to a designated government
body. The Project Director would be selected by a National Advisory
Committee made up of representatives of institutions and offices capable of providing helpful expertise, guidance, and direction.

The Steering Committee would develop the policy directions of the
projects, while the actual research and pilot activities in selected villages
would be carried out under the umbrella of the Information Liaison
Office in each province. It is presumed that prior arrangements would
have been made between the national and provincial authorities.

Description of Probable Project Activities

These activities may usefully be broken up into four main phases. The
first phase involves creation of the Steering and Advisory committees:
the immediate task of the former would be to seek suitable candidates
for the posts of Project Director and Project Researcher; the latter person
would be responsible for questions regarding content issues for the
village-level work program and other inputs that would help the project
attain its objectives.

During this phase, a suitable international expert would be selected for the proposed three-month consultancy. This expert would be
needed to run workshop training in theater-for-development activities
for selected groups of provincial-level Information Liaison Officers.

Phase two is characterized by training and other preparatory work.
The Project Director should now be recruited for an initial period of two
years. In consultation with the Steering and Advisory Committees, the
Director should establish the broad outlines of the proposed work program, as well as compose a precise job description. However, the specific details of the work would be defined and elaborated as the project
becomes operational.

After a brief period of orientation at the national level, the Project
Director would leave for a six-week study tour in Asia. Countries to be
visited should include Bangladesh, India, Indonesia, and Philippines,
all of which have mobilized some of their folk theatre traditions on
behalf of family planning and other development efforts.

The short-term international expert would reach PNG shortly after the Project Director returns from the study tour. Together, they would work to initiate program activities. The Project Researcher is also to be brought into the project at this time and, after a period of orientation, will begin the work.

The Project Researcher's task is to further develop and extend throughout PNG the inventory of traditional media forms (and their individual profiles and assessments for potential use in development programs), which the 1980 UNESCO report covered for just 20 villages in five of the provinces. The final result would be a national inventory. The work is needed less for the sake of pure scientific investigation than for the action-oriented pragmatic requirements of the Project Director, whose future program activities may depend upon it for effectiveness.

A national inventory should generate an organized body of knowledge about the many living folk forms throughout the country. It should provide systematized information about their formal structures, conventions of presentation (styles and techniques), normally accepted content, extent of audience reach, and other helpful details. The inventory should also include informed judgments about those forms which appear to offer good potential for use in development communication work—judgments about flexibility of form or ease of incorporation of development-oriented content without danger of overloading or otherwise destroying their cultural integrity. The completed inventory should also include recommendations on the extension of these folk of forms into the mass media for the broadest possible impact.

Finally, the task of the researcher is to determine, or at least to suggest, training needs for (a) communicators whose skills are needed at the local level in uses of folk media for development; (b) local-level extension workers, whose efforts are to be linked with those of the communicators; and, (c) village performers themselves, who would be involved as performing artists in subsequent project activity.

In research, attention would be drawn to the relevant participation development issues in each geographical area—family planning (in view of the high growth rates in many provinces); health care and nutrition; economic development activities using intermediate and fully developed technologies; integration of women and school dropouts in economic activity; cultural restoration; and political and legal education, among others. Some indication would be needed as to which kinds of messages or issues could be channeled through what traditional forms of communication in each of the regions studied.

Negotiations are to be undertaken with selected provincial authorities (maximum of five provinces at the start) for permission to proceed with village–level activity. Arrangements should be made to work with the Information Liaison Officer in each of the selected provinces. Appropriate development extension officers are also to be identified for later involvement in the pilot work. The Information Liaison Officers would, in effect, become the part-time extension agents or the staff for the pilot project.

The Training Workshop, for both the Liaison Information Officers and for the others involved at the local level, is important to the success of the entire project. It is to be planned by the visiting expert in conjunction with the Project Director and the Project Researcher. The Workshop would run for two weeks. Participants from the selected provinces should include the Information Liaison Officers and those development extension workers who could be useful in the overall program. PNG theater practitioners and national-level development officers should also attend the workshop . Workshop objectives should cover the following topics: demonstration of the potential use of traditional forms of communication in development programs, provision of practical training in organizing and executing such activities effectively at the local level, and in providing a forum for helpful exchange of ideas and for the identification of skills for possible future requirements.

Shortly after the completion of the Workshop, the expert will leave PNG. The project's operations will then systematically be followed up by the Project Director. This marks the end of phase two of the project.

Phase three features three distinct sets of activities leading to a mid-term review. These are: (a) conduct of baseline surveys in villages selected for pilot project work and follow-up evaluations as work is completed; (2) pursuit of actual pilot work in one or two villages in each of the selected provinces and, from this early experience, development of a draft manual as a guide for future activity on a wider scale; and, (c) continuation of the research work by the Project Researcher. The Project Director will need to encourage, guide, and personally supervise all three areas of work.

The Director should make frequent visits to the pilot work sites to boost the efforts of the Liaison Officers and others involved at provincial and local levels. The provincial Government Information Officer in each of the provinces concerned should also be requested to provide required guidance and assistance.

The work program within each village should be determined by the Project Director and the Liaison Officer. Suggestions, offered below, as to how such an activity *might* be conducted are based on the analysis of data generated from village questionnaires in the 1980 PNG study.

Selection of the first pilot village should be made from among those covered in the PNG report's inventory and assessment of "useful" traditional communication forms. Care should be exercised that the neediest of the villages listed be included in the experimental program of activities.

Having previously made suitable arrangements to link some development extension programs—say, family planning, fresh water program, involvement of women and school dropouts in income-generating activity, improved cash-crop production and marketing techniques and services, and application of intermediate technology information to a variety of village-based enterprises—with the proposed traditional media communication work in a certain village, the Information Liaison Officer will then familiarize himself with the suggestions in the UNESCO report regarding approaches to initial penetration of that village. The Officer would work with one village at a time and take on a second village only after a good program has been developed in the first.

The Liaison Officer should consult with the appropriate village elder, councillor, or church leader and try to make arrangements for workshop sessions with village folk media performers (or artists). There may be some 20 to 30 performers in a population of 600 to 1,000 residents. The group would most probably be composed of one or two elderly or middle-aged storytellers or oral historians, about 15 to 20 male and female singers and dancers, and a youthful group of 4 or 5 string band players. In some villages, some volunteer actors might also be willing to help develop a short humorous skit or play.

A period of workshop training would follow, possibly requiring two evenings a week or one evening a day during weekends. This might continue for several weeks to a month, helping to instill an understanding and awareness of the predetermined range of issues, themes, and information items in the performers/artists. Trainers for this preliminary awareness phase would include the Liaison Officer and several extension workers.

A second workshop in the village would follow to assist the performers/artists in turning development-oriented information and issues into vivid scenarios, plot-lines, and theme materials for convincing and moving performances. The process would move from discussions to tryout rehearsals and then to full-scale rehearsals. A production target date should be set early in the sessions.

The Liaison Officer should then develop plans for a special *singsing* performance dedicated to development. A suitable date might be Independence Day or a Provincial Day. The village officials should be encouraged to invite other clans or entire villages to attend.

From time to time, the Project Director may consider it necessary to call upon the practical expertise from among the members of the Advisory Committee.

It will also be most important, as a link-up with ongoing development efforts, to arrange for extension program demonstration exhibits at the singsing, and to make certain that extension personnel are present for discussions on issues and themes.

The village artists, incidentally, should be encouraged to incorporate their own thematic concerns—problems with thefts of pigs, poor roads—into their performances. This will help ensure full commitment by the troupe to the entire enterprise.

Ideally, arrangements should have been made with the National Broadcasting Commission and the Information Liaison Office for recording and video equipment to be in place to capture those parts of the production which could best be extended into the mass media: storytelling and singsing and string band music could prove to be popular on radio, and the entire production could be replayed on video cassette equipment in other villages as a springboard for discussion. Technicians may require technical rehearsal time before the group singsing.

A number of activities should be planned to follow the special singsing or other folk media such as storytelling. A tour by the performing troupe may be developed and certain dates set for studio recording sessions with some of the better artists. Those elements—songs, for example—which become popular, may be packaged on audio cassettes and sold commercially. If national-level competitions for string band compositions, for example, are organized by the Project Director, the Liaison Officer could work with the village band to prepare an entry for submission. Some of the folk artists may become widely known as a result of the experimental work and it may be justified to use their growing prestige to legitimize certain development issues in the geographical region of their popularity. The production of posters, T-shirts, or radio advertisements featuring these artists could take advantage of this potential.

Major attention, however, should be paid to the development processes within the pilot village itself. If the singsing had identified a practical issue with a realizable solution—for example, the need in the village for a fresh water supply—then modest equipment and the simple technology could be provided to tap an underground water source for a pump. In the absence of a visible or concrete follow-up, frustration might be generated given the heightened awareness and raised expectations about improved living conditions.

If the Liaison Officer succeeds in turning on a "light" for development in the village, he may move on to another village marked for similar experimental activity; however, an evaluation of effectiveness of work accomplished in the first locale is necessary. Inevitably, a comparison of the measurements of the earlier baseline survey will be made with those made after the completion of the experimental work.

The Liaison Officer should be required to submit details of their activities in monthly reports to the national-level Office of Information. The project-related parts of these reports should be made available to the Project Director as aids in monitoring field operations.

The mid-term review may provide the first opportunity to systematically assess progress. Even though a six-month report by the Project Director to the Steering Committee is called for, the mid-term review should make available the data needed to judge both progress and difficulties and to suggest corrective action. The monthly reports by Liaison Officers, the observations by the Project Director, the views on the draft of the manual for village-level communication work, the results of surveys and of the first batch of evaluations, the information about the effectiveness of the training activities, and a report on the progress made by the Project Researcher should all be studied during this exercise. The review should help adjust the course of the project, as needed for its second year of operation.

During the fourth phase of the project, activities in the three major areas continue—pilot work, surveys and evaluations, and research. The draft manual should be tested in the continuing village work. If it appears to be a useful guide to future activities, the Project Director should arrange to have the necessary number of copies made available.

As new information produced by the Project Researcher becomes available, the Director may consider expanding the pilot activity in one or more additional provinces, notably in areas where development assistance is desperately needed.

A final review should take place two months before the close of the initial two-year project period. Research reports, observations, and evaluations of effectiveness may help to determine if the project ought to be terminated upon completion or continued and expanded to other provinces for some specified additional period.

Before the close of the initial project period, final drafts of the following materials should be anticipated: the operational manual, the national inventory and assessment of traditional communication systems, and a report to the Advisory Committee. An edited version of this report might later be printed and released to interested governments and international organizations.

CONCLUSION

This project description is but one attempt to put into an operational format the findings of the 1980 Papua New Guinea study. It remains a theoretical exercise to be tested and revised in practice. At the time of this writing the government was still formulating its official reaction to the project outline.

Although the proposed action program is yet to be tried, the research upon which the design was based suggests that there is fine potential to be realized in harnessing selected elements of Papua New Guinea's traditional communication systems on behalf of the national development effort.

REFERENCES

Abrams, Tevia. (1981). *Development of Traditional Communication Systems: Papua New Guinea* (Technical Report Serial No. FMR/CC/FCP/81/180.) Paris: Unesco.

PNG Information Review Committee. (1979). *Report of the Review of Information Services*. Port Moresby, Papua New Guinea: PNG Information Review Committee.

Population Reference Bureau. (1981). *World Population Data Sheet (1981)*. Washington: Population Reference Bureau.

6

The Chinese Revolutionary Opera: A Change of Theme

Chien Chiao and Michael T. K. Wei

Throughout human history, there have been countless examples of efforts by political elites to manipulate cultural activities, especially in Communist regimes. As Weaver (1964, p. 18) indicates, "Communists condemn artistic or cultural expression which deviates from their harsh political line." However, even among Communist nations, the scope and substance of Chinese efforts during the Cultural Revolution stand out.

The Cultural Revolution of 1966 was much more than a revolution in the ordinary sense. Unlike the 1911 Chinese Revolution or the 1949 Communist takeover of China, which involved mainly the change of the political regime, the Cultural Revolution aimed at breaking away completely from the traditional Chinese culture and replacing it with a new blueprint for life. As Chiang Ch'ing, the alleged leader and chief standard-bearer of the Cultural Revolution, explicitly pointed out (*People's Daily*, November 28, 1966), the purpose of the revolutionaries was to sweep away all remnants of the old ideas, culture, customs, and habits of all exploiting classes.

The mission of the Cultural Revolution as such, no doubt, was unprecedented in Chinese history. It attempted to change not only the political structure, but also the whole culture of Chinese society.

The task of creating a new culture, according to Mao, is part of the revolutionary cause. It should include the setting up of "a complete system of proletarian ideology and a new social system (Mao, 1967, p. 30)." However, this was the most difficult part of the revolution. As Roxanne Witke (1977, p. 380) has theorized, the greatest problem for both revolutionary leaders and historians is neither the decay of empire nor the cataclysm of political revolution, but the process by which ideas become social attitudes.

The first task in creating a new social system is to prepare people for a new way of life. Since Mao perceived a complete cultural change as desirable to the revolutionary cause, he started the Cultural Revolution to achieve this long-cherished goal. In effect, the Cultural Revolution endeavored to discard a whole set of traditional values and norms based on the doctrines of Confucius and Mencius and to substitute an entirely new set of principles compatible with the Communist goals through literature and art.

The use of literature and art as component parts of the whole revolutionary machine was the central theme of Mao's talk to the literature and art workers in Yenan in 1942 (Mao, 1967, pp. 214–217). Not only did he emphasize the political function of literary works, but he also urged the use of workers, peasants, and soldiers as the principal characters in these works depicting their feelings, emotions, and aspirations in the course of revolution. His ideas were not implemented until the outbreak of the Cultural Revolution, when his wife Chiang Ch'ing was entrusted with the task of "revolutionizing" the popular Peking Opera.

In the years between 1966 and 1976, Chiang Ch'ing's influences on the Revolutionary Peking Opera became a new page in Chinese literature and art. Despite the fact that none of the Revolutionary Peking Operas produced by her were original works, they were adapted so that their themes, style, and form became the model for all other literary works and are thus called Model Revolutionary Peking Opera.

Chiang Ch'ing's first formal appearance on the political scene was in 1964 when she served in the National People's Congress as a representative from Shantung province (Witke, 1977, p. 311). Before that date, she had been pushing for reforms in the Peking Opera, but to no avail. During the Peking Opera Festival held in 1964, she made her first public speech on the Revolution in Peking Opera (Chiang, 1967). However, she wasn't well-received, and this famous, widely quoted, speech was not published until three years later. This speech (Chiang, 1967) established the orthodoxy of the Revolutionary Opera:

> It is inconceivable that the dominating positions on the stage throughout our socialist country, which is led by the Chinese Communist Party, should not be occupied by the workers, peasants and soldiers, the real creators of history and the true masters of our country. We should create literature and art which protect our socialist economic base . . .

> The grain we eat is grown by peasants, the clothes we wear are woven by workers and the houses we live in are built by them, and the People's Liberation Army is guarding the front line of our national defense. And yet we fail to portray these people on the stage. May I ask which class stand you artists take? And where is the artists' conscience that you are always talking about?

From then and until the outbreak of the Cultural Revolution, Chiang Ch'ing continued her opera reform behind the scenes. She was, at the time, the censor of cultural works for the People's Liberation

Army. It was not until 1967, when she headed a subgroup of the Cultural Revolution group of the Party's Committee, that she gained complete control over the nation's literature and art (Witke, 1977, p. 347). By 1968, she already had produced four model revolutionary operas and two ballets. These became the only shows permitted. All traditional operas were effectively banned by January 1966 (Cheng, 1974). The model operas were later used as the basis for other genres, such as film, drama, or children's pictorial reading. This measure proliferated the influence of the innovation and legitimized the values it carried. Through controlling creative activities, Chiang Ch'ing practically wiped out the "old" and was able to provide the cultural scene with the "new." Ever since, all artists and writers derived and developed their themes from the model operas. Consequently, everything produced during the Cultural Revolution period shared common features.

Throughout the period when Chiang Ch'ing was in charge of the nation's literature and art, she advocated Mao's thoughts as supreme and infallible guidelines for the Cultural Revolution and the revolutionary cause. Thus, all the major themes of the literary works in the discussion below, not surprisingly, are derived from Mao's central ideas on Chinese revolution.

Despite the tremendous change Chiang Ch'ing brought about in literature and art during her stay in power, her efforts were quickly negated the minute she lost power. The year 1976 is probably a landmark in the contemporary history of China. In that year, Chu Teh, Chairman of the National People's Congress; Chou En-lai, the Premier; and, Mao Tse-tung, Chairman of the Chinese Communist Party, died. More importantly, Chiang Ch'ing, Mao's widow, and three other high ranking officials were arrested by the Government one month after Mao's death and declared enemies of the nation. The arrest of the so-called Gang of Four, who rose to power during the Cultural Revolution by advocating Mao's theories, marked the unofficial end of the most turbulent political period in China since 1949.

Although Cultural Revolution is now a term in history books, revolutionary opera is still an interesting area for study because it represents an attempt to use the "revolutionized" folk medium to promote ideological change. Both the medium and, subsequently, its ideology retain little continuity from the past.

Today, folk media and art forms are being used to promote development messages in many Third World nations. Messages are incorporated into dialogues and scripts are written to present new ideas. Nowhere can such a basic change in the medium itself and such a massive effort in promoting a standardized set of plays be found as in the revolutionary drama. Revolutionary drama retained the singing and the music of Peking Opera. There were, however, drastic changes in costumes, stage decoration, and themes. In fact, when themes were brought to focus on the struggle and the success of peasants and workers in a great socialist society, the costumes and other aspects of the opera had to be changed accordingly. It was through a different set of themes that the image of an ideal new culture was formulated and advocated. To better explain what the messages were which bombarded the one billion people in China during the Cultural Revolution, this paper examines the major themes which ran through revolutionary opera and how they were incorporated in the opera plots.

THEMES

Several themes are central to revolutionary operas: the class struggle and contradictions; the need of unity manifest in comradeship and in the close relationship between the part and the whole; the importance of the army and its popular support; and, a bitter past and sweet present. All of these themes have roots in Mao's thinking and will be discussed in that context.

Class Struggle and Contradictions

Of all the themes identified in revolutionary operas, novels, films, collo- quial plays, dramas, and short stories, class struggle is the most promi- nent. The concept of class struggle, from which various associated themes arise, forms the skeleton of almost every literary work. The idea has been constantly and repeatedly developed and expounded in vari- ous settings through different characters.

Mao defined class struggle as a social reality in the historical period of socialism. The people must constantly be reminded of the struggle between the socialist and capitalist camps as well as the danger of cap- italist restoration. Mao personally appealed to the nation in 1962, urging the people to remember class struggle. However, a more effective way to imprint the idea into people's minds is to lend it support in popular literature and art. Chu Lan, a key theoretician of arts during the early 1970s, pointed out that the function of the modern revolutionary Peking operas is to "profoundly reflect the extraordinarily difficult life of strug- gle led by the Chinese proletariat and by the great masses under the leadership of the Chinese Communist Party" (Chu, 1974b, p. 60). He adds that "their goal is to seize political power by force and the operas are also a deep reflection of the life of struggle which is necessary in order to maintain continuous revolution under the dictatorship of the Proletariat."

In another article, Chu Lan (1974a) explains that the revolution in Peking Opera is, in itself, a radical change born out of class struggle:

> The tremendous changes in the last decade are by no means acciden- tal. The revolution in the Peking opera in China is determined by the fact that there are still classes, class contradictions and class struggle

in the historical period of socialism. This revolution is also an inevitable result of the struggle between Marxism-Leninism revisionism, and a proletarian strategic measure, under the guidance of the Party's basic line, for preventing capitalist restoration and consolidating the dictatorship of the proletariat.

Thus, the prime mission of literature is to describe the class struggle, and to describe it well is the political measure of the adherence of all artistic and theatrical works to the Party's basic line.

Some major works deal with this theme. In the first category, the revolutionary Peking opera, *Azalea Mountain*, represents one of the bitter struggles of the Communists against the anti-revolutionary forces in the early stage of the socialist revolution. In 1928, an armed peasant insurrection led by Kei Kang breaks out on Azalea Mountain, but it is a failure, lacking the guidance of the Party. Later, Ko Hsiang, a political organizer sent by the Party, joins the peasant rebels and helps them achieve victory by transforming them into a militant squad. After fierce fighting, the enemy is annihilated. Finally, the squad is incorporated into the Workers' and Peasants' Revolutionary Army. This story symbolizes the first successful attempt of the peasants to overthrow the landlord class and to establish revolutionary bases in the countryside. Other operas included in this category are *Red Detachment of Women*, which has a similar historical background, the *Red Lantern*, and *Taking Tiger Mountain by Strategy*, both of which depict the struggle against Japanese invaders and bandits.

After the establishment of the People's Republic of China, the class struggle, as prophesized by Mao, did not cease. There has been a constant threat of invasion from the Kuomintang (KMT) based in Taiwan. Hence, the socialist regime must always anticipate the return of the defeated enemies. *Boulder Bay* is a revolutionary opera which focuses on the class struggle in China in the early sixties when the Nationalists tried to establish a "corridor" for commando raids on the southeast coast in the hope of reestablishing their rule (Chen and Hsiu, 1976, p. 131). Lu Chang-hai, the Party Secretary and militia leader of Boulder Bay Brigade's battle with Black Shark, commander of KMT commando unit, epitomizes the basic conflict between the millions of China's laboring masses and the landlord-bourgeois class.

Another form of class struggle taking place in China during the historical period of socialism is the struggle between the proletariat and the hidden enemies who always want to sabotage the socialist construction. These enemies come primarily from the wealthy peasantry, the landlord class, and the capitalists who lost their privileges in the new era and who are hostile to any achievement brought about by the new regime. The opera *On the Docks* is a good example of how the class enemy, Ch'ien Shau-wei, attempts to delay a shipment of seed-rice bound for Africa. However, his vicious plan is discovered by Fang Hai-chen, secretary of the Party branch of the Loading Brigade.

These examples bring out two points. First, in spite of the change in the nature of the enemies, there is little change in the nature of struggle. The struggle against the landlord class in the 1930s has the same political significance as the struggle against the still incorrigible landlords who are unwilling to submit to the dictatorship of the proletariat in the 1970s. Second, no one knows who will be the final winner of the socialist revolution class struggle which continues as history progresses. As long as there are classes there will be class struggle and victory will be a long time in coming.

Contradictions Among the People

The process of class struggle contains unending contradictions. In his famous article, "On the Correct Handling of Contradictions among the People," Mao distinguishes between two types of contradictions: "those between ourselves and the enemy and those among the people themselves." The struggle between the people and the enemy is antagonistic, while that among the people themselves is nonantagonistic. Two revolutionary Peking operas, *On the Docks* and *Song of the Dragon River*, have been hailed as models for resolving the non-antagonistic contradiction. Fang Hai-chen of the former and Chiang Shui-ying of the latter both apply the "democratic method" in dealing with comrades who are following the incorrect line, and treat them with great patience and compassion.

However, in the plots of both operas, the non-antagonistic contradictions are secondary; they are only used to support the antagonistic contradiction. Thus *On the Docks* centers on the struggle between the party secretary Fang Hai-chen and Ch'ien Shou-wei who is clearly identified as a class enemy by his background; he has worked for Americans, Japanese, and the Kuomintang before The Liberation. In *Song of the Dragon River*, the dominant struggle is between the party secretary Chiang Shui-ying and class enemy Huang Kuo-chung who was the comptroller of a landlord before Liberation. He concealed this fact by changing his name and moving to a different village after Liberation.

In the revolutionary Peking opera, *Boulder Bay*, there are two scenes devoted to the conflicts between the hero of the opera, Lu Chang-hai, a militia leader, and his wife and the head of the fishing team, Hai-ken, who have forgotten class struggle. These conflicts are between two ways of thinking, that of the one who is vigilant, ever ready to resist the enemy, and that of the one who wishfully thinks of peace and easy life.

Conflicts among the people are, like class struggle, part of the social reality in the socialist era. They occur everywhere among different types of characters. Since the dictatorship does not apply to those within the ranks of the "people," the only way to solve disputes is by means of the "democratic method" as Mao suggested. Through correct handling of the conflicts among the people, the dictatorship of the proletariat can be secured.

Comradeship and Part—Whole Relationship

Closely associated with class struggle, comradeship and the close relationship between part and whole provide the basis for the unity of the proletariat in struggle against the exploiting classes. Comradeship stems from a common class background and it integrates people of the same class into an organic unity. Human nature, according to Mao, is determined by the class to which a man belongs. Only members of the same class can love one another because human nature is rooted in class.

Class affection is particularly strong among the proletariat. They care, love, and trust each other because of their common background. In fact, their bond is stronger than any genuine kinship tie. As Li Yu-ho, the hero of *The Red Lantern* (1972, p. 36) opera explains:

> People say that family love outweights all else,
> But class love is greater yet, I know
> A proletarian fights all his life for the people's
> liberation.

In fact, Li Yu-ho, Granny, and Tieh-mei, the three members of Li's family, have no genuine kinship tie. They came from three different families, and they belong to three different generations. Their common class background and their sufferings in the past unite them. Camaraderie is the bond holding them together in the struggle against the exploiting class.

The idea that comradeship integrates people into an organic unity for collective action is well-developed in the revolutionary Peking opera, *Song of the Dragon River*. The story takes place in the Dragon River Production Brigade in southeast China at the foot of a hill. In order to save 90,000 *mu* of fertile but drought-stricken fields on the other side of the hill, the brigade party secretary, Chiang Shui-ying, mobilizes the members. They fight the drought by blocking up the Nine Dragon River at its middle section to raise its water level and make the river flow back over the hill to irrigate the dry fields. As the river is blocked, the brigade's own fields would be flooded and the brigade would suffer a great loss. At first the brigade leader, Li Chih-tien, opposes the idea but he sees the point when Chiang explains to him (*Song of the Dragon River*, 1972, p. 30):

> The skin on the hands of the poor and lower-middle class
> peasants is all the same skin, the fields before and
> behind the hill are all fields of the people's communes.

The poor and lower-middle class peasants are thus one in the spirit of socialist construction.

The most stirring episode comes at the final stage of the closing of the dam. The current is swift and the waves are high in the middle of the river and it is very difficult to drive the piles into the riverbed. But the river has to be blocked to save the fields. Motivated by the deep concern for the fellow "class relatives," Fang (*Song of the Dragon River*, 1972, p. 22) makes a suggestion:

> The only way is for people to jump into the gap and block
> the flow with their bodies while the stakes are being driven.

In a minute, led by Chiang, the commune members and the PLA men jump into the river and form a human wall to hold the rolling waves. Eventually the dam is closed, clearly showing that comradeship is a crucial element in mobilizing people for the cause of socialism.

Based on the same principle, relationship between the part and the whole is also very important in bringing success to the struggle against evil. Early in 1939, Mao (1956, p. 201) in his article, "The Role of the Chinese Communist Party in the National War," stated the relationship between the part and the whole:

> If a proposal appears feasible for a partial situation but not for the
> situation as a whole, then the part must give way to the whole.
> Conversely, if the proposal is not feasible for the part but is feasible
> in the light of the situation as a whole, again the part must give way
> to the whole. This is what is meant by considering the situation as a
> whole.

Mao's principle is to "subordinate the needs of the part to the needs of the whole." This principle becomes a general guideline governing relationships between entities of all sizes, from a production brigade to the whole world." Compliance with this principle is another popular theme in the works under study.

In *Song of the Dragon River*, we see another illustration of the part and whole relationship. As previously described, the Dragon River Brigade has to flood three hundred *mu* (roughly fifty acres) of its best fields in order to build a dam to force the river water flow up to the communes which are suffering from a critical drought in the rear mountain. There are two diametrically opposed views within the brigade.

Brigade Party Secretary Chiang Shui-ying represents one attitude: the situation as a whole should be considered, and his group should assume responsibility. Brigade leader Li Chih-tien, whose mind is preoccupied with the targets for yields, the bonuses for exceeding the quota, and the losses of his brigade, cannot see why the river should be blocked and why the crops in the area should be flooded. The opposite views held by Chiang and Li represent a typical contradiction between the part and the whole. According to Mao's principle, the only way to solve this contradiction is to let the few sacrifice for the greater good.

What would happen if the part does not yield to the whole? Consider the modern revolutionary Peking opera, *Red Detachment of Women*. The opera, based on the ballet of the same name, strongly suggests that the whole is composed of the parts, which in turn can hardly exist in their own right without being integrated into the whole.

Wu Ching-hua is a bondmaid who has escaped from the cell of a landlord, called the Tyrant of the South, with the help of Hung Chang-ching, the Party representative of the Women's Company. She joins the women's army motivated by revenge on the landlord. In a surprise attack on the Coconut Grove Manor, Ching-hua, furious at seeing the enemy, gives the signal prematurely and the Tyrant is able to flee. Afterwards, she is criticized by the Company Commander for breaching discipline and is relieved of her gun. To imbue Ching-hua with revolutionary consciousness, Hung conducts a political class for the women soldiers.

It is apparent from the story that revolution is not simply a matter of personal vengeance; its aim is the emancipation of all mankind. In this case, Ching-hua's burning desire to take revenge symbolizes the part whereas the women army's mission to liberate the comrades from oppression is the whole. Naturally, the part has to depend on the whole in order for its wishes and dreams to materialize. If the part fails to fulfill its duties to the whole, disastrous results follow, as in this case, when the tyrants fled. Thus, it is essential that the part be loyal to the whole in order that the whole succeed, which in turn directly benefits the part.

The Importance of Army and People's Support of It

The Chinese Communists take a more militant attitude in regard to class struggle than do orthodox Marxists. They believe that proletariat must shed blood and tears in struggle against the bourgeoisie in power before they can be liberated from oppression and exploitation. This attitude is exemplified in Mao's famous saying that "political power grows out of the barrel of a gun," which assumes that the army is the chief component of the political power of state.

The importance of the gun in securing political power is evident in revolutionary operas. *Red Detachment of Women* expresses a view that the only way to save suffering people from oppression is to rebel with the help of armed forces, which should be commanded by the Party. The whole opera centers around the process of a group of former slave girls arming themselves and overthrowing the tyrannical landlord.

Another work carrying a similar message but with a different approach, is the modern revolutionary Peking opera, *Azalea Mountain*. The opera also portrays the armed uprising by peasants against a tyrant landlord, but emphasizes the importance of following the Party's orders and instructions. In *Red Detachment of Women*, Ching-hua is punished for not using the gun in accordance with the Party's order implying that the gun is under the supreme control of the Party. In *Azalea Mountain* this idea is developed further. The opera points out that any armed struggle without the guidance of the Party is bound to be a fiasco. The army is important, but support from the people is crucial to the success of military maneuvers.

In the fourth scene of the modern revolutionary Peking opera, *Taking Tiger Mountain by Strategy* (1972, p. 74) the regimental chief of staff quotes Mao's instruction:

> Long ago Chairman Mao told us: "The revolution war is a war of the masses; it can be waged only by mobilizing the masses and relying on them." Without the masses we can't move a step.

Mao perceives the masses as the determinant of any military action, though he never underestimates the functional value of the gun. His comment that the richest source of power to wage war lies in the masses shows his particular emphasis on the strategic importance of making alliance with the people in armed struggle. His idea of uniting the army and the people in either the class struggle or in production is another prominent theme in the works studied.

A highly recommended work focusing on the same theme is the modern revolutionary Peking opera, *Fighting on the Plains*. It tells how a detachment of the Eighth Route Army led by Chao Yung-kang, with staunch support from the villagers, prevents the Japanese troops from "mopping up" the communist base in the mountains.

Another work which hails the cooperative spirit among the army and the people is the revolutionary modern Peking opera, *Shachiapang*, which tells how a worker successfully hides a wounded soldier of the New Fourth Army wanted by the enemies.

I k'u szu tien or Remembering the Bitterness of the Past and Thinking of the Sweetness of the Present

This is another popular theme included in most revolutionary operas. To a certain extent, it seeks to expose the dark forces that oppressed the people in the old society and to hail the bright future that the Communist Party is bringing to them. This is, in fact, one of the prime missions of literature and art perceived by Mao. He explicitly declared in his Yenan Talks (Mao, 1956, p. 81):

> All the dark forces harming the masses if the people must be exposed and all the revolutionary struggles of the masses of the people must be extolled; this is the fundamental task of revolutionary writers and artists.

One of the most effective ways to achieve the above goal is through storytelling. According to Mao's strategy of revolution, hatred is a driving force which the Communists must make every effort to exploit. One frequently used tactic is to encourage a victim of oppression to tell his bitter experiences. The individual's description of his oppressor's heinous actions will remind others of their own similar suffering. A concerted hatred of oppression, and of the "class enemy," is encouraged and channeled to inspire revolutionary forces. Its purpose is to make people more appreciative of what they have, more grateful to the Communist Party, and to alert them to any attempt by the class enemy to revive the old system.

In the revolutionary Peking opera, *Shachiapang*, Aunt Sha tells her past at the urging of two young soldiers of the New Fourth Army (Shachiapang, 1972, p. 4):

> In the dark days we were too poor to raise our Children,
> of my four boys, two died of hunger and cold, I had to get a usurious loan from the Tiao's in a year
> of famine.
> To pay the debt, my third son had to work for them as a farmhand.
> A poisonous snake, that bloodsucker Tiao had a murderous heart.
> He made my son toil day and night.
> Brutally beaten, the boy died of a mortal wound.
> Szu-lung, my fourth, has such a fiery temper and is fearless,
> He charged into Tiao's house to have it out with them;
> the bloodsucker accused him of breaking in at night for robbery,
> And had my poor sixteen-year-old thrown into prison.

Having told her sufferings in the old society, she becomes happy as she talks about the present.

Another revolutionary Peking opera, *On the Docks*, contrasts the old society and the new. It focuses on the social status and the prestige of the proletariat before and after the establishment of the People's Republic. This is an important comparison in the political education of youths born after 1949 since they know little about what the older generations have suffered.

In addition to the four major themes, ideas such as internationalism, self-reliance, and success in the development effort were frequently portrayed in revolutionary drama and other literary and art works during the Cultural Revolution.

IMPLICATIONS

Although some degree of similarity can be detected between the themes of Peking opera and that of revolutionary opera (Chu and Cheng, 1978), the attempt at renovating central ideas of the plot lines is clear. The differences are, in fact, so pronounced that the themes are hardly comparable.

Today the thoughts of Mao no longer play an important role in literary creation in China. The works of Chiang Ch'ing have almost completely disappeared. Although the revolutionary operas were never officially denounced, people were reportedly tiring of and deserting them (*Sing Tao Daily,* Hong Kong, July 29, 1981, p. 2). Most of the traditional works have returned to the stage.

While the revolutionary opera is entitled to some credit in promoting development in China (Chu and Cheng, 1978), it has apparently failed to take root in the culture. Instead of becoming the expression of a "new culture," it seems to have remained a form of political propaganda which rose and fell with its promoter.

In the use of folk media for development purposes, there are currently debates on one central issue: given the political messages incorporated into the script, could folk media still remain the "people's media," or would they become a tool of government propaganda? There are, of course, numerous factors involved: the nature of the media; the manner of incorporating the messages; the extent of modification; and, the approach in determining changes, e.g., through local participation or central planning. Our study showed that drastic and basic modifications of a folk medium—having little flexibility in its content—in a top-down, one-way communication could hardly achieve miracles in development.

History seldom repeats itself in the exact sense; progress, however, can be made only if people learn to benefit from the past.

REFERENCES

Chen, Hua and Pu Hsiu. (1976). "A True Bastion of Iron—'On Revolutionary Model Peking Opera 'Boulder Bay'." *Chinese Literature 4,* 131–136.

Cheng, Philip H. (1974). "The Function of Chinese Opera in Social Control and Change." Unpublished dissertation, Southern Illinois University, Carbondale.

Chiang, Ch'ing. (1967). *On the Revolution of Peking Opera.* Peking: Hsinhua News Agency-English (May 9).

Chu, Godwin and Philip H. Cheng. (1978). "Revolutionary Opera: An Instrument for Cultural Change." In Godwin Chu (Ed.), *Popular Media in China.* Honolulu: University Press of Hawaii.

Chu, Lan (1974a). "A Decade of Revolution in Peking Opera." *Peking Review 17* (31), (Aug. 2), 4–9.

Chu, Lan. (1974b). "The Splendid Scroll of the History of Chinese Revolution: A Discussion of the Achievements and Significance of Revolutionary Model Opera." *Hongqi 1,* 59–64. (in Chinese).

Mao, Tse-tung. (1956). *The Role of the Chinese Communist Party in the National War.* Peking: Foreign Language Press.

Mao, Tse-tung. (1956). *Talks at the Yenan Forum on Arts and Literature.* Peking: Foreign Language Press.

Mao, Tse-tung. (1967). *Quotations.* Peking: Foreign Language Press.

The Red Lantern. (1972). Peking: Foreign Language Press.

Shachiapang. (1972). Peking: Foreign Language Press.

Song of the Dragon River. (1972). Peking: Foreign Language Press.
Taking Tiger Mountain by Strategy. (1972). Peking: Foreign Language Press.
Weaver, Richard M. (1964). *Visions of Order*. Baton Rouge: Louisiana State University Press.
Witke, Roxanne. (1977). *Comrade Chiang Ch'ing*. Boston: Little Brown, & Co.

7

The Performing Arts and Development in India: Three Case Studies and a Comparative Analysis*

Ross Kidd

This paper examines three Indian organizations active in didactic or social animation theatre: (a) the Song and Drama Division (SDD) of the Government of India; (b) Jagran, a Delhi-based non-government agency specializing in development communication through mime; and, (c) Action for Cultural and Political Change (ACPC), an animation team in southern India involved in organizing popular movements of landless laborers. These organizations represent three different approaches to socially oriented theatre: a government-run, centrally controlled, mass approach involving itinerant performances by regionally hired troupes on government development themes and services; a locally based non-government program involving mime sketches on government services and community self-help action performed by an externally based troupe for slum-dwellers; and, a popular organization approach run by and for oppressed groups in which drama is an integral part of a social transformation process involving "conscientization," organization, and struggle.

Each program is described in its own terms, with a comparative analysis in the final section. The analysis shows that: (a) these programs represent two different interests and purposes—one a form of "domestication" or ideological manipulation and the other, a "liberation" or structural transformation; and, (b) these interests are reflected in the historical origins, organizational structure, program methods and processes, etc. of each program.

*Sources for this study include those cited in the bibliography; interviews with Song and Drama Division staff (1978–81), Aloke Roy of Jagran (1980–81), and ACPC team members (1980–81); and observations of Jagran and ACPC field programs. I am indebted to Dr. Felix Sugirtharaj (ACPC) and Evelyn Voigt for their help on the ACPC and SDD case studies respectively; their weaknesses, however, are my own responsibility.

In the opening section the historical and political-economic context in which the programs were shaped is described briefly.

Political–Economic Context

At Independence, in 1947, political power was transferred to the indigenous bureaucratic and capitalistic classes, but India remained within the sphere of influence of the advanced capitalist countries. India set out on a course of massive industrialization and agricultural transformation, all within the system of bourgeois property relations and with heavy doses of foreign aid (which expanded the enclave of foreign ownership inherited from the colonial period). The various rural development strategies used over the first three decades of Independence were all absorbed and distorted by India's class structure. The beneficiaries were rich farmers and landlords who controlled the social, economic, and political life of the village and appropriated state resources to strengthen themselves, all within the socialist and Ghandian rhetoric of rural uplift and alleviating poverty and unemployment.

During the 1950s and early 1960s the agricultural development strategy consisted of land reform, cooperatives, and community development (CD). The land reform program eliminated some of the huge feudal estates, but was highly unsuccessful in implementing the landholding ceilings and redistributing excess land. CD and co-ops also failed to achieve the social equity objectives; the rich farmers took control of these new structures (the village council or *panchayat* and co-op) and used them to increase their own economic and political power. The jobs, land, and other opportunities promised to the smaller and landless peasants never materialized. The assumption underlying the CD approach, i.e., that all social classes in the village shared common interests and would benefit equally from collective projects was shown to be specious. Agricultural production remained fairly stagnant during this period due to the grain imports from the U.S.A. and other countries.

In the mid-1960s, when food surpluses in North America declined, a "Green Revolution" was launched in the Third World with American backing to achieve food self-sufficiency (as part of the multinational corporation strategy to shift agricultural production to the Third World where cheap labor could be exploited). The new seeds, fertilizer, mechanization, etc., raised productivity (and increased the markets for the multinational corporations). The "Green Revolution," however, polarized the class structure—fattening and capitalizing the rich farmers, reducing the proportion of middle farmers, forcing the smaller farmers into debt, and producing massive landlessness, unemployment, and impoverishment. The rich farmers appropriated the spoils of this program, consolidated their hold over the panchayat and their relations with the bureaucracy (as their means of monopolizing the state resources for the "Green Revolution"), and maintained their domination over, and exploitation of, the poor farmers and landless laborers.

In the 1970s the revolutionary implications of these changes became increasingly clear. The Indian government, again with the backing of the international aid apparatus, moved to contain social unrest with a "mini-Green Revolution," including benefits directed to the smaller farmers and social welfare measures but without any significant land reform (Feder, 1976). These mini-reforms and government services directed to the poor—the basis for Mrs. Ghandi's 20-point program and slogan of eradicating poverty—were aimed at integrating the poor into the system, drawing them away from radical social action, and dealing with some of the contradictions and tensions produced by the capitalist "betting on the strong" strategies. This was coupled with more repressive measures in the mid-1970s (the Emergency) in order to contain more directly the growing tensions and class conflict.

The role of development communication and non-formal education in this overall "integrated rural development" strategy was to promote the mini-reforms and services of the state and to persuade people to accept reformist and government-controlled ways for dealing with their problematic existence—birth–control pills, development loans, house sites, small economic projects, etc.

While the 20-point program made lots of promises to eradicate poverty, the follow-through was rather hollow. The increasing remoteness, insensitivity, and inflexibility of the bureaucracy and its collusion with the landowning classes worked to prevent most of these mini-reforms from being implemented. In response to the continuing failures of government-based development programs and the disillusionment with Ghandian "change of heart" strategies (i.e., attempts to persuade the landlords to be generous and just), and building on the growth of class consciousness in the countryside and urban slums, a number of radical initiatives were started in various parts of the country to organize the marginal and small farmers and landless laborers to fight for what the system was not providing (i.e., minimum wages, abolition of bonded labor and rural indebtedness, other government reforms and services, etc.) and to try to change the system itself (e.g., the abolition of landlordism).

The Song and Drama Division (SDD) was created during the first development period (1947–1964), Jagran during the second (1965–1972), ACPC during the third (1973–present). Each of these programs is described in turn, setting out: (a) their origins and history; (b) their organizational structure; and, (c) the programs contents and process.

SONG AND DRAMA DIVISION (SDD)

Origin and History

The Indian Song and Drama Division (SDD) was created in 1954 as a specialist unit within the Ministry of Information and Broadcasting for development communication through live entertainment media. Its primary task was to promote national unity and to publicize the government's development plans: small savings, agricultural development, national integration, family planning, and prohibition. The SDD was launched during the era of the "Great Campaigns" when newly emerging Third World nations—China, India, Indonesia, Mexico, Ghana, etc.—mounted "mass education" campaigns on agriculture, health, literacy, civic education, etc. Media were seen as playing a mobilizing role in arousing the participation of the rural masses in the reconstruction and development efforts of government.

The choice of the performing arts as one "media" for a program of mass communication was influenced by the success with this medium by; (a) the Indian People's Theatre Association (IPTA) during the nationalist struggle and, (b) community development programs both before and after Independence (Mathur, 1954; Mayer, 1958; Miles, 1961).

The folk performing arts or folk "media"—drama, poetry, songs, dance-drama, puppetry, etc.—were seen as a necessary complement to the modern mass media. They flourish in remote rural areas untouched by newspaper and radio and, as age-old, community-based, and trusted sources of information and enlightenment could be more persuasive than modern mass media. As part of "traditional" culture, they retain the credibility to convince people to overcome "traditional" ways. They could transform national objectives and policies set in planners' abstract language into living images rural people could understand. At the same time, folk media provide the direct, person-to-person contact needed to help people translate these ideas into action. Moreover, the program could draw on the nation's own vast resource of creative talent and help revitalize what some had diagnosed as a dying profession.

In the 1950s the program operated as a small unit within All–India Radio. With limited resources the initial approach had to be indirect, trying to encourage other government departments to use folk theatre as a means of communication and community education at the local level (Mane, 1980). Later on, when more resources became available, the Song and Drama Unit hired private troupes on a commissioned basis for short experimental campaigns.

In 1959, the unit formed its first *full-time* troupe. The performers became civil servants, combining desk jobs with evening performances and touring. In 1960, the unit was given the status of an independent Division within the Ministry and its budget was expanded.

In the 1960s the Division expanded the number of full-time troupes and opened regional offices. Each troupe was assigned to a different area of the country and attached to a regional office headed by a senior officer. The full-time troupes were the major focus of SDD activity because, it was argued, they could produce high-quality performances and respond quickly to government information campaigns. The part-time troupes were (and are) outside the direct control of the SDD—the SDD hires them but the Field Publicity Directorate (another department within the Information Ministry) supervises their work in the field—and it was felt little could be done to improve their quality.

In 1965–1966 a border war with China erupted. Four new full-time troupes were quickly formed and pressed into service to combat Chinese propaganda and instill a sense of patriotism and defence preparedness among the border population. This program was partially motivated by the success of Chinese propaganda troupes on the other side of the border (Richmond, 1973). This work was so successful that many more troupes were formed for "winning the hearts and minds" of villagers along the border.

In the late 1960s the Indian government launched a massive family planning program and the Division contributed to the communication effort. It commissioned many scripts on this topic, and in 1970, set up four new troupes to specialize in family planning themes.

In 1976, during the Emergency, many private troupes, which normally only work for SDD 20 days a year, were pressed into touring months on end as part of the government's massive propaganda drive. During this period the range of themes was broadened to include not only major policies from the Five-Year Plan but also Mrs. Ghandi's 20-point program: house sites for the homeless, land reform, eradication of untouchability, abolition of bonded labor, rural health, etc.

Organization and the SDD Process

At present the Song and Drama Division employs 41 full-time troupes and about 500 registered part-time troupes.[1] Twenty-eight full-time troupes are engaged in border publicity work; four others specialize in family planning communication; and the remainder serve as generalist troupes attached to the regional offices.

The national office of the Song and Drama Division, based in Delhi, determines the overall policy of the Division and it commissions some scripts used by departmental troupes. Until recently it operated in a highly centralized fashion, prescribing the messages and even the scripts to be used in various parts of the country. It maintains a number of troupes for national functions.

Each regional office manages its own full-time troupe and commissions a number of private troupes within the region. An Inter-Media Publicity Coordination Committee at the state level, made up of representatives from SDD, All-India Radio, TV, Directorate of Field Publicity, and the State Department of Information, plans each quarterly schedule

[1]In addition, most state governments have their own Song and Drama Units. For a detailed description of one of these State Government programmes, see Abrams (1975). He noted that in the period from 1971 to 1974 the Maharashtra State contingent had increased from 40 to 80 troupes. In 1971 it was estimated that more than 400 villages (one million people) were reached by this program—out of 55 million people living in 38,000 villages in Maharashtra State.

of programs, taking into account community fairs, festivals, requests from community development staff, etc. It doesn't need to wait for formal approval of its program by central headquarters in Delhi. However, script approval must be obtained from the national office.

Field development of the private troupes is organized by the Field Publicity Directorate—another department within the Ministry of Information and Broadcasting. It has a network of Publicity Officers based in the field who are responsible for a mobile publicity program of films, seminars, exhibitions, and song-and-drama troupes. The Field Publicity Officer decides on the occasion he needs a song-and-drama troupe. The didactic content is agreed on and a schedule of performances drawn up. In the field the Publicity Officer keeps a check on the group, writing a report on each performance.

At the local level the Field Publicity Officer works through the village panchayat and, in some cases, the Block Development Officer to publicize the performance and decide on a suitable venue, normally just outside the panchayat or school. Local dignitaries open and close the program; occasionally the Field Publicity Officer will give a post-performance talk reinforcing the point of the play and inviting questions. The song-and-drama performance is often part of a larger program, which sometimes includes films.

When the Division started, there was no theory of folk media utilization. Theory developed from practice—through experimenting with various types of folk arts and various ways of inserting didactic messages. They discovered, for example, that for purposes of "instrumentalization", folk media can be grouped into three different categories:

- ritual forms (e.g., tribal dances, religious arts) which are appropriate for development communication because of their in-built resistance to the insertion of foreign contents;
- traditional forms on mythological or historical themes whose overall structure is rigid but permit didactic content to be communicated through the jester or narrator in the interludes between epidoses of the traditional story;
- modernized forms ("traditional" or "syncretic") in which a totally fresh story line is possible. (Ranganath, 1979, p. 5)

They also found that a totally didactic approach turned off an audience. So they use a mixed format—straight entertainment items to capture and hold the audience interspersed with message-oriented plays, songs, and social commentary.

Scripting is handled in two ways. Scripts for the departmental troupes are produced on a commissioned basis by regional playwrights. The private parties are expected to produce their own or improvise, incorporating the message provided by government.

A common feature of many scripts is to compare the lives of two individuals or families—one "modern" and the other "traditional." For example, a typical *family planning* play tells the story of two neighbors: one Rama, who ignores the advice of the family planning motivator and subsequently finds it increasingly difficult to feed, clothe, and manage his rapidly growing family; the other, his neighbor Shamo heeds the advice limiting his family to two children and reaps the benefits.[2]

Another common form is the "change-of-heart" plot. For example, in a play on *untouchability*, a *Harijan*[3] bonded laborer (or Harijan midwife) is treated badly by a caste landlord until the day he saves the landlord from drowning, or the midwife saves the landowner's daughter-in-law during labor, after which the landlord has a profound "change of heart."

JAGRAN

Origin and History

Jagran, meaning "Awakening," is a mobile mime troupe formed during the massive population control program in the last half of the 1960s. During this period, there was an influx of foreign aid and intense international pressure to implement a national family planning programme.[4] Communication was a major aspect of this program. Jagran was one of many non-government organizations created to experiment with various media and approaches.

Jagran's founder, an artist named Aloke Roy, was drawn to the development communications field after experiences in relief work in Rajasthan. In 1967, he was approached by a senior family planning official to find a means of communication to cut across all language barriers and propagate the small family norm. This seemed a formidable problem, given the 17 official languages and 208 recognized dialects in India. Roy eschewed the use of traditional drama because of its regionally specific nature and use of regional languages. He turned to the

---

[2]This modern-traditional juxtaposition, the structure for many of the SDD stories (particularly those of Family Planning), has been labelled (by its critics) the "Rama-Shamo" technique after the most frequently used names of the principal characters.

[3]The term "Harijan" refers to the "untouchables," people at the lowest social stratum in India.

[4]Between 1968 and 1972—the period during which family planning became a high priority in Indian development programmes—AID funding for population control escalated four-fold from $34 million to $123 million while the health care funding dropped from $164 million to $60 million. Other multi-lateral agencies followed suit. AID has used its leverage with development grants and food aid to force Third World countries to accept its population control policies.

medium of mime—a bold, non-verbal style which could appeal and communicate to everyone and provide an effective means of entry into the community (Shiveshwarkar, 1979).

Roy was particularly impressed by mime's capacity for caricaturing social behavior: "Mime is recognition of our own dilemmas. When foolishness is held up to laughter, common sense wins and the message is unmistakable." (Jagran leaflet). He identified comic situations faced by people with large families (e.g., the predicament of getting on a crowded bus with a pregnant wife and ten kids), put them into frames with characters and gestures, and produced short sequences to convey simple messages: We pose a common problem, illustrate it with a story, and then suggest a solution, however simple (Personal Interview, 1980).

Roy's approach to mime seemed to work. After the first experiment, he was commissioned by many other agencies to promote family planning, nutrition, and other development messages (e.g., government savings and loan schemes). In this first experimental period (1968–1974), Jagran worked about a half year in Delhi—its home base—and spent the other half on the road touring other states. Funds came from the Pathfinder Fund (American Family Planning Foundation), CARE (with USAID backing), the United Commercial Bank, Caritas, etc.

In 1972 CARE India invited Jagran to participate in a multi-media mass communication campaign on nutrition in the rural areas of Andhra Pradesh and Uttar Pradesh. The campaign was evaluated. Jagran's work was given a high rating. One social worker said: "What we could not teach in six months about health, nutrition, and population education, mime has done in a one hour programme" (CARE, 1974).

During the Emergency (1975–1976) a major event changed Jagran's widely itinerant existence and gave it a permanent role in Delhi. Backed by the repressive powers of the Emergency and the pretext of a Beautification Campaign, Sanjay Ghandi launched a full-scale attack on the slums of Delhi, destroying homes with bulldozers and herding over 700,000 people to an area 20 miles north of the city.[5] The slum-dwellers had been promised new homes, but it took several months before they were "resettled" in new housing areas on the outskirts of Delhi.

The new houses turned out to be one-room tenements, constructed on plots of 25 square yards each. The occupants—construction workers, domestic servants, office cleaners, hawkers, etc.—worked in the factories, kitchens, and markets of Delhi and had long journeys in and out every day by bus. Many were first generation migrants to the cities, having been forced out of the rural areas by landlessness and dwindling unemployment. There were no schools and only a few clinics with inadequate staff. Only basic services were provided—drinking

---

[5]This event was also the pretext for a compulsory vasectomy drive, a campaign so brutal in approach that it provoked fierce resistance resulting in many deaths in police clashes. There was no compensation for the demolished houses even though for some it represented substantial investments in construction materials (Singh, 1977).

water, public toilets, drainage, sewage, and the bare minimum of street lighting.

The Delhi Development Authority (DDA) asked Jagran to mount a motivational campaign to "teach the residents how to use modern services." The DDA complained that residents didn't flush the toilets, often vandalized the taps and waited for the government to fix them. They wanted Jagran to instill a sense of collective responsibility, to motivate a "self-help" approach to the upkeep of these basic services.

Jagran agreed to help and, after some informal research into the problem, produced a number of sketches. One of them emphasized the importance of the water facilities by showing a man taking a shower in winter when the taps are broken. These water and sanitation sketches were performed along with their existing repertoire on family planning, nutrition, and other themes. In one community the performance produced a positive reaction. People offered to raise the money if Jagran would fix the tap (They didn't trust each other with handling the money). Jagran declined, saying it was the residents' responsibility. Eventually the residents raised the money and fixed the tap.

Since 1976 Jagran has continued this work in the resettlement colonies. In 1977 Roy met Paulo Freire. This influenced Jagran's work. New political themes were added to the repertoire—atrocities against Harijans and corruption by social worker/politicians—and Roy started to describe Jagran as a "theatre of the oppressed," leading through a process of awareness to organization and politicization:

> Strategically our aim is to politicize people but we adopt tactics for entry purposes—e.g., through family planning (Personal Interview, 1980).

However, Jagran defines its primary role in terms of *development communication*, rather than community development or organizing popular movements. Its job is to raise awareness, to make people conscious of (a) obstacles to their development, (b) services provided by government, (c) their responsibilities to their community, and (d) their rights as citizens. In the process Jagran attempts to change "traditional habits and attitudes," which they see as the major obstacle (along with ignorance of opportunities for self-advancement through government services) to Harijan self-development. Roy described the "liberation of Harijans" as a

> Long process. The first stage is to bring awareness. People are unaware of the possibility of change. If it is hammered constantly, consciousness may bring about change (Personal Interview, 1980).

Roy however declines an organizing role:

> All we can do is to make people aware . . . the next step must be taken by the people themselves. As outsiders we can only encourage, we cannot take the leadership or organizing role. Leadership must emerge from within (Personal Interview, 1980).

Jagran Process and Organization

Over the years Jagran has developed a large repertoire covering a range of topics—evils of indebtedness, drunkenness, the dowry system, and neglected children; exposed food, nutrition, hygiene, family planning; maintenance of community pumps, water taps, public toilets, etc.; co-operation, civic consciousness, voting rights; ill-treatment of Harijans and the duplicity of social worker/politicians. New themes are added as Jagran identifies new needs or receives new requests from sponsors or development agencies.[6]

Each daily program is a selection of these themes. A typical program would include six to eight items and run for one-and-a-half to two hours. One program, for example, included items on family planning, bank loans, exposed food, community water tap, bank savings, and nutrition. Examples of the plots include:

> Two wrestlers eat some food before their match, one a banana and the other exposed food. The former wins.

> A man tries to get on a crowded bus with his pregnant wife and nine children. After missing several buses he pleads with a bus driver to let him on. The driver is impatient and after allowing a few of the children to get on starts the bus, leaving half of the family stranded.

> A social worker/politician who claims to be acting as a go-between with government for a resettlement colony takes credit for a community center which the colony's youth have built on their own. When they protest this claim, the social worker incites the police to attack the youth.

> An exploited rickshaw puller is persuaded by his friend to stop working for the rickshaw owner and take out a loan from the bank to buy his own rickshaw.

> A child whose diet is lacking in green leafy vegetables is attacked by the Malnutrition Monster and, as a result, becomes anemic. Later when he starts to eat the vegetables, he successfully resists the Monster's attack.

The production of each mime sequence is usually based on some form of topic research drawing on government institutions in the area, formal and informal leaders, government's own surveys, etc. A written scenario is produced, and the actors are trained to perform it.

Performances are normally held in the afternoon. Crowds range from 100 to 1,000 people, and the majority are women and children. The group performs in an open field surrounded by the audience. It is a

---

[6]Occasionally there is a direct request from a community to take up an issue. In 1981, for example, the residents in one area organized a successful mass protest against the hoarding and blackmarketing practices of the colony's government-licensed shop. They pressured the political authorities to arrest the shop-owner. Jagran happened to be performing in this area after the incident and was approached by several residents to re-enact the struggle in mime—as a means of announcing a people's victory (Roy, 1981).

rough-and-ready, highly mobile theatre—no props, no sets, no lighting, no stage—only a bit of white makeup to accentuate the expressions on the actors' faces. The sketches rely heavily on stereotyped characters—the moneylenders, the brahmin, the outcaste, the demon, the harried mother, etc. The action of each mime is reinforced by a narration in the local dialect, using a hand-held battery-powered microphone. In the performance I witnessed, the narrator kept up a steady monologue, cracking jokes and commenting on the action throughout the performance. At the end of the family planning sketch he asked the audience in Hindi, "How many children is best?" and got the expected reply, Do (two).

At the end of the performance there is no organized discussion. There is some informal conversation with a few hangers-on, but from my observation, and that of others, it is fairly limited. The only immediate "follow-up" of sorts is a fairly regular practice of interviewing audience members—but this seems to be more for evaluation purposes than educational reinforcement.

Jagran's troupe has about eight to ten actors, largely unemployed young men. The membership fluctuates with actors leaving for better-paying jobs and new members being recruited and trained to take their place.

In the beginning all of the actors were middle-class, but in the last few years Roy has attempted to recruit some working class youth from the resettlement colonies. Attempts to involve women have been unsuccessful, rough conditions of the work are cited as the main deterrent. The actors are trained as "development communicators," learning the skills of mime and some basic notions of development. Roy, however, does limit their work to communication, asserting that, "they are not community development workers nor political activists" (Roy, 1980).

Roy is the prime mover and the constant factor in Jagran. The actors come and go, but he remains throughout—the manager, fund-raiser, theater director, playwright, trainer, documentarist, publicist, and driver. A brilliant entrepreneur, he has kept Jagran alive for over a decade in the rather precarious business of running a non-government agency. He tends to make all the key decisions, leaving the actors out of management tasks and strategizing about Jagran's work.

ACTION FOR CULTURAL AND POLITICAL CHANGE (ACPC)

Origins and History

Action for Cultural and Political Change (ACPC) was initiated by six young Harijan graduates in Tamil Nadu in 1974. Their aim was to politicize and organize Harijan and other agricultural laborers to fight for

basic rights and better working and living conditions. They were motivated by a deep sense of outrage at the daily humiliation, economic
subjugation, and cultural oppression faced by their fellow Harijans.
They recognized the bankruptcy of conventional methods of development in solving the basic problems of the landless and the sharpening
contradictions between rich and poor accentuated by the Green Revolution and other rural development policies. They also felt that earlier
organizing work among rural laborers in Tamil Nadu by parties of the
left had come to an impasse and fresh strategies and initiatives were
needed.

Their approach was influenced by the "Community Organizing"
(CO) methods of Saul Alinsky, an American labor and community organizer who devised a systematic approach for empowering "have-not"
communities through mass organization and confrontational tactics.
After an initial experiment in an urban slum (1971–3) they decided to
shift their work to the rural areas—the source of the urban squatter
problems—and to supplement the CO methodology with an educational
approach more suited to their potential audience—economically exploited, socially ostracized, and feudally dependent rural laborers.

Paulo Freire's approach met this need. It addressed this audience
and its low self-image and provided a concrete methodology for overcoming fear and dependence and building class consciousness, self-
confidence, and a fighting spirit. It could be used to structure discussion
of the issues and strategies for struggle and to ensure that all participants understood the objectives and implications of each stage in the
organizing process.

They also drew on Ghandi's notion of challenging social systems
that perpetuate injustice and some of his specific tactics for protest; and,
they adopted a Marxist approach for analyzing social situations.

In the first four years (1974–1977) they worked as a team in the
Chittamoor area (Chinglepet District), experimenting and building their
first laborers' movement. By 1978, when the ACPC staff moved out of
Chittamoor, the newly formed agricultural laborers' movement (which
had been created through their efforts, taken over the organizing initiatives, and won two major wage strikes), obtained written agreements
from the landlords to stop all beatings, taken possession of farming land
and house sites, released a number of families from bonded labor, and
successfully petitioned local authorities for many basic services.

At the end of the Chittamoor period, ACPC decided to expand its
work. Four of the organizers each took on a new area, trained a new
team of animateurs, and set up a new animation structure. The other two
organizers remained behind in Chittamoor as resource persons for the
laborers' movement. Their aim was to develop laborers' organizations in
each area which, over time, could develop links and form a broad-based
movement. Each team of animateurs was given autonomy. However,
the four teams remain in close touch. They meet regularly for joint

training, reflection, and strategizing and exchange experienced animateurs, and provide refuge and advice for each other in times of crisis.

Each organization represents a temporary and flexible animation structure. Once an area is organized and a self–reliant laborers' movement formed, the animation organization dissolves and the animateurs move on to new areas. Within each team and the network of teams there is a collective approach to the work; each team member has an administrative responsibility for the area association as well as an obligation to do field work and live in the field.

ACPC Process

The ACPC organizing process consists of a number of interrelated activities: (1) getting into, accepted, and "grounded" in an area; (2) adult education and literacy classes; (3) leadership training and action committees; (4) cultural action programmes and mass meetings; (5) struggles and consolidating a movement.

Getting Started. ACPC only moves into an area on invitation. Its first task is to select good bases for the organizing work—Harijan villages with a large population primarily engaged in agricultural labor and with a history of struggle.

Once a key village is chosen, the animateur finds a place to stay and gets to know its people. He also conducts a study of the area—land ownership, categories of labor (daily paid, contract, bonded, sharecropper), seasonality of work, wage rates, methods of payment, "injustice facts" (i.e., demeaning behaviour demanded of Harijans—such as having to wear the *dhoti* tied around the thighs as a sign of servility), government services, etc. This survey provides some of the themes for the adult education program.

After a month, he calls a mass meeting to explain publicly the objectives and implications of ACPC's work. He explains that the purpose of their work is to build a laborers' movement and not to do economic projects or charity. He says it won't be easy and it will, inevitably, provoke a reaction from the landlords. If the community is willing to accept the ACPC program and its risks, the animateur stays in the village and the adult education classes begin.

Adult Education and Literacy Classes. Literacy is a strategic "entry point"—Harijans express a desire to read and write and this motivates their initial participation. As an innocuous looking activity, literacy conceals the real intentions of the ACPC organizers from the landlords and bureaucrats.

The classes are held in the middle of the village in the open air and are meant to provide a meeting place and a discussion forum for the whole village. The study sessions follow Freire's method of discussing vital socioeconomic and political issues.

Instead of using centrally produced drawings, the group creates its own codes—short improvised skits or role-plays performed by the animateur and group members. Sometimes these skits are worked out beforehand, but often they develop spontaneously in a form of role-play—for example, the animateur might stand up and shout "I'm the landlord and I want some bonded labor" and people spontaneously accept roles and move into the drama. It is highly participatory, rough drama and every one joins in.

After each skit is performed, the animateur leads the group discussion about their own experience of the issues—landlessness, poor working conditions, unemployment, untouchability, lack of services, alcoholism, etc. On each issue the animateur challenges people to explain why the problem remains unsolved, getting them to bring out their fears, their dependency on the landlords and, at the same time, drawing out counterinformation—positive experiences of organizing, of taking action. He gets them to view their own disunity as immobilizing and many of the conflicts within their community as ones created by the landlords. He also helps them to see how their own cultural conditioning—the myths and rationalizations they've accepted—reinforces their submissiveness and passivity. During the same period, the animateur gets people to tackle some small "winnable" issues on which they're all willing to act in order to show them they *can* do something about their situation.

Leadership Training and Action Committees. Leadership on the actions arising out of the adult education sessions is taken by an "action committee." This is formed by the animateur after he has spent about six months in the village. He selects about 10 to 15 people for this committee—highly motivated, selfless young people who have an understanding of the animateur's work and a certain defiant, fighting spirit. (The traditional leaders of the community are rarely invited to join this group since they are largely appointed and manipulated by the local power structure). Their job is to take the priority issues of the community, plan the tactics for each struggle, and mobilize the community's participation in each struggle.

They meet regularly for training, normally late in the evening when the adult education sessions are over. Their study sessions prepare them to analyze problems and strategies in greater depth and to lead the community in taking action on various issues.

An important aspect of the training is to prepare the leaders for confrontations with bureaucrats and landlords. Many will never have been inside government buildings, let alone made demands on government officials. Dramatization or role-playing help to prepare them. The animateur plays the bureaucrat, and the leaders take turns presenting their case to the "official." After each practice session they discuss how they could improve their performance. Through role playing and critique, they work out who is going to speak, what points are going to be made, what reaction they should expect from the official and their counterresponses, etc. They learn that government only responds to pressure and that their approach should be threatening—criticizing and discrediting the officials and pointing out their corrupt practices. When the roles are reversed and a leader plays the role of the bureaucrat, he begins to understand him and loses some of the fear of confrontation.

Struggle and Movement. Struggle is the means by which the Harijans challenge their oppressors. It is the mainspring for building and consolidating their movement: people become more unified, confident, and class conscious through struggling for concrete objectives. In the beginning, the action committee takes up relatively small issues—for example, petitioning local bureaucrats for basic services (e.g., wells, street lights, house sites, a teacher for the Harijan school, and the like).[7] These initial actions are neither massive nor explosive. Their aim is to build up people's unity, confidence, and experience without inviting a major confrontation with the local power structure before they are ready.

After succeeding on small actions, the community moves on to more fundamental struggles using a wide range of tactics—for example, wage strikes, invading government offices *en masse* to press their demands, hunger strikes outside government offices to demand justice, land occupations, flooding public officials with telegrams and/or petitions, and organizing support from urban-based middle-class groups who could publicize their situation and lobby on their behalf during a crisis. This new level of struggle requires a larger mobilization of people—mass meetings are held, more laborers are invited to take an active part, and inter-village action committees are created to plan joint actions and support each other's struggles.

This new stage represents a direct attack on the local power structure and, as a result, provokes retaliation. The landlords harass their employees and sometimes fire them, vilify the ACPC organizers with the government and the political parties, and sometimes openly attack the Harijans. An effective organizer uses this repression, not as a setback, but as the provocation needed to galvanize the laborers into a stronger organization.

---

[7]ACPC has capitalized on provisions in government development plans and legislation for basic reforms and services promised to the rural poor, most of which normally remain unfulfilled because there is little enthusiasm by the civil servants and no pressure on them to carry out these plans. The conventional expectation is that since the rural poor are unorganized they will wait for rather than demand these services. However, these 20-point program promises, development plan targets, and reforms in the statute books provide important "within-the-law" targets for the initial organizing phase.

Cultural Action Programmes and Mass Meetings. These activities are organized at various stages of the process to build solidarity, deepen community discussion and understanding of major issues, get people fired up, clarify the target for a specific struggle, assure massive support, and plan and agree on the strategies for struggle. These meetings are normally held before launching a struggle and often bring together agricultural laborers from a number of neighboring villages. Their aims are double-edged; on the one hand they want to stir people's emotions and rally their support, and on the other hand they want to make sure people understand what they are getting into, e.g., possible retaliation from landlords), so they can prepare for it.

Many of these meetings are conducted in the form of a highly participatory drama in which audience members respond to challenges and questions from the actors and discuss the issues presented in the play.

These dramas are used at different phases of the organizing process. In the initial stage (within the first three months), the drama consists of a number of skits on various problems in the village. Between each sketch the actors discuss the problems with the audience, challenging them to do something about the problems.

A skillful animateur makes use of the disagreements between members of the audience—the defeatist and the more daring—to help people deal with their fear and submissiveness, to raise and overcome some of the conflicts within the community, and to raise people's hopes for change (Von der Weid and Poitevin, 1981, p. 114).

In the second stage, the drama shows a group of people (action committee) coming together and taking action on issues such as water, house sites, and electricity, through petitioning a government officer. There is no attempt at this point to frame the issue in terms of class struggle. The aim is simply to show that Harijans can solve their problems if they get organized. For example, in one drama the women march with their water pots to the government office and demand access to a river in their area (which the landlord has grabbed for his exclusive use). When the bureaucrat refuses their request they smash their pots in front of him, a militant action which prompts him to do something about the problem.

The third stage drama marks the beginning of more fundamental struggles. The class enemy is identified, each of the key powerful figures are caricatured, and their corrupt or exploitative practices exposed. The drama shows the laborers organizing to fight against these injustices. The actor playing the role of a youth leader, who has previous experience of urban trade unions, explains the importance of a laborers' organization and answers people's questions about the organization and the consequences of a strike. Actors and audience discuss the strategies and tactics for a real strike (or other form of struggle) being planned by that community. Sometimes the actors will even role-play the reactions of the landlords meeting together.

The fourth stage coincides with the growth of a broader movement and if often enacted to a number of villages working together on various struggles. It shows that individual struggles are not sufficient—that the laborers need to build links with agricultural workers in other areas. One of the actors presents the objectives and perspectives of the agricultural laborers' movement and everyone (including the audience) questions him. In the course of this discussion, the actor explains new strategies and tactics for broadening the movement—for example, organizing mass rallies of laborers at the district headquarters with a set of demands; organizing hunger strikes in front of government offices to protest injustices done to laborers in other villages; legal prosecution against landlords backed up by mass demonstrations.

Unlike the short skits used in the adult education classes, the "cultural action" program takes a whole evening. The program begins about 7 p.m. with revolutionary songs to attract the laborers returning from the fields. The whole village gathers around the stage area, lit with lights extending out into the audience, and equipped with a loudspeaker. The actors are some of the villagers and a few animateurs. The play is unscripted—the actors have agreed on a scenario beforehand and each improvise his/her lines. Although untrained, the actors have no difficulty dramatizing incidents and characters drawn from their own lives. They caricature their oppressors with real insight into their idiosyncracies—although in the beginning they have to overcome the initial fear that the landlords will find out and victimize them.

The "play" is a number of skits on various problems linked through the principal characters—a clown character (who acts as a narrator/commentator), landlord, landlord's servant, youth leader—who appear throughout the play. Songs are performed between each skit. In the second stage drama observed by the writer, the play showed

- a bonded laborer remaining loyal to his landlord and being tricked into signing a false bond paper
- another laborer approaching the landlord for a small plot of unused land, being turned down, and accepting it meekly
- the landlord in collusion with the government officials, attempting to appropriate drought relief funds meant for the Harijan village
- a trader adulterating his goods (e.g., adding water to milk), hoarding, and money-lending at exorbitant rates
- Harijan initiatives being undermined by religion, alcohol, and manipulation by the landlords
- the bribing of a government official by the landlord.

In the final scene of the drama, actors and audience discussed real plans, to be carried out the following day, to pressure the government into deepening their well. They planned to march *en masse* to the Block

Development Office, and if the official refused to help, they planned to go on a hunger strike outside his office.

Each drama not only shows the problems, but gets the audience talking about them. It is a brilliant example of audience participation and dialogue (and not in the rather contrived fashion of conventional post-performance discussion). The Harijans are just sitting there, resting, tired from the day's work, enjoying the songs and jokes, and slowly becoming absorbed by the drama. Suddenly they are being challenged and drawn into it. One of the characters—for example, the loyal bonded laborer—walks into the open space in the middle of the audience and taunts them about their lack of loyalty to the landlord. An animateur in the audience is the first to argue back, but soon everyone joins in ridiculing him for being so submissive and accepting such bad treatment. This actor-audience dialogue continues for 5 to 10 minutes before shifting back to the stage. Later another actor puts a firm question to them—"Look, your brother is being beaten. Why are you sitting quietly? Why are you allowing this to happen?" This provokes another furious response. Sometimes the discussion shifts totally to the audience.

This kind of dialogue is repeated at various points throughout the drama stimulated by the actors, an animateur in the audience, or audience members themselves. For example, when the bonded laborer is about to sign the false document or the government officer to be bribed there is a huge uproar with everyone trying to warn him—one old woman walks right up to the stage to make her points. When the landlord tries to threaten the laborers (in the audience) into working for him, they shout back: "You do not pay us enough! We will not work without more pay."

In the second, third, and fourth stages the drama constitutes a highly participatory struggle–planning meeting. For example, in the third stage drama after introducing the notion of a strike, overcoming fears, and explaining its consequences, the actor playing the youth leader leads the audience in discussing how to organize it—the most strategic time (during harvest), stopping laborers from other villages from coming for work, winning their support, surviving during the strike, informing the police so their action is not misrepresented by the landlords, the terms and conditions for the strike, anticipating the landlord's divisive tactics and physical retaliation, and so on.

These discussions with the audience that are built into the drama preclude the need for a follow-up mass meeting. By the end of the cultural evening there is a very clear understanding of the issues and a firm commitment to the agreed-upon action. Nevertheless, there is follow-up. After every performance the animateur goes around the village listening to people's reactions. If there is firm support, the action committee meets immediately to plan and to mobilize people.

The reaction of the landlord is also assessed. The drama represents the first time the Harijans threaten the landlords openly—ridiculing and criticizing him and asserting their intention to organize against him. It is important to see which way the wind is blowing—whether the landlord will try to stop the planned action and, if so, how he intends to fight back.

COMPARISON AND ANALYSIS

In this final section the three programs—the Song and Drama Division (SDD), Jagran, and Action for Cultural and Political Change (ACPC)—are analyzed in comparative terms. The origins and objectives, organizational structure, communication model, program content, and program process are examined in turn.

Origins, Objectives, and Audience

SDD was created as one means of consolidating the state's authority, advancing its program, and enlisting support for it. More specifically, its purpose was to propagate the major themes of government's modernization strategy—savings, capital-intensive agricultural production, family planning, etc. While adopting the mass campaign approach of China and Russia, it left out a critical ingredient—mass mobilization and active participation of the people. Without this vital component it has become essentially an exercise in top–down propaganda and bureaucratic paternalism, controlled and run by development planners: "Here is what government can offer you. It is up to you to participate as individuals in making use of the services provided." Development is something that planners/governments do for, and to, rural people through communication. In this, SDD accepts a modernization framework and see its work in terms of (a) changing traditional attitudes and habits which impede development and, (b) informing people about government services and programs.

Jagran is not a state institution, but it does have many of the same social origins, modernization ideas, and goals of the SDD. Its initial economic benefactor was the powerful American-funded family planning lobby, and its initial work was to promote their idea of the "happy small family." Since basing their work permanently in the slums of Delhi, Jagran has added a community development objective (getting people to improve their situation through collective effort such as the maintenance of water taps) and has continued its initial work, on a broader set of themes, of changing traditional or negative behavior and advertising the availability of government services. One new measure over the last few years has been a token objective of conscientization.

In both these cases the use of the performing arts was not seen as a strategy of conscientization, of making the poor challenge their situation. The SDD was devised as a form of mass information, and as a means of legitimizing the policies and practices of the Congress party–led government. In the 1960s, with the growing pressure from the international family planning lobby, SDD and Jagran's media work was seen as an important strategy in getting the rural and urban poor who had been by-passed by other development programs, missed out on the schooling system, and were beyond the reach of other media. The object was to convert them to the small family norm. This was not a broad-based adult education program to increase their skills and socioeconomic possibilities or to raise their consciousness. There was no material economic reason for a mass adult education program which would make the poor more productive. Their growing landlessness, unemployment, massive migration to the cities, and marginalization in the cities required a means of containing their social discontent. SDD's and Jagran's role was to anesthetize them, to socialize them to accept a compliant role in the system (e.g., getting them to work together in maintaining the few community water taps rather than demanding better facilities, blaming themselves for their reproductive habits rather than struggling against the exploitation and unjust structures, and so on). It was a form of self-help social welfare, social control, and population control.

ACPC is concerned with fundamental structural transformation. Its social origins lie in the history of Harijan and other laborers' struggles against exploitation and ACPC's critical assessment and rejection of conventional development approaches of the state and many non-governmental agencies. ACPC's objective is to transform unjust social structures through organizing the powerless to fight against exploitation and for their rights (including services promised by government but not delivered).

It rejects the notion of development as handing out modernization packages and socializing the "illiterate and ignorant masses" to accept the modern packages (contraceptives, fertilizer, toilets, green leafy vegetables, etc.). It views development as a process of social transformation, of overturning unjust structures, policies and programs. Its approach implies confrontation—a notion which is diametrically opposed to the SDD's assumption of a community of interest between various classes in a village.

SDD's focus is broad, attempting to reach the "generalized" masses—all citizens without distinction. Jagran and ACPC, on the other hand, commit themselves to a more strategically defined audience—the marginalized, the powerless, the oppressed. Jagran and ACPC, however, part company over strategy and tactics. Jagran was invited by officialdom to work in the urban slums; ACPC chose to concentrate its energies on the rural workers, having discovered that the source of urban marginization is the increasing landlessness, unemployment, and impoverishment of the rural peasantry. Jagran responds to invitations by official agencies (e.g., Delhi Development Authority, and CARE). ACPC moves into an area only when it has been invited by the laborers.

Organizational Structure and Performers

SDD and Jagran are both hierarchies; decisions and initiatives are made at the top and orders are passed down the line of command to the troupes in the field. The only difference is that Jagran is much smaller in scale, and the "general" often accompanies the troupe in the field. ACPC, on the other hand, is a functional collective; even though there are varying levels of skill, understanding, and experience in the group, decisions are made collectively and everyone has a "front-line" role, working and living in the villages. Structurally ACPC is a decentralized network of local area teams each with full autonomy over initiatives in its own area.

Operationally SDD and Jagran are mobile programs dependent on itinerant troupes who arrive in a community, give a performance, and go. ACPC, on the other hand, works on a sustained basis in each of its communities, and their cultural programs are not dependent on outside professional troupes. The villagers in each community, along with the local animateurs, produce their own drama.

SDD's coverage, in comparison to Jagran's, is relatively sparse; with a mandate to cover all of India, its troupes are only able to visit each of India's 600,000 villages on average of once every six years. Jagran's work is more concentrated, limited to 16 resettlement colonies in Delhi. However, even Jagran's coverage has been criticized by its audience as too discontinuous and community members have suggested that Jagran train a group in each area to do the work (Mehra, 1978, p. 11). ACPC's local teams work on a sustained basis in their communities.

ACPC and the director of Jagran share a moral outrage about the victimization of Harijans. ACPC translates this into a deep commitment which involves giving up the perks and the easy living available to educated Harijans, working and living *with* exploited Harijan laborers, and sharing the physical risks of class struggle. Roy puts his sense of anger into sketches (exposing the corruption of politicians and condemning Harijan atrocities) and takes them to the "forgotten urban poor," but these bold statements are always *for* the Harijans, rather than *with* them. It is his analysis rather than one growing out of the Harijans' own analysis and sense of dissatisfaction with the system.

Roy's conviction and commitment aren't absorbed by his actors. Like the SDD troupes, they take a more mercenary approach to the work. They join Jagran to learn some skills which might be marketable in TV or film acting and to earn some income. In SDD's case, lack of commitment by the performers is admitted to be one of its major problems:

> The performers are associated with the work for monetary considerations. The results that can be achieved are self-evident. The performances go on but no advancement is made. The edge has never been able to achieve a cutting sharpness (Naarayan, 1974, p. 8).

The commodification and commercialization of folk theatre are the main problems; development becomes a business of disbursing contracts and hiring a certain number of troupes for a certain number of performances rather than a complex process of bringing about social change. The performers are graded, hired, given a script or a message, and sent off to propagate something they hardly believe in.

In criticizing this mercenary approach, one can't blame the actors. Their response is totally realistic. There is no economic security in this work, nor is there any attempt to involve them in a way which fosters commitment. In the case of the SDD part-time troupes, the rate of pay is lower than from private shows and government's interest in them doesn't extend beyond their 20 performances of publicity drama each year:

> There has been no systematic thinking and action for their continu-
> ous survival in their own environment, namely villages, fairs, tem-
> ples, the ritualistic festivities (Mathur, 1977 p. 2).[8]

Training is minimal in Jagran's case, and nonexistent in the case of the SDD. Jagran's training is limited to acting skills, no attention is given to developing sociopolitical understanding and analytical skills. The training is functional, geared to a narrowly defined performance context. In contrast, ACPC's training program for both animateurs and village leaders is broadbased, sociopolitical in content, and continuous; it relates dialectically to the process of organization and struggle, guiding and reflecting on it.

The involvement of the SDD and Jagran performers is limited largely to acting. Unlike the ACPC animateurs who take part in all strategizing aspects of the work, the SDD and Jagran performers are left out of the process of selecting, defining, and shaping the message. They are simply expected to reproduce the development messages they are given. There isn't even an attempt to have dialogues with them about their own experience and analysis of the issue (e.g., performers' own lack of literacy skills and experiences with family planning campaigns).

With only financial incentives to motivate them, many of the performers (especially the SDD troupes) do this work in sufferance; their meager income is the price they pay for relinquishing their traditional role as a tribune of popular concerns. However, there is little personal commitment to the ideas they are expected to disseminate. As one song-and-drama performer put it when asked about the effect of his group's performances:

> We don't really know. All we can say is that when we do a good
> script we entertain people and when we do a so-so script we bore

---

[8]A recent conference on folk media in India recommended that government take an interest in the long-term economic security of the performers (and not just their immediate usefulness for government's propaganda purposes) and "educate the folk artists about their rights and help them to avoid being exploited" (Kumari, 1980).

people. About what effect we have in the villages, that's something for the Government to say (Abrams, 1975, p. 404).

They are resigned to their role as propagandists for purposes of survival, but their hearts are not in it—it is not their issue and the performances lack the dynamism of their own creation. As Das (1980) observed that "They will work for any government department, political party, fertilizer company, or local landlord who will pay them." The ACPC dramas, on the other hand, grow out of the situations, experiences, and analyses of the actors who are themselves villagers. They aren't handed centrally produced, prepackaged scripts and told to perform. They create their own dramas out of their own collective analyses of their immediate situation and the deeper structures in which they are embedded. This is a genuine expression of the people.[9]

Communication Model and Program Content

The two "camps" have diametrically opposite approaches to communication—SDD and Jagran are "top-down," "banking" exercises; ACPC is one of conscientization. The former deliver information in a one-way fashion about topics largely chosen by decisionmakers outside the community; the latter stimulates popular expression of, discussion, and action on problems identified within and by the community. The former is an exercise in propaganda—an active source operating on a passive receiver with the object of anesthetizing people and persuading them to accept the legitimacy of the ideas they are receiving from the dominant structure. The latter is a process of engagement, analysis, questioning, and deepening people's understanding and resistance to the dominant structure.

The differences are not accidental, a matter of selecting optional methodologies. They are determined by the ideological framework in which each operates. SDD and Jagran accept the modernization framework of transforming the traditional sector through introducing modernizing inputs. This provides the rationale for their "banking" approach. The poor are poor because they are "backward" or "traditional." It is up to the modern sector (read the developmentalist) to overcome traditional ideas and bad habits and replace them with new ways of thinking and behaving. This is necessarily a one-way approach because the poor have nothing to contribute to the interaction, being "ignorant" and "backward." Their role is simply to absorb new information, attitudes, and habits.

---

[9]One folk media claim is that it is a means through which communities "have a voice." In the case of SDD, it may be their mouthpiece—i.e., the traditional dramas that they are used to—but it is clearly not their voice. By accepting the role as a mercenary, as a paid spokesman for ideas they have no commitment to, the folk artists themselves relinquish their role as a genuine expression of the people. In this propagandists role they are no longer the "carrier of a community's history, values, aspirations, etc."

For ACPC the cause of poverty and underdevelopment is not the "inadequacies" and "ignorance" of the poor; it is the structural relationships which keep the poor powerless, subservient, and exploited. For them the critical problems of the poor aren't "drinking, illiteracy, superstition, uncontrolled family, malnutrition, and insanitation," as listed by one SDD official (Ranganath, 1979, p. 1). These are only symptoms of their exploited and unjust treatment—the effect of their impoverishment, not the cause. For ACPC the key problems are those of exploitation, victimization, ostracization, and injustice.

For ACPC the problems of the poor cannot be solved by merely propagating modern information, skills, and technologies. "Banking" the poor with modern information and ideas will not get at the fundamental structures keeping them powerless and oppressed. "Development as modernization" will only integrate them more successfully into the structures keeping them exploited, stifling their frustration, and growing discontent, converting their anger into self-blame, and redirecting their collective potential into individualized ways for adjusting to the system, or collective actions which do not threaten the system. So ACPC's communication method had to be one promoting an active rather than a passive response, working on people's anger and dissatisfaction with their situation, encouraging them to question and analyze the issues (rather than merely accepting the ideas and directions of the animateurs), and developing their confidence, unity, and fighting spirit. ACPC's approach promoted concrete and confrontational actions demonstrating to the people that they could do something to challenge their victimization if they were organized.

When viewed in detail, SDD's methodology is crudely top-down. This is illustrated by a diagram in Parmar's (1974, p. 6) book, *Traditional Folk Media in India*, showing SDD's vertical communication structure flowing from the urban development planner to the audience in the field. The decisions about content and the choice of messages are all taken in national or district capitals; the job of the artist is to put it across and the audience to listen.

Jagran often claims that its "themes come from the people." An analysis of the history of their repertoire, however, shows that they reflect the history of its varying sponsorships—Pathfinder Fund, (family planning), CARE–India (nutrition), United Commercial Bank (savings and loans), Year of the Child (deprived children), etc. Jagran's repertoire includes few issues which seem to reflect the real concerns and priorities of the slum dwellers. For example, there are no sketches on: (a) the landlessness, unemployment, and impoverishment forcing people to come to the cities; (b) Sanjay Ghandi's slum clearance and sterilization campaigns; (c) the exploitative and insecure working conditions for unskilled laborers; (d) the inadequate services in the colonies; (e) transportation problems in getting to and from work and all of the services based outside the colonies (e.g., schools); and, (f) the problem of dealing with officialdom.

Jagran's repertoire, then, is not a set of Freirian codes. It is a core of prefabricated knowledge defined by experts, which is, in Roy's words, "hammered into their consciousness." This "curriculum" approach to development theatre limits it to the kind of general education available in a school—a well-defined curriculum (read ideology) of those who control the society and not a content growing out of the struggles of slum dwellers for better working and living conditions.

The Jagran and SDD "curriculum" and the mobile nature of their work forces them to adopt a generalized approach to awareness-raising. Their plays aren't a rallying call for specific actions or struggles. Their anti-untouchability plays, for example, give a general picture of Harijan victimization, but fail to bring out the specific injustices (e.g., beatings and rapes) in that particular community around which the community could organize. In contrast, ACPC's plays reflect immediate problems and organizational needs of the local community and serve as a focus for organizing.

The major contrast between SDD and Jagran, on one hand, and ACPC, on the other, is the way they reflect reality. SDD and Jagran present a one-dimensional view of reality incapable of leading people to a deeper understanding of the structural context of their oppression. Each skit presents one neat technical solution for a single problem, often in the form of a service provided by government, with no reference to the sociopolitical context, nor any indication of the sociopolitical implications of the solution prescribed. If you have so many children you can't get on the buses—"Stop at two, more won't do!" If you are exploited as a rickshaw puller, get a bank loan and buy your own rickshaw. If you have an unbalanced diet, eat green leafy vegetables. These easy slogans fail to address, for example, (a) the economic circumstances (needed for labor and old-age security) forcing people to have large families (b) the issue of transportation itself (c) the exploitation of rickshaw pullers (d) the red tape and corruption involved in getting a development loan (e) the underlying political economic conditions which often leave people without any diet, let alone a balanced diet. Instead of giving a broader picture of people's material conditions, the political-economic structures creating those conditions, and the obstacles they face in taking individual or collective actions, an easy technical solution is offered.

There is no use of contradiction, which would make people question and deepen their understanding. The answers are simple: adjust your behavior in a certain way, use the prescribed government services, and work together to maintain the few water taps and public toilets and everything will be lovely. There is no sense of the real limitations on any of these actions, their implications, or of the possibly negative consequences. This is not a form of conscientization to get people thinking. This is anesthetizing propaganda, "educating the masses by influencing their subconsciousness" (Shiveshwarkar, 1979).

Each of Jagran's topics are treated as discrete problems requiring a separate solution; there is no attempt to show their linkages (for example, between Harijan victimization and alcoholism) or their common roots in the underlying political-economic structure. Many of the problems (e.g., deprived children, alcoholism, and malnutrition) have their origins in the exploitative working conditions—yet they are treated separately and diagnosed in terms of the morality or the behavior of the "victims," rather than the unjust social structures which underpin all of these problems.

Without bringing out the connections between problems, the symptoms (heavy drinking, malnutrition, borrowing money, etc.) are presented as the real problems and the crucial underlying causes (low wages, insecurity of employment, inequitable treatment, etc.) are deftly concealed. As a result these are treated as technical problems requiring technical solutions (go to the bank for loans, to the clinic for contraceptives, eat green leafy vegetables), which only provide a partial answer to the fundamental problem.

Coupled with the technical prescriptions and slogans is a "Blaming the Victim" attitude. As agencies serving an implicit legitimation and social control function, SDD and Jagran produce dramas which make the poor feel responsible for creating their own situation. This is done by distracting attention from what the dominant classes are doing to the poor (i.e., by leaving out the historical aspect and economic relationships) and poking fun at the poor themselves. Through the character of Rama in SDD's Rama–Shamo dramas, the poor are ridiculed for their large families, their "traditional" farming methods, their insanitary habits, etc. They are left with a sense of guilt, that it is their backward behavior which is the ultimate problem and not the social system which pushes them off the land and out of a job, deepens their indebtedness and dependence through criminally high interest rates, etc. By restricting the scenes to the domestic situation and ignoring Rama's economic life and social relationships, the whole rationality for producing a large family is subtly removed, and Rama can be blamed for his "irrational," "backward" behavior.

Jagran's use of mime is similar. Unlike ACPC who use ridicule in defiance of the landlords and a means of bolstering the courage of the laborers, Jagran uses ridicule as a weapon against the poor. Although their intentions are positive—they feel that seeing their problems and inadequacies exposed will benefit the poor—by focusing largely on the "defects" and "traditional behavior" of the poor without showing how these are socially produced, Jagran undermines their confidence. People are made to feel inadequate by blaming them: (a) for not eating the right foods and burying their money in the ground, when their pay is so small they can hardly eat at all; (b) for not limiting their families and not sending their children to school, when their survival often demands extra breadwinners and school fees are prohibitive; and, (c) for taking loans from the money lender, when their "salaries are so small it is difficult to manage to the end of the month" (Mehra, 1978), and the national banks do not give loans for consumption or health expenses. It is no wonder that some of Jagran's audiences

> assumed that the purpose of depicting their problems was to criticize them rather than to arouse their consciousness and motivate them to act. Some of these people felt that the problems of rich people should be given equal time (Mehra, 1978, p. 12).

To them they are not the main problem but rather the system which produces their indebtedness, alcoholism, delinquent children, insanitation, etc.

The issue of alcohol, addressed by Jagran and ACPC, provides another point of comparison. In Jagran's dramas, men are blamed for heavy drinking without any reference to the structure which produces and maintains this drinking problem ACPC, on the other hand, shows in its drama (a) how men turn to drinking because of the pressures of their exploited situation, (b) the vested interests involved in alcohol production, and (c) the landlords' use of drinking to maintain their control over the laborers. In the discussions woven into the drama people raise the importance of dealing *collectively* with the drinking problem as a vital aspect of organizing a successful struggle.

SDD's and Jagran's portraits of reality rarely depict class conflict (let alone class relationships). The overall image of society projected in the dramas is that of harmony and cooperation, rather than of conflicts and division. Where conflict is portrayed, it is within the neighborhood between poor people themselves or the conflicts within families. By contrast, in the ACPC case class conflict is portrayed as the core of the drama and provides the basis for dialectical analysis. In limiting their scenes to the colonies, Jagran eliminates the potential use of dialectics and of showing the differences between the working and living conditions of working class and middle class people and relationships between them. Where Jagran does portray class conflict, it is resolved not through dealing with it as such, but through an individualistic solution which itself may pose some problematic class relationships.

In SDD's case, people resolve their class conflict dramas not through struggles by the Harijans to demand equitable treatment, but through the paternalistic, "change-of-heart" response of an individual landlord. In contrast, ACPC's dramas show how unrealistic that solution is: that landlords are locked into their class position, that it is difficult for them to move outside their class interests in order to treat a laborer in a nonexploitative way. They exploit the Harijan not as a matter of will or choice—their position in the system demands this way of behaving. Landlords resist caste reforms precisely because caste discrimination is closely linked with economic exploitation.

In both cases, SDD and Jagran present unrealistic proposals for solving the problems of working class people because they fail to consider the real constraints and possibilities within the power structure. They are too neat, too simple; they assume the bureaucracy will respond quickly to provide the services and the legal provisions promised or that the local power structure will not attempt to interfere with the way these services and laws are implemented. Or they assume that the problems will go away if the poor simply rehabilitate themselves, adopting modern habits and behavior. The ACPC dramas, on the other hand, show that it is unrealistic for Harijans to wait for a landlord's change of heart to get better treatment, or to expect a bureaucrat to provide house sites, bonded labor reforms, etc., without a certain amount of collective pressure. Their dramas show people how to pressure the landlords and civil servants for better working and living conditions. Where SDD and Jagran limit themselves to giving the poor information on government services and reforms, ACPC shows them (in the drama) and actually organizes them to assert their legal rights and demand those services and reforms.

Program Process

ACPC's cultural program is an integral part of a total social transformation process (conscientization, leadership development, organizing, and struggle) and its "actors" are animateurs and villagers. Acting is only one of their tasks and it is integrated into their total animation process. SDD's and Jagran's dramas are "one-off" events, and the actors are primarily performers—their job is to put on a good show and once it's over to hit the road.

ACPC dramas are rough-and-ready sketches acted out by members of the community expressing their problems and provoking discussion on the source of their problems and what needs to be done. Jagran and SDD's dramas are polished "well-finished plays" performed by outsiders presenting both an outsider's view of people's problems and a solution. The former has a rough story line worked out by village actors beforehand leaving lots of room for improvisation, changes in plot, and dialogue with the audience, including many sequences where the audience takes over the drama. The latter is a scripted or, at least, a tightly controlled play with no audience participation. In the former, the audiences work out their own solution in the course of the drama; in the latter, the solution is prepackaged and ready to be consumed.

In the ACPC cultural action program, discussion is woven into the drama, takes place between scenes, and is organized when the dramas are over; the object is to deepen people's understanding of the issues and to talk about what might be done about the problem and organizing to do something. The Jagran or SDD cultural event is structured primarily as a performance. Any form of additional interaction with the audience is a means of message reinforcement. For example, a Field Publicity Officer answering questions at the end of an SDD performance is attempting to persuade people not to raise critical awareness. A Jagran commentator who asks the audience "How many children makes a happy family?" is simply extracting confirmation that the message has been communicated.

In the case of SDD and Jagran, the relationship between the performance and the follow-up action is problematic. For SDD, it largely depends on the enthusiasm of local development workers; SDD staff admit that coordination is weak. SDD and Jagran dramas primarily point towards individual behavioral change. However, Jagran also talks about collective action, but it sees this in a mechanical, linear way flowing out of a long conscientization process:

> Before they can become organized and politicized their consciousness needs to be raised. It's a long process. The first stage is to bring in awareness. People are unaware of the possibility of change. If it is hammered constantly, the consciousness may bring about change (Personal Interview, 1980).

Jagran has no organizational strategy beyond bringing people together for a performance. They seem to believe that once people have been "awakened" and have reached a certain level of awareness, then an organizational process will develop spontaneously and people will take action.

This contrasts with ACPC's work, where organizing is a deliberate process and consciousness and organizing grow dialectically. People cannot be exposed to awareness; it is not something you "hammer" into someone. Social and political understanding is only acquired when put into practice, but, in addition, it is learned *from experience,* from taking action. Action in the ACPC process not only flows out of, but also constitutes, "awareness-raising". Marching on the government office and discovering you can not only make your case, but can argue back when the official shouts at you is as much a part of the growing confidence and class consciousness as sitting in a study circle or participating in an ACPC drama. Learning in ACPC is dialectical, leading to action and in turn being informed by action. Learning in Jagran's case is a static, passive process, uninformed by action or meaningful dialogue.

Jagran attempts to cover itself by maintaining an ambiguous community role. While aiming to arouse community action, it resists taking on organizational responsibility. Its job is to "hammer" in awareness. If the community doesn't take action, they can be blamed for being "apathetic." While maintaining informal contacts with local leaders and organizations, its collaborative work with local residents' associations seems to be limited (Fernandez, 1980). While it is true that they consult local leaders in planning their daily program, there is little attempt to put their "theatre" directly at the service of the residents' association—for example, to rally support for a specific struggle or initiate a community dialogue on an issue.

Jagran and SDD motivate people to make individual use of the available government services. ACPC develops popular organizations to confront government and demand these services which, due to official corruption or sheer inertia, are unavailable or appropriated by the rich landowners. Collective actions promoted by Jagran—e.g., collective maintenance of water taps—are not challenges against the system. They are the classical forms of "self-help" community development used by the state to control people's collective energies and to divert them from pressuring government for adequate services.

CONCLUSION

These case studies have shown that theatre can be used, on one hand, as a medium for dictating the views and prescriptions of the dominant class; legitimizing the system and controlling people's participation in it; shifting the blame for poverty from the oppressive structures to the "self-impoverishing" poor; and anesthetizing people so that they participate uncritically in reproducing the apparatus of domination. However, on the other hand, theatre can also be used as part of a social transformation process in which the oppressed express their problems and grievances, deepen their understanding of the exploitative social structure, and build confidence, class consciousness, and power through organizing and struggling against oppression.

REFERENCES

Abrams, Tevia. (1975). "Folk Theatre in Maharashtrian Social Development Programmes." *Educational Theatre Journal* 27 (1), 395–407.

CARE - India. (1974). *Impact of Mime.* An Evaluation of Jagran's Development Oriented Mime Performances at Okhla Neighbourhood Comprehensive Health and Welfare Project. New Delhi: CARE-India.

Das, Kajal Kumar. (1980). *Burrakatha of Andhra Pradesh.* New Delhi: Indian Institute of Mass Communication.

Feder, E. (1976). "McNamara's Little Green Revolution: World Bank Scheme for Self-Liquidation of Third World Peasantry." *Economic and Political Weekly* (India), 11 (14), 532–541.

Fernandez, Aloysius. (1980). *Evaluation of Jagran 1979–1980.* New Delhi: Jagran.

Kumari, Abbilasha. (1980). "Communication and the Traditional Media." *Communicator* (New Delhi) 15 (3), 12–18.

Mane, V. V. (1974). "Identification of Flexible Folk Drama in Family Planning Communication." Paper prepared for the UNESCO Inter-Regional Seminar-*cum*-Workshop on the Integrated Use of Folk Media and Mass Media in Family Planning Communication Programmes, New Delhi, Oct.

Mane, V. V. (1980). "Traditional Media: Organization and Administration for Development Communication." Paper presented to the Seminar on Communication and The Traditional Media, Indian Institute of Mass Communication, Pune, India.

Mathur, J. C. (1954). "The Folk Theatre as an Instrument of Social Education." *In*

S. C. Dutta (Ed.), *Place of Recreation in Social Education: A Symposium*. New Delhi: India Adult Education Association.

Mathur, J. C. (1977). "A Distressing Aspect of Theatre Development in India." Unpublished article, New Delhi.

Mayer, A., et al., 1958. *Pilot Project: India*. Berkeley, California: University of California Press.

Mehra, Rekha. (1978). *Jagran Evaluation: An Attutudinal Evaluation of the Impact of Pantomime*. New Delhi: Church's Auxiliary for Social Action (CASA).

Miles, Lee. (1961). "Drama and Community Development." *Community Development Bulletin 12* (2), 44–48.

Naarayan, Birendra. (1974). "Puppet as a Medium of Communication for Family Planning." Paper prepared for the UNESCO Inter-Regional Seminar-*cum*-Workshop on the Integrated Use of Folk Media and Mass Media in Family Planning Communication Programmes, New Delhi, Oct.

Parmar, Shyam. (1974). *Traditional Folk Media in India*. New Delhi: Geka Books.

Ranganath, H. K. (1979). "Not a Thing of the Past: Functional and Cultural Status of Traditional Media in India." Paris: UNESCO International Commission for the Study of Communication Problems.

Richmond, Farley. (1973). "The Political Role of Theatre in India." *Educational Theatre Journal 25* (3), 318–334.

Roy, Aloke. [Personal Interview], 1980.

Roy, Aloke. [Personal Interview], 1981.

Shiveshwarkar, Shyamala. (1979). "Theatre of the Oppressed." *Hindustan Times Weekly* (New Delhi), *18* Feb.

Singh, K. M. (1977). "Women and the Family: Coping with Poverty in the Bastis of Delhi." *Social Action* (Indian Social Institute) *27* (3), 241–265.

Von der Weid, D., and G. Poitevin. (1981). *Roots of a Peasant Movement*. Pune, India: Shubhada-Sarswat Publications.

8

The Barefoot Actors: Folk Drama and Development Communication in Asia

Debra Van Hoosen

For centuries, folk drama in Asia has served as a traditional channel of communication, conveying information to rural villagers while providing them with entertainment. Through the use of dialogue, action, music, song, and dance the stage has presented a vitally important view of the cosmos which has implanted basic beliefs and behavior patterns in rural audiences. Of more general importance is the fact that folk drama has remained a flexible medium over the years and has adjusted its content according to gradual social changes. Because folk drama was able to maintain its contemporaneity, it survived and left an indelible mark on sociocultural and historical records. Commenting on the tremendous impact of theatre in Southeast Asia, James Brandon (1967, p. 278) remarks:

> It is not an exaggeration to say that, had the theatre not existed as a powerful channel for communicating to large groups of people, Southeast Asian civilization would not be what it is today. Through the medium of theatre performances, the complex religious, metaphysical, social, and intellectual values of the ruling elite were disseminated to the most unsophisticated villagers in the most remote areas.

Among the wide array of theatre genres found in Asia, folk dramas is the earliest and most widespread theatre form tied closely to religious and agrarian activities prevalent in rural village life. The history of folk performances in India, Sri Lanka, Indonesia, and the Philippines goes back a long time. It is estimated (Gargi, 1966) that the tradition of folk theatre as it is found in India's rural areas today is between 400 and 600 years old. Ritual theatre in Sri Lanka can be traced back by legend to (c. 200 B.C.) pre-Buddhist times (Gunawardana, 1976). At least one theory claims that Javanese *wayang kulit* existed before 1000 A.D. in Indonesia

(Brandon, 1967). The oral tradition of relaying tribal histories in the Philippines predates Spanish colonization.

While some folk theatre forms with strong religious content remained relatively unchanged through time, folk theatre forms with more secular content incorporated changes within the society. Usually, comic characters introduced the village's current topics of conversation. Folk theater became a source of information as new ideas and humorous improvizations were added to traditional stories; these secular elements, indicative of change, are germane to the discussion of the role of folk theatre in rural development.

During the early 1970s, the notion of using folk media to promote development had become an international topic of discussion. In 1972 and 1974 UNESCO organized two meetings in which communication consultants, government officials, and folk media experts met to discuss how folk media and mass media could be used in a particular development program, namely family planning. To date, these two conferences appear to be the most extensive attempt to examine the issue. A renewed interest in the use of folk media for development, however, seemed to be emerging as "newer concepts of development" advocated themes such as local participation and integration of indigenous media and mass media. In light of this recent development, it is necessary to reexamine the communication strategy suggested by some of experts in considering development communication objectives and long range goals.

The strategy to use folk dramas for development follows one of two basic communication models, with or without slight modifications. In the past, most folk media campaigns adhered to a one-way communication model. While the source of the message has usually been government or development officials, the content varies depending on what development campaign is in vogue at the movement. The path of the message is, for the most part, in a one-way direction from the top levels of the development pyramid, gradually filtering down to the bottom of the development spectrum, the urban and rural poor. Messages have been described as "general and sloganistic" (Kidd and Byram, 1978) and usually seem to stop once they reach the intended receivers.

Such a one-way approach to message dissemination largely ignored one major feature of folk media: close interaction between the audience and the actors. Through interaction the media have maintained an up-to-date cultural identity and have continued through decades, and even centuries. But in the past, development campaigns have had no direct line of communication from the receivers back to the source. In other words, the source of the message uses a channel such as the folk drama to send a message to a specific audience; the audience having heard the message has no direct means of communicating with the senders. No exchange of information takes place; no one knows if the message has had an impact or not.

The Red Triangle Campaign for family planning in India is an example of a one-way flow of development communication. In this case, outside professional troupes were brought into the villages to give performances on the need for family planning. The intended "message" aimed at the villagers was to limit the number of children in their families. The campaign was not designed to find out what the villagers thought about the "message" and, therefore, had no need for dialogue. (Wilder, 1977).

In fact, most of the population campaigns which have used folk drama to promote family planning exemplify a one-way communication flow from the imported artists ending when the message reached the intended audience. On Bali, *dalangs* were asked to insert family planning "messages" into traditional shadow puppet performances (Muncie, 1972), and in West Java, dalangs inserted messages in *wayang golek* (wooden puppet) performances, using the *punokawan* characters (clown-servants) to introduce the subject. A slight modification was used in the Philippines. A family planning campaign made use of *zarzuela* and *balagtasan* troupes who had been well-versed in the family planning program prior to their performance. After the performance there was an attempt to continue the communication process through follow-up surveys. An attempt was made to evaluate the impact of the performance, in some cases one week later.

Problems with this method of communication did not go unnoticed. For example, Parmar (1975) developed a model which modified a top-down campaign strategy using India's traditional media. In the existing bureaucratic structure, the source of the message is the Directorate of Field Publicity, which passes the message down through two intermediary groups—the regional offices and the field units—before the message can be transmitted via traditional folk channels to the receivers. As Parmar indicates, the problem with this model is that there is a large gap between the source of the message and the receiver. The policy makers are frequently out of touch with their target audience. Parmar proposes the addition of a coordinating board, comprised of artists and script writers who know and understand the target audiences and have the competence to transform the intended messages. This procedure would bridge the gap at the grassroots level, the strategic point of entry for the intended message. In addition, an impact study group to evaluate how the message is received and to give feedback to the policy makers is suggested. It is possible to improve and modify the information and assist in its flow from the policy makers, through proper administrative channels, and to insure that the intended message reaches the receivers. Thus, the impact study group is linked to the source. With this model the message conveyed through traditional media will be as effective as the policy makers and the coordinators can make it.

Ranganath (1977) has suggested a similar model in his working manual, "Folk Media for Population Communication," the content of the message being modified to meet the objectives of the communicator.

Ranganath suggests also that, because the use of a folk form for development purposes is a delicate matter, the use of the folk form should be determined by artists.

The second communication model in current use, is a two-way process of communication. In this model the folk drama facilitates an exchange of ideas. As Kidd and Byram (1978) explain:

> (the) performance is the catalyst for discussion. The purpose is no longer simply to put across information; it is to help people develop a critical awareness of their situation and a commitment to collective action.

In order to discuss a two-way communication model and its application to folk drama and development, we must briefly review the work of Paulo Freire on the process of conscientization and action. Freire's method revolutionized teaching and literacy programs for rural illiterate poor in Brazil and Chile. Applying his model to folk drama offers exciting possiblities for development work. In Freire's model the receivers are the poor, the members of the "silent culture" (Haviland, 1973, p. 282):

> The "silent culture" is made up of those people who have been called the masses, the illiterate, the unskilled, the uneducated, the undesirable elements of society. They are the subjugated who make up the greatest percentage of the people in the developing world.

These are the people who supposedly benefit from development programs, but for the most part see little improvement.

Freire's teaching methodology stimulated these people's natural curiosity, and they were able to learn to read in a phenomenally short time. They became aware of the social, economic, and political conditions affecting their lives. They were able to identify problems they faced regularly and to plan ways to solve them.

Freire's methodology can be described as a two-part process of conscientousness and action (Haviland, 1973, p. 281):

> men come to understand the realities of their existence (conscientization) and . . . from those realizations (progress) to a course of action designed to liberate them from the forces which limit their capacity to act as human beings.

To facilitate conscientization Freire advocates using a picture, or drawing to represent village realities. "Codification" and "decodification" occur in this part of the process (Haviland, 1973, p. 283):

> This image is called a "codification." It is a static representation of one part of village life . . . The dialogue which follows the introduction of the image seeks to investigate the reality which it represents . . . and probe the reasons why things are as they are.

Freire's teaching methodology stimulated communication between both senders (the educators) and receivers (the villagers) and, as a result, both were able to gain from the exchange of information. In this case, the medium which stimulated the dialogue was a photograph, but there is no reason why other media could not be used. For example, dramatizations could facilitate the exchange of ideas and provide an arena for learning.

As mentioned earlier, most development campaigns have employed a top-down strategy for disseminating messages. But some development campaigns used folk drama and did not resort to one-way communication. A two-way flow has been tried with folk drama using villagers as actors instead of bringing professionals into rural areas. These villagers have had no previous "acting" experience, only a desire to participate. An example of this is found in the Philippines with the Kulturan Tabonon's use of dramatic conscientization.

In this instance, folk theatre has been used to try to raise the villagers' overall social consciousness. Plays were not intended to implant a development message, but they attempted to bring about an awareness of some of the social factors affecting the lives of the audience. Besides being tried by *Kulturang Tabonon Sa Dabaw* (the Brown Culture Drama Group of Davao), a grassroots community theatre group, the Kabalaka Mobile Theatre in Capiz (*Kabalaka* is a local term for social consciousness and social action) advocates dramatic conscientization. The Kabalaka troupe recruits youths and adults from the barrio to be the actors, along with six technical staff members. Originally, the Kulturang Tabonon was formed by a group of local artists, but eventually included about twenty students and young adults from the community (Morante, 1977).

The Kulturang troupe first presents a play and, afterwards, conducts small group discussions with the audience. This is followed by a social analysis of conclusions reached by the small groups, so that the entire audience hears a consensus of opinion. The plays focus on either sociopolitical themes—such as the struggle of the oppressed for liberation, collective fights for people's rights, and the historical struggle against former colonial rulers—or on morality themes—such as adaptations of biblical stories, e.g., the Good Samaritan, the Last Judgment, or the Beautitudes. The one-act plays are low cost, require few props, are performed in local dialect, and are portable, so that performances can be staged anywhere. Their objective is a better understanding of the social environment and they have been found to be one of the more effective means of awakening awareness and understanding.

Similarly, the Kabalaka Theatre group presents community problems in dramatic form, but their initial approach is different from the Davao group. Cast members spend about two days in the barrio talking to leaders, local people, and development workers to find out what the problems are. The plotline is based on the results of these discussions and on what the cast has learned from other performances. After a few rehearsals to define the roles, the story is established. The aim of the Kabalaka theatre is to help barrio people transform themselves into socially conscious individuals, capable of realizing their own potential for growth. They address themselves to the need for better social relationships, values, and attitudes. Although there has been no formal evaluation of this group's activities, the general opinion is that there is a positive reaction to the plays. The performances elicit a sense of audience participation, because the audience realizes that the actors are portraying some of their very own realities (Rimon, 1975).

Another example of using drama to achieve conscientization, based on Paulo Freire's success with a two-way communication process, is found in Botswana with Laedza Batanani. Its use, however, is not without side effects (Kidd and Byram, 1978, p. 10):

> Without care its power as spectacle can overwhelm its usefulness as a tool for education and action. There is also a need for fresh ways of working with communities in order to produce a truer representation of the situation in communities and not merely a reflection of the concerns and interests of the dominant class. Only when these problems are resolved will popular theatre become an effective conscientizing force and make a real contribution to progressive social change.

Although there are problems in using this approach, there are benefits. The process requires no memorization, minimal rehearsal time, simple costumes, and relies on the enthusiasm, improvisation, and creativity of nonprofessional performers. It is based on the principle, "that anyone can learn to play a role, improvise dialogue, or handle a puppet" (Kidd and Byram, 1978, p. 4). It is a new process which has worked in Africa, and, with some modifications, can be applied to development elsewhere.

Despite the fact that a particular communication model may be effective in successfully conveying development information, the struggle to achieve development is always a long, continuous process. As Fuglesang (1973) emphasizes, the communication process itself will not change the way people behave, regardless of whether dramatizations are used or not:

> When the NEED for behavioral change is there, people change and learn new skills with ease. But the need arises only when new opportunities for action appear and when rewards that mean something to people are offered (p. 116).

The success of development work is contingent on whether or not people perceive a need for change. Part of the problem of determining real needs comes from the lack of participation and input from the people affected. It has been argued that those who are sick or malnourished will not be able to participate on any level of a development program, and that there isn't enough time or resources to develop a grassroots approach to development on a nation-wide basis. But, given the time and resources that have been spent in the past and the lack of success of development efforts in most developing countries, can governments and international aid agencies afford to further widen the gap between the rich and the poor? For development to become a reality, it must begin where the problems and the needs exist. Has folk drama as it has been used in development campaigns facilitated the development effort or has it hindered development? To answer this question it is necessary to look at how dramatic performances have been evaluated.

Evaluation

In India, where folk drama has been used for development purposes on a massive scale, evaluations have not been based on statistical analysis. Though a questionnaire was sent out between 1960 and 1961 by the Research and Reference Division to survey the Song and Drama Division's program, there has been no definitive assessment of the impact of this or of later programs (Parmar, 1975, p. 34). In general, if the majority of the audience responded favorably to a production, government officers considered the performance to be successful. But there have been additional factors which reaffirm the block officers' observations and indicate that programs have been successful (Abrams, 1975, p. 399):

> Measurement of the effect of these live entertainment programs upon the population could not be obtained from any official source, but state-wide figures showing rapid increases in adoption of family planning methods and in totals of personal small savings provided officials with some indications of the value of the utilization of folk forms, especially in the context of the combined use of mass media and traditional folk media programs.

Methods of evaluating performances outside of India seem to follow the same general pattern.

The reason folk drama has been successful in some instances may be the appropriateness of the medium and the message. In other cases, the medium may be inappropriate or the wrong approach to the development problem have been taken. For example, in view of folk drama's capacity to encourage villagers to work together, the employment of folk drama can be considered to be one of the few short-term success stories of the community development plan. The approach was successful, support was solicited at the village level, and the folk performances reflected villagers input. During the family planning campaigns, folk drama was used with some success to promote family planning messages, and folk drama performances have been credited with helping the overall success of several family planning communication strategies. In these cases, a one-way, top-down approach proved effective, the medium suitable for the content of the message.

There have, however, been examples where folk performances did not have a positive impact on family planning. Ranganath (1977, p. 30) notes three examples which backfired. In one case, at a Yakshagana performance, the audience did not take the jester's message about family planning seriously. In another instance, the religious Yellama songs were inappropriately reworded to include population themes and as a result upset the audience. In another example, a ballad program intending to publicize Family Planning Week was scheduled for adults in one poverty area. Instead of attracting an audience of fertile couples, the adults stayed home, and sent the children out to watch the entertainment, so that they could seize the opportunity for privacy. These three examples exemplify inappropriate approaches to development, and, as a result, the improper use of the folk drama medium. Had the approach included input from the target audience, the results would have been different. Past experience has showed that, although there is great potential in using folk drama for development purposes, problems can occur because of the way of using it. The problems, however, are not insurmountable and demonstrate the need for input from the village level, careful planning, and continued follow-up.

Folk media expert Abrams offers the following assessment of the effectiveness of using Tamasha for family planning in Maharashtra state, India (Abrams, 1975, p. 407):

> much improvement can be made by sharpening scripting and staging techniques. A delicate balance between good, recognized artistry, the new and traditional conventions of the Tamasha form, and modern message content must be struck if greater effectiveness of the social use of the form is to be gained.

Certainly these suggestions are applicable to other forms of folk theatre for use in family planning and other development objectives.

Another factor contributing to the failure or ineffectiveness of folk theatre campaigns has to do with determining the needs and concerns of the target areas. The apporach used by both the Kabalaka Mobile Theatre and the Kulturang Tabonon troupe from the Philippines involves the local community and obtains its input on community problems. But, what are the political ramifications if folk drama takes on the additional role of organizing the community, and decision-making power is given to people at the grassroots level?

Political Considerations

Folk media experts attending the UNESCO organized meeting in New Delhi in 1974 acknowledged (Yount, 1975, p. 2):

> 1) that many urgent problems lie in the villages and 2) that for their solutions, the villagers should be involved in the planning, participation, and implementation of programs, with the folk media— linked to the mass media—as the immediate vehicle of communication.

But, this recommendation was not an endorsement that decision-making power be granted solely to the villagers. The experts indicated that a one-way flow of information was sufficient, particularly if the dramatic artist served as a leader to help sway public opinion (Folk Media in Development, 1975).

Because the use of folk drama in development has been applied with some success in top-down communication strategy, and has helped to limit population growth in Indonesia and elsewhere, this model will continue to be followed in future campaigns. In short, from the government's viewpoint, this model can be controlled easily, but a two-way communication process, where the input originates at the grassroots level is not as easily directed. Those in power may want the monetary gains brought in by development programs, but, paradoxically, may feel threatened by development efforts to change the status quo. It seems appropriate to mention that Freire's work in North East Brazil was so threatening to those in power that he was jailed for over two months and then expelled from the country (Shaull, 1972). That scenario has been repeated in other parts of the world. In Mexico, students employing Freire's techniques were machine-gunned by the army because they threatened those in control (Ohliger, 1972). In India, using theatre for political purposes to promote the independence movement resulted in restriction and censorship by colonial authorities (Richmond, 1973).

It may not be politically feasible to give decision-making power to those who disagree with the ruling class. Although the governments of many developing nations are facing the challenge of modernization, authorities wish to avoid possible dissension, riot, or revolution. Thus, the use of folk drama to develop "silent culture" and to give people the tools to determine their destiny may not be readily approved.

Advantages and Disadvantages

In using folk drama in development programs, its advantages and disadvantages must be considered. First, folk drama is an easily understood, existing channel of communication in South and Southeast Asia. It is a trusted source of information which can portray politically and socially sensitive issues through fictional characters and/or puppetry. Performances can generate interest in moral, political, and social issues and can expand or reinforce face-to-face communication by extension workers.

But, by far the biggest incentive for using drama is that it is a flexible medium, easily altered through additions or deletions according to local need. The medium is versatile and adapts easily to culture-specific problems and audience preferences. Plays are not limited by physical surroundings, nor do they require film projectors, television sets, or cinemas to be seen. The medium is portable and low cost, and is capable of reaching a small group of people or an audience numbering in the thousands. Folk drama fosters a sense of unity and cooperation in prosperous times, as well as during adversity. It is a medium that works with and through a cultural tradition, not against it, a problem with other modern mass media. These are the major advantages of using folk drama for development communication; but what are the disadvantages?

Perhaps the most difficult problem confronting the use of local folk theatre in conjunction with development work is that it takes a tremendous amount of time and energy to implement a project from start to finish. The time factor is important because if a project is too time-demanding for the people involved, who may have families and basic survival matters to tend to; then the effort will fail. Each situation is unique, and the guidelines are mere suggestions of what to do. The use of folk drama requires an innate ability to adapt, improvise, and create with what is available.

A second problem is that dramatizations are geographically limited to a specific area. If transportation is not a problem, then topography may be. In the Philippines and Indonesia clusters of islands and miles of ocean complicate matters. Language variation and different customs and religious beliefs contribute to communication problems. Transfer of an idea to several villages may be difficult. Another potential problem in using folk theatre is that financial support is needed, either from government sources or from other outside aid agencies.

The quality of folk drama or folk theatre varies, with the subject matter and performance style being unique to the cultural milieu of a particular area. Performances can be further distinguished by audience informality and occasional, spontaneous audience participation. Folk drama may employ "professionals," such as the *dalang* in *wayang kulit* and *wayang golek* performances or the actors in *yakshagana*, actresses in *zarzuela*, but performances are not restricted to professionals. The cost of using professionals is a consideration if budgets are limited. Evaluations and cost/benefit analyses are needed to determine the overall efficacy of using folk media, and this is also costly.

Until the track record of folk media in development is improved and its value is understood, money will continue to be put in developing mass media because some believe they are easier to deal with, more effective, and soon to be found everywhere. Dramatizations, unless videotaped or photographed, are a transitory, fleeting art form. Once the curtain comes down the show is over, and only the images which remain in the minds of the audience determine whether or not the performance has had any impact. Audience reactions and actions have have been the only available means of measuring effectiveness.

Perhaps the most serious objection to the use of folk theatre for development comes from those who believe it is subversive. Any attempt to change the status quo can be threatening to authorities, and may constitute reasons for censorship. The result, instead of moving forward in the direction of development, might instead be taking three giant steps backward.

Yet, the possibilities of using folk theatre for development communication are endless, limited only by imagination and resourcefulness. Dedication and commitment are essential if the goals of development are ever going to be achieved.

REFERENCES

Abrams, Tevia. (1975). "Folk Theatre in Maharashtrian Social Development Programs." *Educational Theatre Journal 27,* 395–407.
Brandon, James R. (1967). *Theatre in Southeast Asia.* Cambridge: Harvard University Press.
"Folk Media in Development." (1975). *Instructional Technology Report.* Randall Casey (Ed.), No. 12, Sept.
Fugelsang, Andreas. (1973). *Applied Communication in Developing Countries: Ideas and Observations.* Uppsala, Sweden: Dag Hammarskjold Foundation.
Gargi, Balwant. (1966). *Folk Theatre in India.* Seattle: University of Washington Press.
Gunawardana, H. J. (1976). *Theatre in Sri Lanka.* Sri Lanka: Department of Cultural Affairs.
Haviland, R. Michael. (1973). "An Introduction to the Writings of Paulo Freire." *Adult Education 45,* 280–285.
Kidd, Ross, and Martin Byram. (1978). "Popular Theatre as a Tool for Community Education in Botswana." *Assignment Children 44,* Oct.–Dec.
Morante, Melchor. (1977). "Theatre of the Small People: Experiments in Community Theatre in the Philippines." *Asian Action 7,* (March–April), 42–43.
Muncie, Peter C. (1972) *Doctors and Dukuns, Puppets and Pills.* Washington, D.C.: World Bank Group.
Ohliger, John. (1972). "The Struggle for Birth and Rebirth: Introduction to Bibliography." *In* Stanley M. Grabowski, *Paulo Freire: A Revolutionary Dilemma for the Adult Educator.* (Occasional Papers, no. 32.) Syracuse: Syracuse University Publications in Continuing Education, (Nov.).
Parmar, Shyam. (1975). *Traditional Folk Media in India.* New Delhi: Geka Books.
Ranganath, H. K. (1977). "Folk Media for Population Communication, A Working Manual." Unpublished manuscript, Bangalore University, Bangalore, India.
Richmond, Farley. (1973). "The Political Role of Theatre in India." *Educational Theatre Journal 25,* 318–334.
Rimon II, Jose G. (1975). "Reviving Folk Media." *Population Forum, 1* 2–7.
Shaull, Richard. (1972). *In Pedagogy of the Oppressed,* by Paulo Freire, transl. by Myra Bergman Rano. New York: Herder and Herder.
Wilder, Frank. (1977). "The Red Triangle in Retrospect." Unpublished paper, University of Chicago.
Yount, Barbara. (1975). "Using Folk Media and Mass Media to Expand Communication." *Information, Education, & Communication in Population IEC Newsletter,* (No. 20), 1–16.

PART III

CONTINUITY AND CHANGE IN COMMUNICATION SYSTEMS

Overview—Part III

Georgette Wang

The studies which make up Part III demonstrate the continuity of communication systems in the midst of change as shown in different cultures and a variety of media. It was pointed out earlier that planned change for the future cannot be effected smoothly without adequate consideration for the past. The first chapter, on communication dualism in Iran is an extreme case, where change was manipulated by a small elite and imposed on the masses. As a result, the tightly controlled mass communication system became alienated from its audience and served as a government mouthpiece. On the other hand, the traditional communication networks were conveying different messages with the aid of modern inventions such as audio cassettes and telephones. The eventual failure of the modernization attempt was inevitable.

The Iranian case exemplifies the outcome of an attempt to change without giving due consideration to cultural continuity. Change without continuity is not compatible with the rules of evolution. The communication technology that stimulates change may be the same everywhere, but the way the technology is accepted, used, and defined varies from one culture to another. Folk media, popular literature, and cultural values and practices all find their way into modern communication media and channels. The chapters on Indian cinema, televised bag puppetry in Taiwan, and chivalric stories in Hong Kong mass media are three such examples.

India has the largest movie industry in the world. Indian movies, however, differ considerably from those produced in Hollywood and in other nations. With a rich tradition of folk drama to draw upon, Indian cinema can be seen as a new outgrowth of an old tradition. Technology is used to present fantasies and types of imagination which are centuries old in visual form, while important features of drama, such as music and songs, are given a new lease of life in the modern cinema.

Integration of folk media and mass media is often found in countries where folk media are popular. In an effort to preserve folk media, and/or to keep a balance between locally produced and imported programs, television broadcasters have incorporated folk media into the program content, and some of these programs have become very popular. The chapter on televised bag puppetry in Taiwan analyzes the influence of television on this particular folk medium.

Mass media are double-edged swords in developing nations. They introduce Western values and lifestyles, but at the same time they can reinforce and reflect cultural traditions and values. Chivalric stories, as a form of popular literature, have captured the interest of Chinese readers for centuries. However, they have never been as popular as they are in Hong Kong today, thanks to their promotion by the mass media. The chapter on chivalric stories in Hong Kong mass media examines the historical background of chivalric stories, the social factors involved in their popularity in the mass media, and the value changes reflected in some of these stories.

Communication system can be viewed as part of the overall sociocultural system. Therefore, changes in one system are intimately related to changes in the other, and this is especially true at the interpersonal communication level. The chapter on the Korean village meeting is a unique case, in that *Saranbang*, the original traditional communication channel and network, failed to persist after the Korean War. However, two other forms of village meeting emerged based on the same spirit. The two functions of the traditional network—decision-making and entertainment—were maintained through the new forms.

These chapters demonstrate, not only continuity in change, but also change in continuity of communication media and channels. What is observed, therefore, is not a simple phenomenon of continuity or change, but the complementary interaction of the two in the process of evolution.

The chapter on organizational communication in ASEAN nations examines continuity and change at the interpersonal level from another angle. As pointed out earlier, communication system can be viewed as a subsocial system; therefore, the interpersonal communication style and networks are largely patterned by the social structure. Despite some regional differences, paternalism has dominated ASEAN societies for hundreds, or even thousands, of years, and, at the same time, influenced the communication patterns among people. With rapid social change, new institutions, such as business corporations, emerged. These institutions usually perform functions which are similar across cultures. It was found, however, that the traditional interpersonal communication philosophy and pattern is still pervasive in such corporations, although certain changes can be expected in the future.

Of all non-Western societies, Japan is probably the most often cited example of an ideal mixture of the traditional and the modern. Indeed, Japan is now taking the lead in many branches of communication technology. One very important development in recent years is the experimentation in interactive television. The change brought about by such an experiment is an outgrowth of an existing system, and not the imposition of one imported from another culture. This study describes the system, as well as the way in which it has been accepted as one new element in the existing culture.

Many have argued that when the information age dawns, "indigenous communication systems" will eventually disappear. The last chapter in this book is an attempt to visualize the future, seeking an answer to the question of whether indigenous media and channels will disappear under the impact of new communication technology.

9

Dependency and Communication Dualism in the Third World
With Special Reference to the Case of Iran*

Majid Tehranian

The purpose of this essay is twofold; to present an argument on the emerging dualistic structures of communication systems in the less developed world, and to support this theoretical perspective through an examination of the Iranian experiences that led to the traditionalist Islamic Revolution of 1979. It is argued that despotic modernization, as exemplified by the cases of Iran and those Third World countries that inhibit participatory democracy, has pitted the modern mass media systems, often controlled by oligarchic interests, against the traditional communication channels that are often controlled by traditional opinion leaders. Where opinion leaders also happen to belong to an extensive and powerful religious communication network, the traditional system can employ informal channels and smaller communication technologies to mobilize an effective opposition movement. The emergence of radical (right as well as left) religious ideologies in a diversity of historical situations (Fundamentalist Islam in the Middle East, Moral Majority in the United States, Theology of Liberation in Latin America, and the resurgence of Roman Catholicism in Poland and elsewhere in Eastern Europe) thus may be viewed as popular protests against the depersonalizing and alienating effects of the modern mass media and the bureaucratic structures they represent. Traditional communication systems, if linked to a populist cause and popular institutions, can thus undermine and sometimes overthrow dominant political and communication systems based on the more advanced technologies.

*The author is grateful to Georgette Wang for her thoughtful editorial suggestions in the writing of this essay, drawn from a number of his previously published and unpublished articles.

DEPENDENCY AND DUALISM: A CRITICAL PERSPECTIVE

The historical transition from an agrarian to an industrial economy, society and polity, invariably described as "modernization" or "development," has been viewed from at least three different theoretical perspectives. First, there are those theorists who have viewed the process essentially in terms of a *pluralization* of society, economy, and polity. Liberal political economists and their theoretical descendents largely subscribe to such a view. The increasing levels of division of labor, differentiation of society into distinctive structures and functions, diversification of interests groups, and the achievement of a dynamic balance among the competing groups and interests, is the essence of the pluralist, liberal-democratic views of development (Tehranian, 1979).

By contrast, a second school of thought on development has placed its emphasis largely on increasing levels of *rationalization* as the key element in the process. Hegel and the Hegelians, with their emphasis on the role of reason in the process of historical development; Marx and the Marxists, with their views on the key role of technological advances in the progressive unfolding of history; and Weber and the Weberians, with their concern with the rationalization of culture and bureaucratic authority as the twin engines of social progress, may all be considered to belong to this theoretical tendency. The deification of the State as the repository of all authority and legitimacy, characterized by the totalitarian views of modernization, also may be considered as a vulgarization of this theoretical model.

A third school of thought, latent in both the first and the second, has emerged with the rise to historical self-consciousness of the peoples of the Third World. The central concept here is that of *liberation*. Liberal theorists, Marxists as well as Freudians, have provided some of the theoretical insights for those in the Third World who view modernization essentially as a process of liberation from foreign colonial domination, domestic elite exploitation, and an internalized bondage to self-images of inferiority and depravity brought about by years of colonial conditioning.

All three schools consider religion, however, as an element of traditional society that would have to be destroyed or, at best, modified to pave the way for what Weber called rational-legal structures and belief-systems. The Marxists go farthest in their critique of religion by considering it basically as a fraud or, in the celebrated words of Marx, as "the opiate of the masses." The liberals are more tolerant but no less contemptuous of the obscurantism of religious dogmas which have created real obstacles for true scientific progress. Although most Third World theorists tend to understand sympathetically the vital part religion can play in national struggles for independence and cultural rehabilitation, they begin to dismiss it once it encroaches upon the authority of the newly-independent state.

Most theorists of modernization, from whatever theoretical persuasion, tend to agree, however, that industrial society ultimately would be a graveyard for most religions and religious dogmas. For Marxists, religion is a form of false consciousness that the class struggles of the capitalist society would demystify and subsequently destroy with the abolition of all classes in the post-capitalist societies. For Freudians, religion is an illusion that like all other illusions of psychic life would give way to ego-rationality and reality-principle. For Weberians, traditional religions would be modified to incorporate and legitimate the principle of rational calculation, the hallmark of capitalist and, indeed, all industrial societies. For most modernizers and Westernizers in the Islamic World (from Mohammad Ali in Egypt ot the Pahlavi Shahs in Iran), religion and, particularly, Islam have presented an even greater anathema on their path to industrial progress and a national, secular culture.

All three schools of thought and the modes of political action that have flowed from them are more or less grounded on the "Idea of Progress" which itself emerged out of the optimism and rationalism of the eighteenth and nineteenth century West. In the meantime, however, the fundamental assumptions on which much of the idea of progress was based have come under some serious questioning. The infinite perfectibility of man, the unlimited bounties of nature, the unquestionable ability of human reason, science, and technology to save man from the fetters of life and the depravities of his own nature, the organic view of society as a homeostatic and self-correcting mechanism, and the evolutionary views of history as a teleological process of necessary change towards some predetermined goals, are all assumptions cast into serious doubt by the bitter experiences of the twentieth century. The primacy of *homo economicus* and *homo faber*, dignified by the rise of ideologies of industrial society into irrefutable conceptions of human destiny, have fallen apart in the face of twentieth century mass movements that have glorified the mystiques of race, nationality, and history. Even religion and its metaphysics of salvation have re-emerged with considerable gusto in the industrial as well as pre-industrial, the socialist as well as the capitalist societies, to fill the lives of ordinary citizens with a meaning and an emotionality that has proved wanting in the routinized and calculating tempo of modern life. The death of religion might be said to have been somewhat exaggerated by the great Liberal and Marxist pundits.

The scientific approach to the understanding of religion has often underestimated the perennial religious functions, which are not only to awe, attract, and mystify, but also to provide a vital and necessary cushion against the vicissitudes of human life. While it is true that the conditions of predictable material comfort, as promised and delivered by the industrial system, tend to lessen the importance of such emotional cushions, the anxieties and uncertainties of rapid social transformation call urgently for such ideological amenities. While secular ideologies may satisfy the human needs for certainty, identity, and community, they have failed to fulfill the ontological function of traditional faiths, which is to bestow meaning upon the perennial experiences of death, suffering, and evil. In other words, modern science and technology and their concomitant ideologies of progress have failed fundamentally to respond adequately to the finite fragility and morality of the human condition. For this reason, if no other, great contemporary scientists, such as Albert Einstein, have always recognized and acknowledged profound ties between the scientific and mystical traditions.

Old ideas do not die, they just linger on in a variety of different apparitions. The idea of progress, a fervent hope of mankind for worldly salvation, reappeared in the post-war period in the guise of theories of modernization and development as applied particularly to the case of the less developed world. However, the Third World has been seduced by the First and the Second Worlds with a dream that has gradually turned into a nightmare. The set of imageries held up to the Third World under the utopian rubrics of "the classless society" or "the age of high mass consumption" have proved to be powerful worldly myths. They bear a striking resemblance to the Cargo Cult of some remote Pacific Islands in their promises of peace and plenty. During World War II, the planes that crashed into these islands brought such a temporary abundance of consumer goods and freedom from hunger that an expectation of a Second Coming has lingered on ever since in the form of Cargo Cults. Theories of modernization and their ideological expression in "developmentalism" have also provided a new and powerful mythology which tends to underestimate and legitimate the human costs paid by those who undergo the sufferings of the historical transition, and they do so often for the benefit of a few who are culturally as remote from the natives as were the pilots of those cargo planes from the natives.

Despotic modernization, imposed either by colonial or post-colonial secular elites, has often dislocated the traditional society without necessarily substituting a new rational and humane order; it has undermined the self-sufficiency of the indigenous economy without providing for productive interdependence; it has destroyed the legitimacy of the old polity without constructing a new peace and justice; it has homogenized and depersonalized the old cultural patterns without giving a new sense of cultural autonomy and creativity. In ideological terms, few if any new perspectives have yet emerged to replace the paradigm of progress and the primacy of instrumental reasons, to provide hope without euphoria, realism without cynicism, guide to action without obscurantism and self-centered righteous indignation. The Third World thus stands somewhere in the twilight of tradition and modernity, suffering the worst consequences of both without benefitting much from their blessings. The obscurantism and timidity of traditional societies are thus mixed with the greed and ceaseless anxieties of modernity to produce an atomized society held together by the fears and shame of backwardness.

To begin to understand the problems of modernization, it is necessary, first and foremost, to recognize that the great historical transition has always entailed heavy human costs. Despite the considerable benefits modernization has bestowed upon man and the marvels it has achieved here on earth and out in space, it has also set into motion some irreversible forces which have destroyed the traditions of civility and weakened the bonds of human affection. Modernization has never been a unilinear, deterministic, stage-by-stage, movement along certain preconceived notions of material progress and human welfare expressed by such indices as *per capita* income, *per capita* consumption, or officially declared arrivals at certain historical epochs. On the contrary, the processes of modernization have shown an inherent tendency under different historical settings to be multilinear, probabilistic, and replete with social, economic, political, and cultural contradictions. Nor can modernization be achieved by a complete break with the past. Tradition and modernity, it is true, are often in conflict throughout the period of transition from rural or tribal to urban and industrial social structures, but no country has managed to arrive at an integrated modern industrial society without a reconstruction of its past traditions into new molds that could maintain a sense of persistent identity and continuity.

In fact, in the Third World, where modernization has been experienced mostly as Westernization, the tasks of integration of tradition and modernity have proved to be doubly difficult. The Third World has experienced modernization as a double curse. The dislocating effects have often been experienced also as cultural depersonalization. The processes of modernization began, in the first instance, with Western domination, national humiliation, and a gradual erosion of traditional societies and cultures. The shame of defeat was thus exacerbated by profound feelings of cultural inferiority, self-doubt, and, in more serious cases, self-hatred. The objective realities of subjugation and the subjective acceptance of an internalized self-image of inferiority imposed from outside led to a gradual process of cultural depersonalization typical of the master-slave psychological syndrome. The master's projection of his own feelings of insecurity into an image of the White Savior, and the slave's acceptance of a self-image of depravity and inferiority have persisted into the post-colonial period. However, the colonizer-colonized syndrome has been gradually internalized in the form of elite-mass dependency.

To state the case in more formal theoretical terms, modernization may be viewed as a heuristic, probabilistic, and dialectical process in which *three* contradictory/complementary forces are at work. We may identify these forces as the process of *accumulation, mobilization*, and *integration*. The processes of accumulation may be defined as a top-to-bottom process of increasing concentrations of wealth, power, and information, while the processes of mobilization represent a reverse, bottom-to-top process of increasing claims on wealth, power, and participation on the part of those layers of population that feel dispossessed. From this point of view, the processes of integration represent, therefore, those attempts at the reconstruction of communities of interest, authority (legitimacy), and identity undermined by the contradictions of accumulation and mobilization (Tehranian, 1980).

As a primary carrier of modernization, the processes of accumulation have been carried forth by increasing levels of domination and manipulation of nature and society (often considered the essence of imperialism), of technological production, bureaucratic rationalization, and cultural secularization. These forces have, in turn, produced, on the whole, conditions of alienation of labor, atomization of society, bureaucratization of authority, and homogenization of culture. Modernization in this first sense has also brought about conditions of exploitation, transcience, anonymity, rootlessness, and anomie for modern men. In the Third World, where the processes of accumulation have taken place mostly through dependency on foreign powers and corporations, they have also resulted in the creation of dualistic economies, societies, and cultures. The economies are often characterized by a traditional and subsistence agricultural sector that has few linkages with the extractive or consumer industries tied to the international marketplace through transnational corporations. The societies are often divided into a secular, metropolitan elite tied in its standards and style of life to the most advanced world metropolitan centers, and a traditional and religious mass, mutually alienated. The cultures are, furthermore, increasingly divided into an international "pop" culture adopted by the Westernized elites and indigenous belief-systems and practices, stagnant and yet resilient and resistant to the foreign encroachments. Although there exist some middle groups of industries, and social and cultural groups that operate as linkages between the two extremities, they are often too weak to be of much consequence.

By contrast, the processes of mobilization (identified as pluralization by the liberals and differentiation by the sociologists) represent a secondary carrier of modernization set into motion by increasing levels of division of labor, urbanization of human settlements, stratification of society into social and professional classes and groups, pluralization of life-worlds and individuation of the human psyche. Increasing levels of physical (geographic), social (vertical as well as horizontal), and psychic mobility thus galvanize those layers of population that have suffered the consequences of accumulation to demand greater shares in wealth, power, and information (participation). However, in the Third World, where processes of accumulation have often taken dualistic forms, social and political mobilization frequently leads to polarization of society into isolated and alienated elites allied to foreign powers, on the one hand, and xenophobic mass movements on the other.

The processes of integration thus represent a tertiary carrier of modernization aimed at the resolution of contradictions which arise inevitably from the forces of accumulation and mobilization. Wherever the processes of accumulation have been indigenous, gradual, and relatively slow (as in the historical experience of the West), the rate of mobilization also has been commensurately slow and manageable. The processes of integration have thus managed to reconstruct modern industrial society in the West around values and institutions which incorporate both change and continuity. The bonds of traditions of civility thus serve the causes of modernity. Wealth, power, and information are also increasingly shared through the modern institutions of mass education, mass consumption, mass communication, and mass participation. New communities of interest (interest groups and political parties), authority (science and government), and identity (nationality and ideology) establish the bonds of civility that mitigate violence and violent power struggles. However, when the rate of mobilization exceeds the rate of accumulation (as under revolutionary conditions anywhere), processes of integration would fail to match the measure of supply to demand, opportunities to claims and level of consensus to conflict. A new revolutionary ideology and leadership emerges and is often left with the task of reconstruction of society on the basis of some new conceptions of community interest, authority, and identity. In the Third World where forms of accumulation are often alien and the processes of mobilization have polarized society into traditional and modern sectors, the new revolutionary ideology and leadership, also, often fall short of the tasks of integration, and society is fragmented into its pre-modern and modern, as well as its ethnic, racial, linguistic, and religious constituent elements. In a bi-polar world system, where sources of technology and military hardware are limited primarily to the two Super Powers, the tendency for small, less developed nations is to turn to either of them to reimpose some measure of order and stability upon fragmented society. But with the increasing international polycentrality of power, it is conceivable to withdraw from Great Power struggles and to concentrate on a self-reliant and indigenous strategy of development.

However, the enemy is often within. Years of colonial conditioning and elite alienation from indigenous languages, religions, cultures, and peoples have undermined the possibilities for creative dialogue and cultural regeneration. Social and cultural elites in Third World societies thus have been dispossessed of their own cultures without having necessarily gained roots in the alien cultural traditions. Black faces and white masks, to use Franz Fanon's apt phrase, often characterize their schizophrenic social and psychological conditions. A physician that cannot heal himself thus fails to provide credible prescriptions to those plagued by the same malady. The masses, still steeped in their own living indigenous cultures and traditions, yet plagued by the imposition of seductive and alien cultures, soon develop the same schizophrenic symptoms. For them, however, the possibilities of attaining of the living standards of the alien culture are so remote that feelings of repulsion overtake those of attraction. If a traditional leadership force (the Ulama, the voodoo doctors, the Catholic priests) is still available to move into the leadership vacuum, social and cultural movements of considerable force and momentum emerge. If not, traditional and modern societies are condemned to live side by side with few linkages, a great deal of friction and little hope for social, cultural, and political integration.

Modern man may be said to face three competing/complementary sets of identities, which we may label as *primordial, status* and *civil*. Primordial identities consist of the most basic and natural sources of human identification, i.e., race, sex, age, language, and culture. Status identities, by contrast, consist of those layers of human self-definition programmed into each individual through his/her social class and professional status. There are, however, those tertiary layers of personal identity expressed in terms of the all encompassing ideological or political abstractions which define one's civil status in life as a citizen of a given political entity (Tehranian, 1980).

Clearly, the modern nation-state system has tried to integrate all three layers of identity within the all-encompassing concept of the nation in order to facilitate its claims to total power and loyalty. In those circumstances where there is some homogeneity of population in terms of race, language, religion, and culture and also a sufficiently high rate of accumulation of wealth to co-opt the dissident elements in the mobilized lower classes, national/civic identities have succeeded in superceding the differentiation of status and primordial identities. However, in those circumstances where we witness a heterogenous population and rapid mobilization overtaking the rates of accumulation of wealth and power, social and primordial identities reassert themselves (Geertz, 1963). The appeals of liberalism, Marxism, and religion as alternatives to nationalism for the ideological integration of society lie in the fact that they provide universalist conceptions of the political community. Among the heterogeneous populations, therefore, they have a more integrating ideological apparatus than nationalism which tends to be divisive. In an age of nationalism, however, claims to cultural and political autonomy among the primordial groups are strong and cannot be easily resisted by the intellectual appeals of liberalism and Marxism. Where sources of social support for these two ideologies are also weak (as in the Third World countries characterized by the weaknesses of the bourgeoisie and working class movements), religious ideologies prove to have the strongest appeal as an integrating force.

The set of reactions characterized as "countermodernization," whether expressed in religious or secular terms, are not, however, unique to the Third World. It seems to be a universal reaction typical of the earlier and later stages of industrialization in which costs tend to outweigh benefits. In the earlier stages, a nostalgia typically sets in for the "natural" harmony and cohesion of the traditional society, which is undermined by the tensions and contradictions of industrial life woven together by the "cash nexus." In the later stages, typified by the coun-ter-culture movements of post-industrial societies, the protests against an over-stratified and over-bureaucratized society call for the disman-tling of the industrial society in favor of a return to "nature" and its gifts of harmony.

We may also call this set of reactions as "the Rousseau effect," because it was Jean–Jacques Rousseau who first formulated them philo-sophically to attack modernization from a radical point of view. But the romantic themes Rousseau introduced into the literature of moderniza-tion recurred in the early stages of industrialization of most societies. Revolution against urban squalor and decadence, the idealization of rural life, the myth of the "noble savage," nostalgia for a mythical gold-en age in the past, and a tendency towards fusionist rather than pluralist conceptions of the nation (Rousseau's "general will" [*volonté generàle*] vs. "the will of all" [*volonté de tout*]) aroused by the regret for the loss of community, are typical of this set of reactions. Jefferson's conception of a decentralized rural democracy, Thoreau's Walden, the Russian Narod-nik's idealization of rural life, Gandhi's rejection of industrialization and advocacy of a return to Indian rural industries, the Wahhabi movement of eighteenth century Arabia for a return to pristine Islam, which has inspired the Muslim fundamentalist movements throughout the Islamic world, all aim at a recreation of the glory and purity of the golden past here and now. They also represent similar ideological tendencies under different historical settings.

The feverish search for identity that ensues under such historical circumstances has contradictory social and political consequences. Poli-tics of *identity* as opposed to *interest* or *status* politics is a double-edged sword. It can be, under favorable circumstances, an integrating force. But it can also serve as an instrument of political extremism and mass violence. In contrast to interest politics that centers on accommodation of material interests, and status politics that focuses on considerations of prestige, identity politics tends to be totalistic in conception calling for the extermination of the enemy. Such modern tragedies as the persecu-tion, expulsion, and massacre of the Jews in Germany, the Armenians in Turkey, the Biafrans in Nigeria, the Chinese in Southeast Asia, the Kurds and the Palestineans in the Middle East, are reminders of the extremes to which the fetish of identity can go. The reconstruction of society along a totally novel or primordial state of purity, as exemplified by the Year Zero mentality of the Pol Pot regime in Kampuchea, or Ayatollah Khomeini's call for a purist Islamic society (Fallaci, 1979), inevitably calls for the elimination of all those elements of human frailty and deviation that stand in its way. Particularly, when done in the name of religion it can also lead to a corruption of the religious institutions by considerations of worldly gain and power, as well as depreciation and demythologization of the religious faith.

In the Third World, where the new traditions of science and tech-nology are largely imported along with the social, political, and economic institutions of modern bureaucratic domination, the problem of identity is made doubly intense. The processes of modernization and technological acceleration are added to the indignities of cultural depersonalization mixed with colonial and neo-colonial overtones. If the prevailing social and economic system also suffers from grave conditions of injustice, the search for identity then assumes ideological formations that combine xenophobia with fundamentalism and populism. Where traditions are strong and proud of their claims to a historic worldview and style of civilization, as in the Islamic world, the new social movements also may be the birth pangs of a more authentic, just and, ultimately, liberating style of social, economic development. Some measures of obscurantism and xenophobia will also have to be suffered along the way.

COMMUNICATION DUALISM AND THE ISLAMIC REVOLUTION

The case of the Islamic Revolution in Iran, although extreme, is very significant for an understanding of the dynamic forces of modernization in the rest of the Islamic World, and perhaps in all of the Third World. In a profound sense, one could say that the upheavals in Iran represented a crisis of communication rooted in the political, economic, and cultural cleavage between the elite and the mass that had emerged over the last 170 years. This cleavage has led to a schizophrenia in the cultural identity and historical consciousness of the Iranian people. It has split them into two worlds of secular and religious beliefs, centering on pre-Islamic and Islamic symbols for their ideological/mythological sustenance.

The Cultural and Ideological Cleavage

Modernization for Iran, as for many other less developed countries, has entailed a triple curse. In the first place, modernization came to Iran as to many other African and Asian countries primarily in the form of Westernization. It meant, therefore, the uprooting of Iran's indigenous social, economic, political, educational, and legal institutions in favor of their Western counterparts. Thus, the cohesion and coherence of a traditional corporate society was gradually replaced by the tensions and contradictions of a society undergoing modernization, but with few indigenous modernizing institutions of its own. The indigenous institutions had very little time or opportunity to respond to the Western challenge by adoption and adaptation; they largely recoiled in reaction.

Second, the processes of Westernization have bred and pampered a political and cultural elite that showed a missionary zeal for the complete overhaul of Iranian society in the image of the most "advanced" sectors of Western society. For some members of this elite, who were much in evidence in the seventies, this image reflected Southern California in all its seductive trappings. The dreams and utopias of this elite thus increasingly set them sharply apart from the rest of the Iranian society.

The elite's historical consciousness was this-worldly and secular, but its cultural identity was rooted in a mystification of Iran's pre-Islamic past and its promises of power and pre-eminence. In contrast, the historical consciousness of the masses was based primarily on oral traditions, which conveyed in mythopoetic terms the historical and cultural continuity of Iran from its pre-Islamic to post-Islamic past. In their utopian yearnings for redemption, justice, and deliverance, the masses identified themselves primarily with Islam's archetypical heroes and martyrs. The slogan of "The Great Civilization," as the expression of the ideological and cultural ethos of the ruling elite, was thus pitted against the slogan of an "Islamic Republic," which became the rallying cry of a mass revolt.

Third, the cult of the state as the embodiment of all that is true, good, and beautiful (i.e., Reason and Order) plagued Iran no less than other modernizing societies with totalitarian tendencies. The Iranian state did not recognize any truth beyond itself and could not tolerate any challenges to its authority. All other institutions were to serve its purposes and designs and had no claim to any purpose and design of their own. Any whisper of opposition was considered as the ultimate treason, leaving little room for the natural development of contradictions, and their resolutions.

The Centralized Bureaucracy

In Iran, the forces of modernization—particularly in the 54 years under the Pahlavies (1925–1979)—thus represented a relentless drive towards the Westernization and centralization of authority buttressed by a modern army and policy apparatus, an expanding and parasitic bureaucracy, and the support of Western powers. In this process, the indigenous institutions of social and political participation (the village community, the guilds, the tribes, and voluntary associations such as the sport houses, the *zurkhaneh*, or the sufi houses of worship, the *khanegha*) were destroyed without being replaced by modern institutions of participation.

The parliament, the press, the labor unions, and the professional and voluntary associations which could provide such vehicles were kept largely under central control and manipulation and this produced sham results. The absence of mass support, however, meant that the pretensions of totalitarian power (one command, one party, one book, one ideology) were not matched by totalitarian organization and efficiency. Imperial pretensions increased as the substance of power diminished.

The processes of atomization, bureaucratization, and homogenization have been achieved in Iran largely through rapid economic growth, the unfolding of an acquisitive consumer society, and a high rate of urbanization; and great drives towards secularization, mass education, mass communication, and mass consumption. The effect was disintegration, and the social system was not able to cope, particularly after the so-called "White Revolution" of the early 1960s. What seemed to many foreign observers to be a showcase of enlightened dictatorship and development was in fact the making of a national tragedy. The financial corruption, social injustice, political repression, and intellectual arrogance of the regime, given a new edge by the quadrupling of oil revenues in 1973, only deepened the resentments of a society undergoing the agonies of change.

In this context, therefore, it was no wonder that for a new leadership Iranian society turned to the sector which was least affected by the corrupting influences of modernization—namely the *Ulama*, the learned men of Islam. In a survey conducted in 1974 among three social groups in Iranian society (i.e., the communication elite, the professional broadcasters, and the university students), the trend towards strong religious sentiments was already quite unmistakeable. More than 60% of the students and 30% of the other two groups, when responding to a list of 12 different ideological orientations, expressed a preference for a fundamentalist Islamic position. The highest preferences among all three groups, however, were accorded to egalitarianism, Islamic modernism, and moderate nationalism. (Tehranian et al., 1977).

Under the Pahlavies, the Ulama had been progressively stripped of their control over the legal, educational, and endowment *waqf* establishments. But they still retained their spiritual powers through the mosque and the *minbar* (the pulpit). They had therefore both the cause and the means to stir the opposition. Twice in this century, the Ulama had entered into an alliance with the Bazaar merchants and the liberal intellectuals to limit the monarchy. In both cases (the Constitutional Revolution and the Oil Nationalization Movement), it was the liberal intellectuals and the Bazaar merchants who led the way. In the Islamic revolutionary movement, the situation had been radically different. It was now the most radical elements of the Ulama who led.

It is ironic that the monarchy has largely brought this change about by destroying all possible forces of mediation between itself and the masses. In other words, the regime outwitted itself by a thoroughly successful campaign of repression, which discredited all those who argued for a liberal constitutional monarchy. By centralizing the powers of the state in its own hands, the monarchy left few independent and credible politicians, with a social base of power loyal to the regime, who could lend support in the hour of need.

Dissonance and Dualism in Communication

The increasing dualist structure of Iran's social and economic systems revealed itself, perhaps, above all in the communication system. We can best examine the salient features of this dualism in terms of the two competing religious and secular ideologies, structures, and the processes of social communication—living autonomously side by side with immense frictions wherever and whenever they collided.

Secularization in Iran, as in the rest of the Islamic world, has faced the formidable obstacle that Islam recognizes no separation between spiritual and temporal authority. Muslims of all sectarian persuasions believe that the Prophet Muhammad established an ideal Community of Believers in Medina within the short period of ten years from his exodus in 622 to his death in 632.

In Islam, it is not the birth of Muhammad which is celebrated as the beginning of the Islamic Era (in contrast with Christianity, which is dated from the birth of Jesus). It is rather the *hegira*, the Exodus of Muhammad from Mecca to Medina, together with a small band of his disciples, which is celebrated. The Islamic Shari'a Sacred Law is based on the Quran, on the *sunna* (tradition) of the Prophet (particularly during this crucial period of unity of the spiritual and temporal realms), on *qiyas* or the principle of analogy, and on *ijma*, of the principle of community consensus. Muslims of the Sunni faith extend their conception of the Ideal Islamic State to the period of rule by the four *khulafa al-Rashidum* (the Rightly-Guided Successors of Muhammad), while Muslims of the Shi'a faith maintain that succession rightly belongs to Muhammad's cousin and son-in-law Ali, the fourth Sunni Caliph of Islam, and his direct descendants.

The differences in doctrine have been of considerable historical importance up to this day. Because the Shi'ites have often been in a minority, they have generally been favorable to revolutionary action. During the sixteenth century and the rise of the Saffavids in Iran, Shi'ism was declared a state religion and gained a majority position. But its doctrines remained potentially revolutionary.

Today, the majority of Muslims, over 80%, are Sunni. In Iran, however, the majority of the 35 million population are Shi'ite Muslims. In matters of ideology and organization, Shi'ism continues to be distinct from Sunni Islam in two important respects. First, the doctrine of *imamat* in Shi'ism transfers the *temporal* as well as the spiritual authority of Ali to his direct descendants. The various Shi'a sects hold different beliefs about the transference of this authority. The largest sect, known as the "Twelvers," hold that the transfer of powers ceased with the disappearance of the Twelfth Iman in 878. Another sect, the Ismaili Shi'ites, or the "Seveners," hold that the authority has been transferred through the Seventh Imam to his current descendant, the Aga Khan. The "Twelvers" believe that the Iman will one day return to save the world.

Until then, the Ulama hold its powers, and all temporal power is considered as illegitimate to be tolerated only when and if exercised in accordance with the rule of the Shari'a as judged by the body of the Ulama. Shi'a doctrine thus gives the Ulama a considerable veto power over the temporal authorities. It also maintains the eschatological hopes for a second coming of the Mahdi, the Twelfth Imam. Time and again, Mahdism has served revolutionary purposes in the Islamic world.

The Ulama's position of strength in Shi'a doctrine is supplemented in Iran by the strength of the country's religious organization. Given the right cause, this communication network can mobilize (as we have seen recently) vast numbers of people, each imbued with religious indignation and inspired by a single-minded purpose.

The relative autonomy of the Ulama within the state, buttressed by their independent sources of income from religious endowments and taxes, has placed them very close to the mood of the people and has made them powerful potential leaders of political movements. Historically, the Ulama have used this power to act as mediators between the ruling elites, the counter-elites, and the masses. Their close association with the Bazaar merchants and the liberal intelligentsia provided them with strong claims to political power. Under the Pahlavies, however, the relentless policy of Westernization and secularization increasingly alienated the Ulama from the monarchy. The Ulama's educational, legal, and charitable institutions were considerably weakened by the encroachments of the secular and secularizing state.

However, another feature of the Ulama's religious organization—namely, its polycentrism—gave them both, the power to resist this repression and the ability to act when and if a unifying issue arose. The opportunity came after the bloody riots of June 1963, led by Ayatollah Khomeini. The Ulama and the monarchy were polarized as symbols for two diametrically opposed visions of the future of Iran.

These two visions differed on almost every possible ground. The Islamic vision stems from an impulse to return to the purity and sacred justice of pristine Islam. The secular vision attempted to revitalize the pre-Islamic memories of Iranian nationalism in order to recapture the power and glory of Iran's imperial past. Not only did both visions thus conflict in their utopian and retrogressive impulses, but their positive images of the future also clashed. The Islamic vision is inextricably tied to Iran's ties with the Arabs and the rest of the Islamic world. The secular nationalist vision, however, wished desparately to wipe away all memories of Iran's subjugation to the Arabs, to purify the Persian language and to revive pre-Islamic memories and political symbols. Responses to the Western challenge have also been markedly different. Secular nationalism has rejected Western political domination but has accepted and indeed welcomed Western cultural values. In extreme cases, the former was enamored of the West to the extent of Westomania (Gharbzadegi), while the latter has been characterized by xenophobia. All these ideological rationalizations derived from the increasing gulf that separated the lifestyles of the Westernized elite and the deeply religious masses.

A central element of the Pahlavies' cultural policy was the reconstruction of Iranian historical consciousness around the memory of its imperial past, and the destruction of everything that might stand in its way. The choice of the dynasty name of Pahlavi, after Iran's dominant pre-Islamic language, was itself symbolic. The organization of an Academy of Iranian Languages to purify Persian; the return to the grandeur and massive architectural style of the Archaemenids; the forced adoption of Western clothes, breaking the continuity of the country's traditional religious and lay clothing styles; the celebration of Persian kinghood on the 2500th anniversary of the Persian Empire and the 50th anniversary of the Pahlavi dynasty; the changes of calendar, first from the Islamic lunar to the Persian solar and then from *hegira* (1357) to *shahanshani* (2537), were all aspects of the same policy of revived purification. Memories of the constitutional revolutionary period, and of the period of 1941–53, when a quasi-liberal parliamentary system was in operation, were severely repressed. The only major books on the history of the Mosaddeq era that remained in circulation were those of the Shah's autobiography, *Mission for My Country*, and a few histories which glorified His Majesty's role in the recapture of Azerbaijan and in the nationalization of oil.

A nation without a historical memory is a nation lost. But historical memories cannot be altogether suppressed. Persians have never had to rely entirely on historical documentation for their memories. This age-old talent is why Ferdowsi's epic poem, *The Shahnameh,* and the legends of the martyrdoms of Hossein and so many other saints, are part of Iran's oral tradition of vivid drama and meaning. But the cultural policy of historical vivisection did lead unwittingly to historical schizophrenia. The 50% of the population that was below the age of 20, by and large lost the memory of the liberal constitutionalists; but it was reinforced in its memory of the martyrdom of legendary heroes, while simultaneously acquiring a quasi-Marxist revolutionary ideology through hearsay and underground publications.

The massive demonstrations in the Autumn of 1978 were remarkable, among other things, for being predominantly made up of the younger generation and for the singular absence of any references to Mossadeq, the charismatic liberal constitutionalist leader of the early fifties. Instead, large portraits of Ayatollah Khomeini and the martyrs of the new urban guerrilla struggles were prominently displayed everywhere. The underlying theme of the demonstrations was the expectation of a second coming.

For years, the greatest festival spontaneously celebrated by the people was neither Norouz (the Persian New Year, dating to pre-Islamic Zoroastrian times) nor the birthday of the Prophet. It was, as banners throughout the country declared on those blessed occasions, "the sacred birthday of His Majesty Imam Mahdi." Two legitimacies, one spiritual and utopian, the other temporal and ideological, ruled Iran in the name of two competing monarchies.

Themes of Political Communication

The emergence of two nations with two belief-systems revealed itself perhaps most dramatically in the two separate but intertwined modes of political communication. The secular view was profoundly Westernized, and couched in Faustian terms: a remorseless search for power by means of the mastery of science and technology. The Shah himself typified such an attitude by his love of gadgets (particularly military gadgets); his fetish of high, capital-intensive, technology (e.g., nuclear energy, in a country endowed with immense resources of oil and natural gas); and his ambition, flaunted with missionary zeal, to transform Iran within 20 years into the world's fifth major industrial power. Symbolic throughout, one of his first acts after returning to power in 1963 was to change the name of the Ministry of Defense to the Ministry of War. But all this show of strength was undermined by a tragic undercurrent of mysticism and martyrdom, a constant appeal to the unseen powers who protected his life in four assassination attempts, a steadfast call to meet his destiny, and in the end a resignation to "accept the inevitable" instead of engaging in a bloody counter-revolution.

The same themes of power, blood, and martyrdom also ran in the religious opposition' worldview, but as a major note. The unconscious choice of Dr. Mosaddeq and Ayatollah Khomeini as the opposition's charismatic leaders in less than a generation reveals a profound continuity of historical archetypes. The historical consciousness of Iranians has been always deeply moved by the memory of those heroic martyrs who achieved positions of spiritual power through acts of defiance against tyrants, by shedding their blood to redeem the weak and the oppressed. The legendary Siavosh in *The Shanameh*, Imam Hossein in Shi'a history, and Hallaj in Sufi memory, represent such archetypes. Dr. Mosaddeq's combination of apparent weakness and determination, and Ayatollah Khomeini's injured but righteous cause, represented similar drives to power through righteousness and martyrdom.

Competing Communication Systems

These two competing worldviews, based on two rival epistemic communities, were also equipped with two parallel communication systems. Through a rapid acquisition of the modern technologies of broadcasting, as well as of information storage and retrieval, the state had acquired— particularly in the 1970s—a formidable arsenal of monolithic information transmission and control. SAVAK's extensive domestic and foreign network of intelligence gathering, estimated to have employed some 50,000 people, was only the most notorious element in this system. The Imperial Court and the military and civilian branches of the government, each had its own units for gathering information. The Royal Inspectorate in the Court, the Second Column in the Army, and the police in the Municipality, as well as a number of ministries and organizations in the civilian branches, were responsible for reinforcing the power of the state to watch over the lives of citizens.

The division of functions, however, never lessened the preponderance of the security units. The Ministry of Information and Tourism was primarily responsible for checking the press (which was ostensibly private and independent, but in fact largely subsidized). But the security offices issued daily bulletins to publishers, telling them what news to print and how to arrange the columns. Each of Tehran's four major daily newspapers began to look the same—drab, monotonous, and faceless. Despite Prime Minister Amouzegar's appointment of a professional journalist to be Minister of Information, and his promises of a liberalization policy, in 1977, the practice of the daily bulletin from government to the press for obligatory publication was not discontinued.

One particular article, written by the security offices and pushed through the ministry as a routine message to be published in the press, so inflamed the religious opposition by its insults to Ayatollah Khomeini that its publication in *The Ettela'at* may be credited with the rapid escalation of the opposition's struggle after December 1977. The Minister of Information feigned ignorance of the article; he also claimed to have stopped the publication of further abusive articles he received from the security offices. By this time, however, it was too late to stop the tide of opposition.

The Ministry of Art and Culture was nominally responsible for the censorship of films and printed matter. Yet, here again it was often the security offices which acted in the ministry's name. Books and films were censored or refused publication or showing for a variety of reasons, mostly in connection with claims about the security of the regime and the inviolability of the monarch. Sometimes the prohibitions took on arbitrary, or sinister or even comical turns. *Macbeth* and *Hamlet* were prohibited because they showed the murder of a king. The color "red" was treated with circumspection in the titles of books and films because of its revolutionary portent. Sometimes, "subversive" books were placed in bookshops in order to catch the culprits unaware. The showing of a film directed by Dariush Mahhjouii, *Daere-ye Mina*, was not released for some time because it dramatized the criminal activities of a real-life commerical gang, which, in collusion with some medical staff, sold the injected blood of drug addicts to hospitals.

TV and Radio Lose Credibility

In contrast, National Iranian Radio Television (NIRT), the national broadcasting monopoly, enjoyed some measure of independence from both the government and the security forces. This autonomy grew partly from the managing director's direct political links to the throne, his reputation for loyalty and patriotism, his liberal inclinations, and partly from the professional nature of broadcasting itself. This relative autonomy and insularity, however, did not prevent NIRT from including SAVAK-sponsored programs. Early in the seventies, when the urban guerrilla movement had just begun, a high security official took long hours on television to deliver political lectures on "the sinister designs of the subversives." Subsequently, some captured guerrillas were brought before the cameras to be interviewed as they confessed their misdeeds. These interventions tainted the early reputation of NIRT's autonomy and lost it considerable political credibility.

The news bulletins, meanwhile, were primarily devoted to the activities of the royal family, supplemented by a reasonable coverage of Western and Third World news. Domestic news was kept to a minimum, and mostly confined to ceremonial occasions. Whenever NIRT attempted to break through this restriction—for instance, by interviewing people in the streets on such vital issues as inflation or corruption—it faced inside opposition. Entertainment programs probably had an even more disastrous impact. Both domestic productions and imports imposed the cultural tastes of an urban elite, and their metropolitan preferences, upon a premodern population that inevitably experienced strong feelings of impropriety. The rapid expansion of broadcasting coverage (to virtually 100% for radio and 70% for television) brought these programs into the sanctified domain of almost every Iranian family.

Few days passed without some outraged remarks from the pulpit, the parliament, or the press on the immorality and violence of NIRT's television programs. At the same time, with effects that were more subtle but no less real, the television protrayal of upper- and middle-class standards of living must have augmented the sense of injustice, envy, and outrage felt by the poor and the devout. The unparalleled spread, in 1978, of political protest and violence through the entire country, even in the remotest towns and villages, should be considered in some measure as the unintended consequence of this penetration of mass media. Mass communication was considered by the regime as a substitute for real political communication. The political parties, broadcasting, and the press were used to promulgate, legitimate, and persuade rather than as channels for agenda-setting, social feedback, social participation, and the social reconciliation of conflicting views and interests. Television, in particular, was used as a device to awe, attract, and mystify. The direct broadcasting of the Shah's coronation, the festivities of the 2500th anniversary of the Pahlavi Dynasty, as well as all the *Salaams*, the ceremonial occasions on which the Shah gave audience, were deliberately aimed to impress. The major channels of political communication were the Shah's frequent but formalized interviews and the lectures he delivered to officials or to large mass rallies.

The power of television to demystify was thoroughly forgotten. The king increasingly appeared as a jester, with no clothes at all. The absence of intermediary channels of communication between the state and the people meant that messages often fell on either deaf or incredulous ears. It was Premier Sharif-Emami who shrewdly recognized the extent of the credibility gap: "If we say it is daytime when it is daytime, people will deduce it is nighttime."

The technological feat of covering this vast and mountainous country by a large microwave communication network was, within a decade or so, largely countercommunicative. Meanwhile, in direct contrast, the traditional religious communication system was thriving. Its success depended on several factors. It used informal channels and small, as opposed to big, media. Its message was familiar and designed in terms of the archetypical legends of Persian historical memory. And it was credible, because it corresponded to the living reality of its audience and delivered by legitimate opinion leaders.

The network was organized around some 200,000 mullahs (clerics), who had come from small towns and villages to be trained in Qum, Najaf, or Mashhad, and then go back to their towns and villages. Whereas the professional broadcasters and journalists were mostly Westernized urban dwellers, the mullahs retained organic ties with the lower- and middle-classes and knew their hopes and sufferings.

The *Madrassah* (theological seminary) at Qum alone could claim a student population of some 12–15,000 *talabehs,* mostly of peasant origins, who led a life of monastic simplicity on small stipends from the *ayatollahs* (ayatolla means, literally, the sign of God, or religious mentors with the right to *ijithad,* the making of new interpretations and edicts on the Sharia). The talabehs were the hard core of the religious revival, increasingly radicalized by the widening gulf between rich and poor, between the religious and secular life, and the heavy burden of political repression. After 1963, it was Ayatollah Khomeini's fundamentalism and Ali Shariati's special blending of Shi'ism, Marxism, and Existentialism which captured the imagination of this religious intelligentsia.

The communication network on which this increasingly volatile and revolutionary group depended was as old as Islam itself. It was based on some 90,000 mosques, ranging from the city centers to the smallest settlements. These mosques were increasingly supplemented by numerous new religious lecture halls (*hosseinieh*), by informal meetings at people's homes where the Quran was read and interpreted, and by religious processions (*dasteh*) and religious mournings (*rowzeh khani*). The most well-known of these religious centers was the Hosseinieh Ershad in Teheran, which became the thriving intellectual center of a modernist movement in the late 1960s and early 1970s. But the center was soon closed down, the movement repressed, and Ali Shariati, its leader, was detained by the government.

Small Media for a Revolution

The movement soon found other outlets, and made the most imaginative use of "smaller" media. Small-scale publishing thrived more than ever: *Maktab Islam,* a serious religious journal, sold over 50,000 copies, an impressive total when compared to the 3,000 copies sold by *Sokhan*, the country's most prestigious literary journal. The number of periodicals published abroad, in exile, rose to 35.

The newer electronic devices provided opportunities for many novel uses. The introduction of transistorized audiotape machines greatly increased the sale of prerecorded religious messages. Tapes were used both for strictly religious and political messages. Most of Ayatollah Khomeini's messages sent from exile (from 1963 to 1979) came in the form of tapes of *elamieh* (pronouncements) mimeographed or xeroxed on a massive scale.

The communication blackout that lasted from November 1978 to mid-January 1979 (precipitated by strikes of journalists and broadcasters) led many people to put the telephone to a number of ingenious uses. If one dialed several numbers abroad to give and recieve latest news or rumor of the domestic scene, the friendly local operator would be obliging enough to charge the call, not to oneself, but to the telecommunication authority. Messages of political importance were relayed externally as well as internally by telephone, and then taped and duplicated on a wide scale. Various campaigns of terror and counterterror also used the telephone network to threaten the opposition, government officials, strikers and foreign residents.

Several clandestine radio stations were set up, mostly abroad, to relay to Iran the messages of diverse opposition groups, ranging from the Tudeh (Communist) Party to the National Front and the new revolutionary guerrilla bands. The BBC World Service's Persian programs also were prominent during the communication black-out as a source of both straight news and rumors. Motivated, perhaps, by the twin objectives of regaining its former popularity (lost during the Mosaddeq era) and of winning themselves a few points, the BBC's broadcasts mixed news and rumor, hearsay and conjecture. It did not live up to the reputation won during the Second World War, best exemplified by Hitler's remark that he listened to the BBC "whenever I wish to know how we are doing."

In the Autumn of 1978, with the unleashing of the opposition strikes, the most popular form of political communication was the xerox. Dozens of newsletters and elamieh were issued everyday. And all the time, from the beginning to the end, the most reliable of all forms of communication, the rumor circuit, was used to pass on not only news and conjecture but—even more importantly—the deep hopes and fears of a harassed people.

The mass demonstrations of Autumn of 1978 shocked only those who had been hibernating in a winter of political negligence. Even so, their massive size (the estimates ranged from one to three million demonstrators, at the various occasions), their extraordinary discipline and their predominantly religious quality were justifiably sources of surprise and wonder. Here was a revolution that was uniquely Iranian, with no precedents in form or substance in the history of other nations. It required a special approach, a special understanding.

COMMUNICATION AND MODERNIZATION: SOME THEORETICAL IMPLICATIONS

When Daniel Lerner's classic study of communication and modernization, THE PASSING OF TRADITIONAL SOCIETY, was first published in 1958, there was a prevailing sense of optimism about what the mass media can do for national development. His provocative title suggested an inevitable historical process in the erosion of "tradition" in the less developed countries to be hastened by the impact of mass media. Lerner's hypothesis that there is a positive correlation between urbanization, literacy, exposure to media, and political participation (as measured by electoral participation) caught the imagination of many students of communication and development. The "multiplier" effects of media on empathy and psychic mobility were assumed by Lerner, and a generation of researchers after him, to be a generating force for modernization.

The experience of the last several decades in Iran, and elsewhere in the Third World, have cast, however, considerable doubt on the validity of that perspective. Rapid urbanization, of course, has taken place virtually everywhere in the Third World. But we have not seen the kind of urbanization that Lerner had in mind. The influx of large numbers of illiterate or semi-literate peasants into the expanding cities of the less developed world, compounding their problems of unemployment, poverty, and slums, and taxing the cities' resources to the utmost, is not the kind of urbanization that could possibly lead to higher levels of wellbeing, except for the very few.

As for exposure to the media, there has certainly been a great deal of it. Wilbur Schramm has called the sixties "the age of the transistor radio," and the seventies and eighties, "the age of satellites." Most developing countries have already set up or acquired radio and television services, while some with higher incomes have insisted on the conspicuous consumption of color television facilities. Together with the national airline and a steel mill, television and radio are the status symbols of a country's arrival in the modern age. But has this exposure to media, assuredly greater than ever, led to higher levels of literacy and political participation? The example of Iran supports the idea that, for dictatorial governments, mass communication (or is that a contradiction in terms?—can we indeed communicate with an inert mass?) has created the illusion of power and control over minds by means of sending uniform messages to undifferentiated audiences. It shows further that the potential of the mass media to be countercommunicative is exacerbated wherever and whenever broadcasting and the press fail to act through secondary and tertiary channels of informal communication and opinion leadership.

What about political participation? Here, the Lerner hypothesis exhibits both its greatest weakness and its greatest potential strength. If political participation is defined in ethnocentric terms simply as electoral participation, then the concept is devoid of all scientific meaning. But when defined as genuine interactive communication, sympathy, empathy, psychic mobility, or cognitive participation in the decision-making, then the concept begins to be relevant to the processes of social change.

The mediacentric views of communication and development, as characterized by the Lerner–Schramm–UNESCO models of communication systems, will, therefore, have to give greater recognition to the crucial role of informal communication channels and small media. Lerner and Schramm, as well as UNESCO, have already taken cognizance of these emerging trends by reconsidering their earlier preoccupation with big media and communication indicators. The new tribalism in the world, focusing on the separate identity, legitimacy, and ideology of smaller national communities (e.g., the Kurds, Pashtus, Scottish, Welsh, French-Canadians) is taking increasing recourse to small media and to channels of informal communication. If they are to serve their profession, communication specialists can no longer afford to be concerned exclusively with technological advances and technologically determinist views of history. Communication is a process of humanization, and it cannot be divorced from those delicate and subtle bonds of human society which are called art, language, identity, legitimacy, and ideology.

When modernity is understood as a discrete concept, and set against tradition, as so many theorists of modernization have conceived it to be, the chain of empathy is tragically broken. Modernization from above, accompanied by a good measure of cognitive tyranny, treats its objects of manipulation (man, nature) as things to be molded into a new and different cast, against their will and against their sense of history and well-being. For this reason modernization's first task so often is to rewrite history, to obliterate the historical memories which stand in its way. In spite of its different ideological manifestations, the basic phenomenon is no different with Stalin or Attaturk or the Shah. If the tragic case of Iran teaches us one lesson, it is that the traditions of civility are inextricably tied to a country's myths, legends, archetypical heroes, religious beliefs, and, yes, superstitions. To debunk them altogether in the process of modernization is to reject the possibility of all communication, and all civility.

CONCLUSION

Communication dualism in the Third World should be considered as an aspect of the more general phenomenon of socioeconomic and cultural dualism with deep historical roots in the colonial and neo-colonial modes of development. However, the revolutionary transformation of Third World societies from tribal and agrarian entities to quasi-industrial ones has assumed an ever-accelerating pace. This has produced, particularly in contexts suppressing political participation, conditions of transience, abstraction, anonymity, and alienation. In the meantime, the communications revolution that began with the invention of the printing press has also accelerated to provide a multimedia exposure to a complex variety of lifestyles, values, and ideas, as well as access to the small media for purposes of personal explorations and small group communications. The fusion of these two phenomena and their compression in time has produced severe identity anxieties, facilitating a rejection of the rational abstractions of class and national identity definitions and a focus on the more concrete and affective, primordial (i.e., sex, race, religion, language, and ethnicity) identities.

Confronted with the multiple identities that modern life imposes upon the individual, and the difficult demands it makes for integrated social and personality systems, the impulse to return to some simple self-definitions has also been very strong. The inexorable drive toward the equality of conditions paved the way for social and political movements in the twentieth century that have gleefully sacrificed individual freedom at the altar of democratic equality. However, what De Tocqueville (1835–1840) could not have foreseen was the extent to which the processes of technological acceleration and despotic modernization (undertaken by colonial, neocolonial, and postcolonial elites in the Third World) would produce such great measures of rootlessness and identity anxiety that both freedom and justice could be easily sacrificed to satisfy the demands for a sense of identity, even though anachronistic. The desperate yearnings for meaning and community in this historical context bear the potential both for creative social reconstruction, as well as for destruction of all traditions of civility. As the Iranian revolution illustrates, these yearnings have the possibility of leading to more autonomous, free, just, and humane societies, but if the identity anxieties of the uprooted are exploited for the advantage of new authoritarian leaderships, they can also degenerate into new forms of political corruption more pernicious in consequences than the tyrannies they set out to correct.

REFERENCES

De Tocqueville, Alexis. (1835–1840). *Democracy in America,* 4 vol. Trans. by Henry Reeve. London: Saunders & Otley.

Fallaci, Oriana. (1979). "Interview with Ayatollah Khomeini," *The New York Times Magazine* (Oct. 7), pp. 29–31.

Geertz, Clifford, (ed.), (1963). *Old Societies and New State.* London: Free Press of Glencoe.

Lerner, Daniel. (1958). *The Passing of Traditional Society.* Chicago: Free Press.

Tehranian, Majid. (1979). "Communication and International Development: Some Theoretical Considerations." *Cultures 6,* 29–37.

Tehranian, Majid. (1980). "A Need for New Indicators." *Inter Media 8,* 19–23.

Tehranian, Majid. (1981). "The Fetish of Identity: Communication Revolution and Fundamentalist Revivals." *Media Asia 8*(1), 35–39.

Tehranian, Majid, Farhad Hakimzadeh, and Marcello L. Vidale. (1977). *Communications Policy for National Development.* London: Routledge & Kegan Paul.

10

Televised Puppetry in Taiwan
An Example of the Marriage Between a Modern Medium and a Folk Medium

Georgette Wang

The arrival of the modern technology of mass communication has often been considered a threat to the survival of folk media. Though deeply rooted in traditions, customs, and beliefs of the parent culture, folk media in recent years seems to be losing ground in industrializing societies. Their roles in entertainment, education, and communication are being taken over gradually by mass media. As pointed out by Hidetoshi Kato, in the early 1930s, hundreds of street singers and traveling storytellers in Japan were replaced by radios and phonographs (Kato, 1978, pp. 256–157). A similar case was found in Iran where stories formerly told by storytellers are now broadcast on radio, television or made into films (Motamed-Nejad, 1979). In Taiwan, the number of puppet theatre groups dropped from 700 to approximately 300 after the appearance of electronic media.

The significance of folk media in communication and socialization is now recognized by social scientists, but mainly in rural areas where illiteracy is high, living standards remain low, and mass media are absent. When modern means of communication fail to convey the message, folk media are recommended for promoting ideas and programs in family planning (Adhikarya, 1975), public health, etc. The question is, what will happen to folk media when their last stronghold—villages—disappear in the process of modernization? Will folk media eventually disappear, one by one?

According to Kato (1978), broadcasters in developing nations are often reluctant to design combinations between folk media and mass media, basically for economic reasons. While a local production of a single thirty-minute television program could cost $3,000, a series of thirteen one-hour programs can be purchased for several thousand dollars. The popularity of American and Japanese television series in Asia, shows that many broadcasters in developing nations of this region turn to foreign films to fill in the hours. This dependency on foreign films may be a solution to broadcasters' financial problems, but it also leads to a concern with "cultural imperialism," which ultimately may result in a cultural discontinuity. On the other hand, even if advertising revenues can justify the production costs involved, incorporation of folk media does not guarantee cultural continuity, unless it is carefully and thoughtfully planned. Folk media, though deeply rooted in the parent culture, may lose much of their charm in the face of the animation and excitement offered by modern media. In order to attract an audience large enough for survival on television, certain modifications in folk media presentations may be necessary. The modifications not only need to make folk media more attractive to the audience, but must also involve the functions and features of both mass and folk media. Neglect of either may lead to failure. The case of televised bag puppetry in Taiwan is a good illustration.

Bag puppetry was televised for the first time in Taiwan in 1970. Within a few months, the show became one of the top-rated television programs, with advertising revenues pouring in. The success was phenomenal. However, no research was conducted to understand its significance to the future of folk media, or how television might have changed bag puppetry. This paper looks at bag puppetry in Taiwan, especially the factors contributing to its sudden rise in television popularity, and its later downfall.

Puppet shows were one of the most popular forms of folk media in Taiwan before the arrival of electronic media. While the history of Chinese puppetry dates back some 3,000 years, bag puppetry in Taiwan is a relatively recent "immigrant," coming from Chuan Chou of Fukien Province approximately 300 years ago. According to a folk tale, bag puppet shows were invented by an unfortunate scholar in the Ming Dynasty. Having failed the nation-wide examination for a high position in the royal court, the young intellectual started playing with dolls to express his sorrows. With a solid background in literature and drama, a pastime or hobby eventually developed into a sophisticated form of folk media.

Whether bag puppetry is indeed the invention of an unfortunate scholar is unimportant, but early forms of bag puppetry did have a touch of high culture. While most of the plots were based on famous classical fiction and on historical stories, dialogue between puppets often included verses composed by the puppeteer himself.[1] Combining poetic and sometimes humorous dialogue with vivid, delicately performed puppet acts and soft traditional background music, bag puppet shows were at one time the favorite entertainment of upper-class Chinese families and the common people of Fukien and Taiwan, particularly at joyful occasions, such as religious festivals, birthday parties, and

---

[1]The educational background of later puppeteers seemed to be much poorer, as many of them were in fact illiterate.

weddings. To common village people, largely illiterate peasants, laborers, and small businessmen puppet shows introduced the world of literature and history—a world which they fancied, but were unable to reach by themselves. As one man suggested, watching puppet shows was like taking history lessons.

Another type of bag puppetry developed after it came to Taiwan— the now popular *kung fu* (or sword) bag puppet shows. Kung fu puppet shows differ from the earlier forms of puppetry in their action-oriented content. Instead of attracting audiences with elegant verse and soft music, kung fu bag puppet shows are fast-paced, noisy with gongs or other loud musical instruments, and full of fighting. The puppet shows which later became popular on television were closer to this genre of bag puppetry.

Bag puppetry can be performed by only one player, and with very little equipment. As pointed out by Malkin, the "portability" of puppet theatres is important because, as primarily a folk medium in China and elsewhere, they are forced to travel to the audiences rather than the other way around (Malkin, 1977, p. 96).

The earliest stage for puppet shows was called a "four-cornered pagoda." It was easily dismantled, packed away, and carried in a large bamboo basket. Later, more sophisticated stages, such as a "six-cornered pagoda" and a "colorful penthouse," appeared. The basic structure, however, remained the same. In his study of Chinese puppetry, Obraztsov (1961, p. 10) had a detailed description of one stage he saw:

> . . . The whole thing [the stage] is easily carried about on a "beam" or "yoke" which rests on the actor's shoulders, and is therefore referred to as a "portable booth." This beam also serves as a support for a charming little house with a covered terrace—the proscenium.
>
> . . . the rear of the house is generally placed against a convenient fence, the wall of a peasant house or the village temple. A length of cloth is attached to the "foundations" of the house, as it were, and reaches right down to the ground on three sides, thus concealing the puppeteer who stands under it.

The "portable booth," as described by Obraztsov, is still in use in Taiwan when puppet theater groups are called on to perform at religious festivals or parties. After the recovery from the Japanese occupation, bag puppet performances were also shown regularly at puppet theater houses. Though unable to "come to the audiences," shows performed at theater houses featured better sound effects, lighting, and stage decoration. At one time, puppet theater houses could be found in almost every small town and village in Taiwan. Unfortunately, with the decline of bag puppetry, only a handful of theater houses are left to struggle for survival.

As noted above, the "portability" of equipment and the small number of people involved in the performance contributed to mobility. Obraztsov, a Russian puppeteer himself, was amazed to see a Chinese puppet show performed by just one person. In fact, one-man puppet shows were common. A single actor would travel from village to village with big bamboo baskets full of puppets and other materials necessary for his performance. Upon arrival at a new place, he would choose an open ground, set up the stage, and go around the village sounding his gong to attract people's attention to the coming performances. When the crowd gathered, he would start the performance, handling, talking, singing, manipulating the puppets, and making occasional sound effects. He also played the role of cashier at the end of each performance, collecting money from the audience.

While bag puppetry could be performed by one person, a puppet theater group usually consisted of seven to eight people, including the puppet master, one or two assistants, and five musicians. Cheng Yi-hsiung, the head of the Five Continent Puppet Theatre Group in Taiwan, claimed that in order to stage one of his plays, thirty puppets were shown at one time on a three-level stage, requiring up to ten assistants.[2] This caused problems when he was asked to perform in remote villages. However, for the great majority of puppet theatre groups, mobility was assumed. It was the mobility that made the puppeteers such effective communicators in the pre-mass media era. Through casual conversations with local villagers, the performers played the role of reporters, carrying news stories from one village to another.

Bag puppetry had been a popular folk medium, but like other folk media, it was struggling to survive in the face of competition from modern mass media. With rapid economic growth and decreasing illiteracy rates, the newspaper, radio, and television became daily necessities for people in Taiwan. The function of bag puppetry, as communicator, was taken over by mass media. The entertainment and education functions remained, but seemed less significant in a modernized setting. Bag puppetry was, therefore, fading out when a sudden revival came, with the help from its primary rival, television.

Television emerged during the 1960s in Taiwan. As in other developing nations, the dominance and the effects of imported programs (mainly American television series) became a concern for many people. A policy regulating the ratio between imported and domestically produced television programs was instituted by the government to protect the audience from an overdose of foreign-made detective and Western television series.

The regulation, however, presented a problem for broadcasters. As indicated by Kato (1978), the cost of producing a program is usually much higher than buying imported films. In order to minimize expendi-

---

[2]One feature of Chinese bag puppetry is that only one person—the puppet master—handles all the talking and singing in the show even when there are thirty puppets on the stage. Precise coordination is therefore an essential requirement for successful performance.

tures[3] and the risk of audience rejection, producers of TTV, the Taiwan Television Company, turned to the already well-known puppetry.

With the popularity of puppetry diminishing, TTV was cautious in this venture, and puppet shows were, at first, shown only twice a week. The viewers' reactions, however, soon turned the experiment into a happy surprise for the broadcasters. Within a month of the first showing, TTV received thousands of letters from the audience, with a majority praising the ingenuity and creativity of the show. Though no figures were released, bag puppet shows were reported to be a target of competition for advertising agencies, and one of the best money-making programs. Within three months, the shows appeared five times a week. Witnessing the success of TTV, the other two television stations soon followed suit. Before long, people were reported putting their work aside after the lunch hour to watch bag puppet shows on television. An informal estimate of audience size guessed that over 70% of all television viewers in Taiwan were watching these programs (Kuo, 1971).

Several major changes in the televised puppet shows enhanced their popularity and success. Some changes had taken place when puppet theatre houses emerged and stage manipulations (including lighting and sound effects) became possible. However, Huang Jiung-hsiung was responsible for synthesizing the modifications made by individual puppet masters and creating a new form of bag puppetry for television. Huang was a recognized talent in his profession, of a third generation puppetry family. By the time he was contracted by TTV, Huang had 18 years of experience in the business, and was convinced that bag puppetry could attract television audiences only if changes were made.

One major difference between traditional puppetry and the televised version produced by Huang was the scripts. Usually, there was no script involved with traditional bag puppetry. They used classic fiction or historical stories as source materials, apprentices learned the plot and all the dialogue by memory. The advantage of not having written scripts was the flexibility, which allowed room for each puppeteer's own creativity and spontaneity. Failures of memory and the poor educational level of many puppeteers, however, resulted in increasingly impoverished resources for bag puppetry. On the other hand, increased literacy in Taiwan meant that more and more people could read classic fictions and history books, without relying on puppet masters to tell them the stories. In view of these changes, Huang decided to do away with tradition and to use entirely new scripts. The new scripts, of course, had to be able to attract a large audience and, at the same time, make the best use of puppets in "achieving fantasy" (Bussel, 1968, p. 15). To Huang, who complained of not being able to do much with the puppets' "expressionless faces," the solution was a mixture of kung fu

[3]See Jan Bussell (1968), p. 15: ". . . third advantage; an economy of space and manpower."

and mysteries, which attracted audiences by their suspense and fantasy. Characters in this new generation of bag puppetry were able to do things beyond many people's imagination, such as starting an earthquake by blinking their eyes, or hurting someone on another planet by a blow of the fist.

Though appearing to be "super-superhuman beings," the puppets remained dear and close to the audience, partly because of their language. Unlike the traditional puppets who "talked" in a literary tone, Huang used everyday street language for his puppets, using popular slang, and also making some slang popular.

Other notable changes were made in the background music, the puppets themselves, and in the stage decorations. Traditional bag puppet shows were accompanied by strictly classic Chinese music. Background music for the shows put out by Huang, however, was a mixture of Chinese and Western music. Rock and roll music and movie themes, which had never been heard in puppet shows before, became the trademark of this new bag puppetry. This combination attracted the younger generation; to them, the marriage of rock and roll and bag puppetry meant that the shows were no longer antique pieces belonging only to their grandfathers. Huang also adopted the use of modern electronic devices, such as tape recorders and stereo systems, to replace the usual five-man classic Chinese music band.

As most of the traditional bag puppets portray characters in classicial fiction or historical stories, the puppets, like actors and actresses in a Peking opera, have painted faces to signify different personality characteristics. Examples of the symbolic meanings of colors used in the painted faces are described by Malkin (1977, p. 97):

> . . . a white face blending into a rosy pink on the cheeks or brows signifies notability and a strong sense of honor, while a face that is pure white reveals a duplicitous and deeply villainous nature. A red face indicates loyalty, honor, and courage. The black-faced character is even more loyal—often to the point of self-sacrifice.

This symbolic face-painting was gradually de-emphasized by Huang, since new characters created by him and his writers did not necessarily have clear-cut personalities; on the other hand, some physical features were exaggerated. For example, one popular character in Huang's shows had two big front teeth, and was nicknamed "Two Teeth." Besides de-emphasizing the face-painting tradition, Huang enlarged the size of his puppets. In traditional puppetry, the dolls were between eight and fourteen inches tall. The small size of the puppets made it impossible to have a large audience. It was believed, however, that small sizes were necessary to achieve balanced proportions of head and body for the puppets, taking the size and movement of the hand into consideration. Huang decided that it was worthwhile to sacrifice some head-body proportion for the visibility of backseat viewers. Huang's puppets, therefore, were as tall as three feet. In order to take advantage of close-up camera shots, available only with television, Huang equipped his puppets with special devices enabling them, for example, to smoke a cigar or to draw a sword. Other innovations by Huang included three–dimensional movable stage decorations, and special effects such as fire and smoke.

Many of the changes Huang made or adopted were essential to the success of bag puppetry on television. But it was television itself that made the phenomenal success possible. Although bag puppetry was a popular folk medium, its audience had been limited to, at most, several hundred people. With television, tens of thousands of people could be watching comfortably in their own living rooms at the same time. Television also made it possible for the viewers to see the details of puppet movement through camera manipulations. Thus, a fantasy world of bag puppetry was created.

The audience's reaction to this modern version of an ancient folk medium was enthusiastic. According to letters from the viewers, many were impressed by its fresh new look; some were fascinated by the use of rock and roll music; others found great interest in the stories. The novelty, unfortunately, gradually wore off as the audience was "bombarded" by similar bag puppetry shows from all three television stations almost every day of the week. Without good plots, audiences grew tired of heavy fighting and killing. Also, some of the changes in Huang's shows began to draw severe criticism.

At one time bag puppetry was regarded as a valuable medium of education and socialization. The classic fiction and historical stories on which the plots were based strongly emphasized traditional Chinese values, such as filial piety, honesty, uprightness, and loyalty. Like the Javanese *wayang*, another ancient folk medium, bag puppetry offered models and examples of good deeds to the audience, especially to children. On the other hand, the socializing function of television has long been recognized by social scientists. As indicated by Bandura in a discussion of social learning, "models presented in televised form are so effective in capturing attention that viewers learn the depicted behavior regardless of whether or not they are given extra incentives to do so" (Bandura, 1971, p. 7). This theory was supported in a more recent study by Comstock and Fisher (1978) who found that, while observation of real-life behavior is more potent, television presents a strong stimulus to learning, since it requires a more specific focus of attention. Research conducted on audience uses of media, such as the study on listeners of radio daytime serials (Herzog, 1944) and Japanese historical drama (Makita, 1979), suggests that audiences often use the shows as sources of advice. They learn ideas and how other people deal with problems, and then seek applications of what they have learned in their own lives.

Although no survey was conducted to find out what kind of influence televised bag puppetry had on its audience, the shows which featured far-fetched fantasies and non-stop fighting and killing with no special emphasis on traditional values seemed to have lost the original message the folk medium was expected to convey. The potential of televised bag puppetry to influence its audience became a major concern for many people, including parents, teachers, and social scientists. A school boy was reported to have named one puppet character as a "national hero" in an essay, and cases of children talking in undignified "puppet slang" and imitating puppet characters' ways of acting were found in almost every corner of society. In an open letter to Huang Jun-hsiung, a mother of three complained that her children became near-sighted from excessive viewing of bag puppet shows on television, and that they not only imitated puppet stars in talking and acting, but also insisted on buying expensive puppets from the stores.

Another line of criticism focused on the format of Huang's bag puppetry. With a finely carved "colorful penthouse," classic Chinese music, and delicately carved, painted, and dressed puppets, bag puppetry had once been considered a unique combination of several folk arts, as well as one form of folk medium. Huang's new version of bag puppetry, no matter how exciting at the beginning, seemed to have lost the artistic touch. Although the electric movable stage decoration produced dramatic effects, it was no match for the beautiful "colorful penthouse" in the eyes of the artists. On the other hand, the "mixed-blood," background music he used became an embarrassment to many people, especially those who consider bag puppetry a representation of Chinese folk art.

The peak for televised bag puppetry lasted approximately three years. The China Television Company was the first to drop bag puppetry, partly due to failures to get ahead in the severe competition, and partly due to heavy pressure from public opinion (Kuo, 1971). Several months later, the China Television Service, CTS, also chose to stop broadcasting puppet shows in reaction to a new government policy limiting the total hours of television programs broadcast in dialects. TTV, the station which discovered Huang Jiung-hsiung, supported his shows for over four years. The pressing need for change and improvement, though, was clear to Huang himself. In 1972, he had the idea of making one of his best-known puppet stars into a "James Bond-like" detective, hoping that a new emphasis on the battle of wits could avoid criticisms of the shows as being violent. The ideas were never realized. A year later, Huang put another form of puppetry on the screen incorporating cartoon features into the show. The show has, according to a newspaper commentator, kept the essence of bag puppetry, but adapted the animation and lively style of Western cartoons (Liu, 1973). When his contract with TTV expired, Huang produced two more bag puppet series with CTS; all three series used Mandarin for dialogue in order to go along with the government policy of promoting the language, but none of them achieved the popularity of the earlier ones.

Some thought that the days of televised bag puppetry were gone for good, but in February 1980, a contract was signed to make the stories of Huang Hai-tai, the father of Huang Jiung-hsiung, into a dramatic series. Although bag puppetry is not the only element in the series, it is taking an important role. For the broadcasters, this new series could be used as a test of the audience's attitude toward more televised puppetry.

Televised bag puppetry had its rise and fall. For the several hundreds of bag puppet theater groups which never had the chance of working with the broadcasters, there seemed to be little change in their business, only a steady decrease.

Some suspected that Huang's popularity had done more harm than good to the already declining folk medium since many people preferred to stay home and watch bag puppet shows. More viewers in front of television sets meant fewer people in front of the "portable booth" or in the puppet theater houses. When the viewers got tired of watching the shows on television, it was even less likely that they would return to the "portable booth." Before the emergence of televised bag puppet shows, changes such as the use of electric movable stage decorations and tape recorders had been adopted by some puppeteers. But Huang, apparently, made these changes much more popular by using them on television. To many people, this widespread "reform" downgraded the folk medium and took away its indigenous flavor. On the other hand, puppeteers writing their own scripts became common, but, unfortunately, unlike the ancient times, when the puppeteers were intellectuals and many in the audience were not, the puppeteers faced a better educated and more demanding audience. At times, when they were incapable of writing satisfactory stories for the audiences some of the shows were laughed at, when mistakes in commonsense knowledge were obvious. Huang's new version did not solve the problems of bag puppetry, and it created some new ones, but his style was so popular that only five or six bag puppetry theater groups are still struggling to maintain the old traditions. These groups are marked by the old age of both the puppeteers and their devoted group of audiences.

The prospects for bag puppetry in Taiwan are indeed alarming. A survey conducted in 1975 (after the peak period of televised bag puppetry) showed that only 3% of the sample reported watching bag puppet shows frequently, and the majority of these people were poorly educated, elderly rural dwellers. With smaller audiences, puppet theater houses were closing down, and more and more puppeteers were either forced to change their occupation, or to perform on a seasonal basis with supplementary income from part-time jobs. The few who persisted found that the skills handed down to them from their ancestors no longer interested the young. A champion in a bag puppetry contest once stated that, although puppetry had been a family business for generations, he would take in whoever was willing to learn, since his own son had gone to college and probably would never touch puppets again. Although Huang and his group are still making efforts to promote the folk medium, some people suspect that their version of bag puppetry will deviate more and more from the traditional form. The prospect for reviving traditional puppetry is therefore dim.

Conclusions

The case of televised bag puppetry in Taiwan has several implications for the incorporation of mass media and folk media:

1. Mass media could be helpful in promoting folk media.
2. In order to take advantage of the features of mass media and make folk media more acceptable to a better educated, more demanding audience, certain changes and modifications may be desirable.
3. The modifications, however, should be made without changing the basic feature and function of folk media.

Traditional puppetry, however unattractive to the audience today, represents an indigenous folk medium form. Its educational implications may seem negligible, but the emphasis on traditional values helps to maintain cultural continuities. Given the audiences' enthusiasm several years ago, a new and lasting peak could be expected when the folk medium uses a modern medium, and reasonable modifications are made. Huang's innovations were creative, but unfortunately some of them were made at the expense of the original features of bag puppetry. As some pointed out, a good writer is very seldom hampered by organizing the plot of a story around traditional values. In other words, new scripts could be written without disrupting the cultural continuity of a folk medium. Along the same line, the artistic aspects of bag puppetry do not have to give way to electronic devices. A finely carved "colorful penthouse" would look more interesting when decorated with equally finely carved and painted moving background scenery.

As pointed out by Kato (1978), "to establish continuities between traditional media and newer electronic media will be a great task for the people of these [developing] countries." The case of televised bag puppetry in Taiwan showed that designing continuities between folk and mass media is not simply a question of financially motivating the broadcasters, it involves a far more sophisticated approach and the close cooperation of artists, writers, experts in modern drama, and broadcasters. Whether such an effort will be undertaken now seems to be the determining factor in the future of bag puppetry in Taiwan.

REFERENCES

Adhikarya, Ronny. (1975). "Communication Support for the Family Planning Programmes: the Potentialities for Folk Media in Indonesia and the Problems Involved in Pre-Testing and Evaluation." *Asian Population Studies Series No. 27*. Bangkok: UN/ESCAP.

Bandura, Albert. (1971). *Social Learning Theory*. Morristown, New Jersey: General Learning Press.

Bussell, Jan. (1968). *Puppets.* London: Dennis Dobson.

Comstock, George A. and Marilyn Fisher. (1975). *Television and Human Behavior.* Santa Monica: Rand.

Herzog, Herta. (1944). "What Do We Know About Daytime Serial Listeners?" In Paul F. Lazarsfeld and Frank N. Stanton (eds.), *Radio Research, 1942–1943.* New York: Duell, Sloan and Pearce.

Kato, Hidetoshi. (1978). "Global Instantaneousness and Instant Globalism—The Significance of Popular Culture in Developing Countries." In Wilbur Schramm and Daniel Lerner (eds.), *Communication and Change The Last Ten Years—And the Next.* Honolulu: The University Press of Hawaii.

Kuo, Da-Jin. (1971). "Indigenous Art—the Modified Puppet Shows' Merciless Swords Logic." *The New Life News* (March 11). (In Chinese).

Liu, Lon. (1973). "Another Television Innovation by Huang Jiung-hsiung." *The Taiwan Daily News* (April 18). (In Chinese).

Makita, Tetsuo. (1979). "Television Drama and Japanese Culture with Special Emphasis on Historical Drama." In Heniz Dietrich Fischer and Stefan R. Melnik (eds.), *Entertainment: A Cross-Cultural Examination.* New York: Hastings House.

Malkin, Michael R. (1977). *Traditional and Folk Puppets of the World.* New York: A. S. Barnes and Company.

Motamed-Nejad, Kazem. (1979). "The Story-Teller and Mass Media in Iran." In Heinz Deitrich Fischer and Stefan R. Melnik (eds.), *Entertainment: A Cross-Cultural Examination.* New York: Hastings House.

Obraztsov, Sergei. (1961). *The Chinese Puppet Theatre.* London: Faber and Faber.

11

Indianness of the Indian Cinema

Binod C. Agrawal

It is a Sunday afternoon; the streets are full of men, women, and children in the industrial city of Kanpur, a Hindi-speaking region. It is difficult to walk straight ahead in the surge of humanity on the streets without being pushed, tripped, and sandwiched between others. At one of the crossings in a busy commercial center, the crowd is even more dense; hawkers are shouting and selling sweets; men and women are converging from all directions. In a nearby cinema a popular Hindi movie, *King of Destiny*, is in its tenth week. The signboard in front of the cinema theatre reads in English "House Full." However, tickets are available for the current show; one has to just keep his eyes and ears open to find a scalper, a devious looking character, who might "whisper," loud enough to be heard in the maddening rush, "Five for ten," meaning tickets costing five rupees are available for ten. In Ahmedabad, a Gujarati-speaking industrial city, on the same afternoon another Hindi movie, *Don*, is creating a similar hubbub in the middle of town.

In a Tamil-speaking Madras city, a new film is to be released. The usual full contingent of ritual specialists are at the cinema gate to perform the opening ceremony by chanting religious hymns, offering flowers, sweets, vermillion, and coconut. The star, an actor-turned-politician, is present at the ceremony, and is an added attraction for the throngs waiting to get a glimpse of their favorite hero. Police are on hand to protect him from the mob of enthusiastic fans.

The same evening, in Bombay and Delhi, many middle-class and upper-class residential areas look deserted. By six o'clock the children are indoors and most housewives are out of the kitchen. Household servants choose to stay in their employers' homes even though they are free to leave. Everyone is eagerly awaiting the "Sunday Evening Hindi Movie," a regular telecast. In most of these homes, the television is only turned on during weekends because that is when commercial films are telecast. These regular broadcasts represent a threat to the Indian cinema (Agrawal and Sinha, 1981) once secure in a unique position. The fascination with film is so strong that families and other groups rent video cassette recorders to see the telecast film again (Agrawal and Baradi, 1981).

These displays of enthusiasm have been repeated constantly over the past 75 years. When the first full-length silent movie was released in 1913, it was commented that the showing of *Rajah Harischandra* in Madras brought, according to one observer, an almost phenomenal crowd (Barnouw and Krishnaswamy, 1980, p. 16). This was also observed in 1931, when only 27 films were released, and in 1980 when more than seven hundred films were premiered.

In the past 50 years, there has been a steady growth in film production in all major languages of India: Assamese, Bengali, Gujarati, Hindi, Malayalam, Marathi, Oriya, Punjabi, Tamil, and Telugu. Lately, however, the production rate in four Dravidian languages, Kannada, Malayalam, Tamil, and Telugu, has increased more than that in other languages (Dharap, 1979, p. 396).

The Indian cinema has always been an urban phenomenon in a predominantly rural country. About 37% of some ten thousand cinema halls, located primarily in the cities, are touring cinemas, a phenomenon peculiar to the Indian scene (Dharap, 1979). These touring cinemas literally camp in urban centers, where they are a prominent and unique feature.

More than two hundred thousand persons are employed in film production, distribution and exhibition. It is estimated that more than ten million viewers go to the movies on any given day. The entertainment tax collected by various states and local bodies was more than 2,060 million rupees (about 260 million dollars) for the 1974–75 fiscal year (Dharap, 1979). Today, the capital invested in the film industry is estimated at 800 crores (one billion dollars). Almost 75% of this money is concentrated in Bombay, the film capital of India, where the majority of Hindi films are produced (Dharap, 1979). The rest is spread among the other film producing cities: Calcutta, Madras, Bangalore, and Hyderabad. Today, invariably, all newspapers and magazines carry news and features on cinema and cinema personalities. More than a hundred film magazines are published in various Indian languages and in English, and keep the interest of moviegoers alive by providing them with glimpses into the lives of their favorite film stars, including details about their romances, hobbies, and general idiosyncrasies. Movie posters fill almost all wall spaces in the urban landscape. Railway stations and public places are full of posters on which even illiterates can identify their favorite heroes and heroines. In urban middle-class homes, cinema personalities are discussed more than anybody else.

The Indian cinema is accused of excessive extravagance, because of the phenomenal fees paid to its stars, as well as the large scale under-the-table deals and rampant corruption involved in the making of its gory and glossy products. What is Indian about Indian cinema? Is there anything special about the content, production, and direction? Is it a genre, artistically and technically? Answers to these questions cannot be found in the research conducted so far on the Indian cinema (Hurley, 1975). To date there is no empirical data compiled on the profile of the Indian cinema viewer. Little is known about the economics of film-making; there is no systematic documentation of the history of the Indian cinema (Barnouw and Krishnaswamy, 1980; Dey, 1981; Dharap, 1979; Kumar, 1981; Paul, 1977; Rangoonwalla, 1979). Overall, communication researchers, sociologists, and anthropologists, have not been interested in doing a sociocultural analysis of the Indian cinema, although, recently there have been efforts made to analyse the characteristics of the cinema viewers in a few given regions (Agrawal and Sinha, 1981; Exposure of Youth to Mass Media, 1979; Telugu Films, 1981). Because cinema is a technological extension of art forms and theatrical traditions, this paper explores Indian cinema in the context of Indian civilization.

The Indian Civilization

India is one of the oldest literate civilizations of the world. The concept of literate civilization, rather than culture, is used here as a point of departure because civilization implies an extra increment of scope of elaboration. In this regard, the literate civilizations of the world are those which have been literate long enough to have accumulated a wealth of written documents of all sorts and a set of rich intellectual traditions: religious, historical, legal, scientific, and the like (Hsu, 1969). It should be noted, however, that at no given time in the history of India were the majority of Indians ever literate. Hence, Indian civilization can be divided between literate and illiterate categories of people, each having separate means and channels of communication. For literates, information and knowledge is preserved and transmitted in written form, whereas illiterates use memory and word-of-mouth. The information exchange between the two classes is verbal and through personal contact.

Various art forms such as dance, music, and painting are essential elements of Indian civilization, which have had a permanent and profound influence on the emergence and evolution of Indian civilization. The manifestation of art in the literate class is highly codified, formalized, and internalized according to specialized *jatis* (castes). The learning of art forms has been part of the *jati* guild in many parts of India, although particular forms have not been restricted to any one group (Vatsyayan, 1980, p. 11). The same holds true for the illiterate class where art can also be a means of livelihood and thus assumes even greater importance.

The concept of *Natya*, generally translated as "drama," is different from the original Greek drama. It is a visual characterization of human experience supplemented with verbal and nonverbal symbols. Contrary to Greek drama, where emphasis is laid on the fable or the plot, Indian drama gives more importance to stage sets, costumes, makeup, dance, song, and instrumental music (Rangacharya, 1980).

In the Indian civilization, "there are traditions, and not one tradition, of the performing arts, in the vast geographical area. All are characterised by a staggering multiplicity of genres, forms, styles and techniques" (Vatsyayan, 1980). But the spatial distribution and tradition of art forms differ according to their historical association with a particular class or *jati*. The arts developed in a framework of local or regional distinctiveness which cuts across socioeconomic stratification. There is a dialogue and interaction between varying levels, and often there is much overlap. The movement is two-way, not merely the penetration of "great art" into popular levels. Tribal and village forms also affected and continue to affect "high art." Also, there is a clearly identifiable pattern of communication among regions at particular levels. Thus, there are two broad patterns: one, a vertical movement among forms of a particular region at different levels and socioeconomic groupings; and another, a horizontal movement among regions where themes, content, and forms have developed in a framework of continual communication at particular levels (Vatsyayan, 1980, pp. 4–5). Any attempt to classify these art forms creates several difficulties (Vatsyayan, 1980). Confusion is compounded as various authors have used the same term to cover different kinds of art forms, such as "traditional folk media" (Parmar, 1975), "traditional theatre" (Vatsyayan, 1980), or "folk stage" (Rangacharya, 1980). While a hierarchy of artistic value is not being suggested here, operationally, three forms of theatre or dramatic tradition can be identified. These are literate, folk, and regional traditions, all of which coexist in Indian civilization and continually influence each other. However, each of these flourishes with its own strength and has the ability to create, recreate, and express its own ideas and traditions. Of course, folk tradition, in most cases, acts as a bridge between literate and local traditions. The role of the literate tradition, also called *Sanskrit* or "classical" drama, is aptly expressed in *The Natyasastra:* "There is no wise maxim, no learning, no art or craft, no device, no action that is not found in the drama" (Ghosh, 1967, p. 15, stanza 116). In literate drama, all elements of human feeling and emotions are expressed: duty, lovemaking, laughter, hate. Literate drama is expected to provide love to those who are eager for its fulfillment: courage to cowards; energy to heroic persons; wisdom to the learned; composure to persons who are troubled; and self-restraint to those who are disciplined. According to *The Natyasastra,* "Drama is a mimicry of actions and conduct of people, which is rich in various emotions, and which depicts different situations. . . . [IT] will thus, be instructive to all, through actions and states depicted in it, and through sentiments arising out of it" (Ghosh, 1967, p. 15, stanzas 111–113).

Each linguistic region in India has a tradition of folk drama, and these works are performed even today. Although they were not written down originally, they nonetheless reflect the historical continuity of Indian civilization. *Nautanki, Natch, Tamasha,* and *Gigipada* are some of these folk drama works (Parmar, 1975). At least one authority, Vatsyayan, does not accept these art forms as a part of folk tradition. In her opinion "they are neither folklore nor classical, but overlap with both of these categories" (Vatsyayan, 1980, p. 9). However, these art forms are currently included in the folk tradition of their respective linguistic regions, and are transmitted by word-of-mouth among illiterates. Various forms of devotional singing, dramatization of local myths, and religious mythologies fall within the category of "regional tradition," of which *PuruliyaChau* of West Bengal; *Rasdhare* (Mewar, Rajasthan); *Sannata* in North Karnataka; *Chavittu Natakam* performed by the rural Christians of Kerala are examples.

The Indian cinema, from the very beginning, relied upon various art forms and cut across all three traditions. The *Natyasastra,* and various works of folk and local drama traditions, found a new means of expression through celluloid. However, very few efforts have been made to analyse the exchange between cinema and drama traditions. The remainder of this chapter explores the influence of drama on the Indian cinema with special reference to folk drama.

Advent of Indian Cinema

The advent of Indian cinema is closely associated with the period of British domination. Cinema, like other technology, came to India from Europe and was initially identified with European culture, primarily French and English. In 1896, cinema was thought of as connected with the fairies of the foreign land and was considered entertainment for the English-educated elite. At the same time, the literate drama tradition of India was discredited by the European literary traditions. The local drama tradition was languishing due to increasing poverty, and the folk drama tradition, especially in the rural areas, was fading. At that time cinema, the technological marvel of the century, was incomprehensible to the members of the illiterate class and also to many members of the literate class. Its impact was limited to a small portion of the urban, Western-educated elite, who watched the "moving pictures" to know more about European cultures.

The potential of a cinema for the masses, which cut across three traditions had occurred to many, however. For this reason film-making was adopted by such a person as D. G. Phalke (1870–1944), whose education was rooted in the literate tradition and who had also been exposed to photography as well as to Indian art forms. Phalke initially tried to use photography in the era of silent cinema to portray the literary tradition. However, when Phalke chose a story from that tradition, he cautiously chose the one which was also common to local and folk traditions: the Hindu myth of *Rajah Harischandra*. A letter written to the editor of *Kesari,* dated May 6, 1913, accurately describes this indigenous approach to film-making:

> The images in his [Phalke] films are Indian and are drawn from *Purans* and are thus familiar to all. Mr. Phalke made a complete film of 3000 ft. in which he has shown the entire play "*Harischandra*" . . . All the movements and expressions of the characters on the screen were so realistic that the spectators felt that those moving characters were also speakers . . . They have come out so well that the Harischandra and Taramati of the screen bring tears to the eyes of the spectators (Studies in Film History, 1970, p. 15).

From this modest beginning, the genre of Indian cinema evolved. In the last three-quarters of a century, it has attained some distinctive features, which can certainly be called culture-bound characteristics. There are three primary components in any film industry: production, exhibition, and audience. With respect to the Indian cinema, the first two have been analysed and described. There is little empirical data on the Indian audience, however, this chapter makes reference to the little there is. It also analyzes the use of story and music and song in production, and the techniques of film-making. Finally, it discusses the interplay between film exhibition and class and view characteristics.

The Plot

The plots of the Indian cinema are taken from two sources: myths, which traditionally provide the base for both the literal drama and drama of the two other traditions, and history, which has been a foundation for folk and literate drama. Roughly from the Asoka period, or the 4th century B.C., until the advent of British rule all the folk heroes and heroines were taken from history. A third category of films, which can be termed, "contemporary concerns," covers the broadest spectrum of stories spanning a period dating from the beginning of British rule until the present.

Mythological Films. Religion has been inextricably linked with development of Indian civilization, especially as regards the literate class. Even today, it would be extremely difficult to separate religion from art forms, in which the recreation and repetition of various prototype figures are the norm. In the local and folk drama traditions *Ramlila, Krishna Lila, Garhba,* and *Katha,* a few of the dramatic works are used to transmit religious information and to reinforce religious beliefs. In the illiterate class, word-of-mouth, especially in the Bhakti movement, and songs communicated this information.

The first Indian feature films were mythological epics and these same myths are filmed today. Their influence has spread to other genres, too, as they are used again in thinly disguised forms (Rangoon-walla, 1979, p. 16). The cinema audience has not yet been weaned from myths. Indeed, the craving for mythological films has even gained momentum in the 1970s, and *Salutations to Mother Santoshi* became a phenomenal hit in 1975 throughout India. The characteristic has not been altered by changing sociopolitical forces in India or abroad.

Historical Films. In the Indian film context, history means a description of the lives of kings and queens, and their feuds, intrigues, wars, politics, and general glorification. The historical films as nonfiction are supposed to be based on the truth, but the Indian cinema assumes that its representations need not be strictly factual (Rangoon-walla, 1979, p. 28).

Historical films gained popularity in India for two reasons. First, the medium provided a handy visual device for showing grandeur through palaces, processions, and battles, which meant language was no barrier (Rangoonwalla, 1979, p. 28); second, very powerful movies were produced that cut across class barriers. The feudal life style of centuries ago was known to all classes. Hence, it was possible to comprehend and circumvent history. Attempts were also made to incorporate a few non-Indian historical characters, such as Alexander the Great, who had invaded India. However, due to the availability of innumerable historical personalities and events, history on the Indian screen remained indigenous.

Contemporary Concerns. More than 70% of the films produced in India are classified as "social." Almost all films reflecting contemporary concerns would qualify as such. These social films include stories based on love affairs, family problems, socioeconomic and political issues, conflict between modernity and tradition, spying, and the general feats of daring. The most characteristic feature of these films is that the time span of the story covers one or two generations or several reincarnations of lives. Even if a story is about war, spying, or smuggling, it ultimately centers on a family. The story must create some conflict between one character and members of his family, community, village, or society at large. In its narration, the literate drama tradition is followed. The story proceeds through emotional, situational conflict to a serene resolution that restores harmony and creates a happy ending. *Devdas*, produced several times in many languages, including Bengali and Hindi, and other similar films reflected the inherent conflict between individual love, and community opposition. *Madhumati* reinforces the concept of reincarnation. Several movies since then have been made on reincarnation. Some folk and local drama traditions have had an even more permanent influence on the stories of contemporary concern. Several films center on the family and some of the problems of the extended family, including the domestic. Even when Western stories are adopted, the contents resemble a folk drama more than their foreign origin would suggest. *Sweet and Sour*, for example, adopted from an English movie *Yours, Mine and Ours*, in no way resembles the original movie.

This section would not be complete without mentioning the new consciousness created by Satyajit Ray who used the language of cinema without recourse to any of the theatrical conventions of the studio-made Indian film (Bahadur, 1978, p. 11). However, even Ray's triology *Song of the Road, The Unvanquished,* and *The World of Apu,* focused on the life of a family over a generation in the folk tradition of rural Bengal.

Melodies in Cinema

Cinema has retained dramatic traditions, and the contribution of cinema to Indian culture seems to lie in synthesizing, integrating, and invigorating all three dramatic traditions. By taking inspiration from classical folk and local musical traditions of songs and dances, Indian cinema provides a new medium of entertainment and communication which has something to offer to everybody.

Song and Dance. An Indian movie is incomplete without some classical and folk dances, both solos and duet. By the early 1950s, song became essential to a successful film. Another sociological factor responsible for strengthening the position of songs is that music in Northern India had remained the monopoly of courts and *kothas*. The only music available to the masses was either the devotional music of Kathas, Kirtan, and Bhajans or that of Qawalis, Mushairas, or Shehanai. Cinema changed this and gave an unexpected gift to Indian music (Mahmood, 1974, p. 87). It is no accident that the first talkie, *Beauty of the World*, had a dozen songs, and that *Court of India* had over seventy. The Indian talkies unlike those of any other land, used music from the beginning. In doing so, film tapped a powerful current, one that has given it an extraordinary new impetus, and that went back some two thousand years (Barnouw and Krishnaswamy, 1980, p. 69). As songs and dances are found in all the three drama traditions, they were, in this new form, quite acceptable to the Indian cinema viewers. Beeman (1980, p. 82) observed that to understand the structure of music in contemporary Indian film, an understanding of the nature and use of music in the contemporary folk theatre is necessary. From east to west, north to south, all major folk theatrical forms in India involve the total integration of music with other performance elements in a manner that is very different from Western performance tradition.

Playback Singing. Another characteristic feature of the Indian cinema is playback singing and the cinematic handling or pictorial depiction of songs. Ray (1976, p. 74) characterizes it as a "strange practice . . . the public blindly accepts . . . that whoever breaks into song in a film does so in the voice of one of a half-a-dozen popular singers who seem to have cornered the play-back market."

The influence of cinema songs is all-pervasive in contemporary India. *Vividhbharti,* the commercial station of All-India Radio, broadcasting from all major cities, plays film songs for more than 12 hours a day. Records and cassettes of these songs are sold widely in the market. The melodies and even the lyrics of a number of film songs are borrowed from the folk drama and folk songs of various linguistic regions, with the result that these regional and folk songs get national exposure. Several such folksongs have become accepted in the literate drama tradition.

Techniques of Film-Making

In cinema it is possible to perform oracles and miracles, to diminish and enlarge human size, to reduce the dimensions of time and space, to make gods and goddesses fly from earth to heaven and to lands below the earth, and to convert the human body into other forms. Assisted by this extraordinary power of cinema, depictions of *Ramayana* and *Mahabharata* have become more authentic and real for the viewers who could only imagine the divine powers of the gods and goddesses. Movies are also able to reinforce ancient qualities and values such as the duties of a son towards his parents, the sacrifice of a woman for her husband and son, and the virtues of chastity.

Similar techniques have been used in historical films to reinforce the belief that our ancestors were very powerful and strong, as well as the established assumption that the golden age of the Indian civilization was in the past. *Tamil* and *Akbar the Great* are good examples of films which portray a past as could not be depicted otherwise.

A variety of cinematographic techniques have been used to depict the Indian belief of reincarnation of soul. In films of contemporary concern such as *Madhumati, Meeting, Palace,* and *Month of March,* heroes and heroines are presented. Similarly, characterization of identical twins, either getting lost after birth or having two opposite characters, is one of the popular plots in the Indian cinema and has its origins in literate and folk drama traditions of antiquity. New techniques evolved to suit the needs of such films. All these efforts have led to the indigenization of production techniques.

Class in Cinema

The hierarchical civilization of India maintained its class characteristics in almost all forms of recreation including drama. *The Natyashastra,* for example, while discussing the constructional theatre, clearly specifies where various classes should sit. In the medieval period one observes a similar phenomenon. When foreign films arrived in India in 1896, the hierarchy-oriented Indian culture adjusted itself very quickly in conformity with its established norms by providing different price tickets for different classes of viewers. Barnouw and Krishnaswamy (1980, p. 5) observe that by the end of July, 1896, the showings had acquired two indigenous aspects: Reserved boxes for Purdah Ladies and their Families were announced late in July, and a broad scale of prices was introduced. For the first showing there had been a single admission price of one rupee, but later prices ranged from a low of four *annas* to a high of two rupees. This wide price range was to remain a feature of film exhibition in India, important to its future growth and range of appeal.

Even today, in various parts of India, separate seating arrangements are made for men and women, and there are three or four classes of seats with different price ranges. Observations indicate that the price of a ticket is associated with the class, though often desperate viewers must buy tickets of higher classes. But in the dark, who knows who he is sitting next to? Money is the only factor in deciding who will watch in which class. Lately, it has been pointed out that in Kerala, in the southwestern corner of India, higher priced balcony seats are occupied by the new rich who have petrodollars in their pockets instead of by the old elite

Such changes are quite in line with the folk drama tradition. In the context of traditional theatre, Vatsyayan (1980, p. 185) observed that "the democratizing role of the theatre is obvious, particularly in details of performance and audience where the prince and the pauper rub shoulders with each other. The theatre in India is indeed a fifth veda with no class or caste barriers."

This exploratory analysis clearly supports the view that Indian Cinema is linked to the art forms and the theatrical traditions of the Indian civilization, but at the same time it has developed as a distinct genre of cinema.

REFERENCES

Agrawal, Binod C. and Hasmukh Baradi. (1981). "The Fifth Channel: A Challenge for Media Planner." (Mimeographed.) Ahmedabad: Space Applications Centre.

Agrawal, Binod C. and Arbind K. Sinha. (1981). "Future of Cinema in India." (Mimeographed.) Ahmedabad: Space Applications Centre.

Bahadur, Satish. (1978). "The Context of Indian Film Culture." *In Film Appreciation: Study Memorial Series No. 2.* Pune: National Film Archive of India.

Barnouw, E. and S. Krishnaswamy. (1980). *Indian Film* (2d Ed.) New York: Oxford University Press.

Beeman, William O. (1980). "The Use of Music in Popular Film. East and West." *India International Centre Quarterly* 8(1), 77–87 (Special Issue).

Dey, Ajoy Kumar (Ed.). (1981). *50 Years of Indian Talkies 1981.* Calcutta: IFSON, Indian Film Society News. Editor: R. Chattopadhyay (Special Issue August 1981).

Dharap, B. V. (1979). *Indian Films 1977 & 1978.* Pune: Motion Picture Enterprises.

Exposure of Youth to Mass Media. (1979). *Communicator* (New Delhi) *14*(3), 1–7.

Ghosh, Manomohan. (1967). *The Natyasastra.* Calcutta: Manisha Granthalaya Private Limited.

Hsu, Francis L. (1969). *The Study of Literate Civilizations.* New York: Holt Rinehart and Winston.

Hurley, Neil (1975). "Indian Cinema—Correcting A Misapprehension." *Indian Journal of Communication Arts* (Sept.), 7–10.

Kumar, Pavan. (1981). "Themes and Trends in Telugu Cinema." *Interface* (Hyderabad) *5*(2), 9–12.

Mahmood, Hameeduddin. (1974). *The Kaleidoscope Indian Cinema.* New Delhi: Affiliated East-West Press Pvt. Ltd.

Parmar, Shyam. (1975). *Traditional Folk Media.* New Delhi: Geka Books.

Paul, Ramesh. (1977). "Punjabi Cinema: A Survey and a Plea." *Indian Journal of Communication Arts* (Aug.), 9–11.

Rangacharya, Adya. (1980). *The Indian Theatre.* (Second ed.) New Delhi: National Book Trust, India.

Rangoonwalla, Firoze. (1979). *A Pictorial History of Indian Cinema.* London: Hamlyn Publishing Group.

Ray, Satyajit. (1976). *Our Films, Their Films.* Bombay: Orient Longman Limited.

Studies in Film History, A Compilation of Research Papers Devoted to D. G. Phalke. (1970). Pune: Film Institute of India.

"Telugu Films: An Attitude Study of Hyderabad Film-Goers." *Interface* (Hyderabad) *5*(2), 5–8.

Vatsyayan, Kapila. (1980). *Traditional Indian Theatre.* New Delhi: National Book Trust, India.

12

Changing Ways of Communication With a New Medium
The Case of Hi-OVIS In Japan

Isao Araki

Television has a thirty-year history in Japan dating from 1953, when two stations began broadcasting in Tokyo. During this period it has become the most influential of mass media. However, the situation is now undergoing a gradual and serious change, due to the appearnace of the so-called, "new media." The advent of the new media is crucial, not only for television, but for all of us, because they will replace the central role of mass media in communication; consequently they will impact upon every sphere of our social life.

CAPTAIN (Character And Pattern Telephone Access Information Network) system, VRS (Video Response System), CCIS (Coaxial Cable Information System), and Hi-OVIS (Highly Interactive Optical Visual Information System) are representative examples of communication systems which should be included in our classification of new media (CATV Study Group, 1978). These new communication devices were developed to meet increased and varied demands for information which the mass media alone could not supply. Moreover, these systems provide two-way communication, made possible by recent technological developments in the fields of computer science and communication engineering.

The introduction of these new systems will lead to changes in social, educational, economic, and political spheres. The main concern of this chapter lies with the process by which these new media affect communication and how people react to the medium. An appropriate way to illustrate this is to select and observe an area where the Hi-OVIS has been installed. The audiences or users of the system are not any particular client or organization, but are residents in a community. Both ordinary television programming and new information services are included in the telecasts. The operation is an example of the transformation from mass media to demassified media (Toffler, 1980, p. 158).

There are three fundamental cultural levels of the Hi-OVIS project. This chapter includes discussion of the technological level of the Hi-OVIS system; the programs and information exchanged through the medium, referred to here as the mental level; and, the behavioral level, constituted by audience reactions to the medium and messages. These levels correspond respectively to artifacts, mentifacts, and socifacts, which are often considered as the fundamental components of a culture (Bidney, 1967, p. 130).

We begin with an overview of the general state of television broadcasting in Japan, the environment in which the new media appeared.

Television Broadcasting in Japan

One of major characteristic of the broadcasting system as an insitution is that there are two types of stations, from a financial viewpoint: Commercial stations, privately owned and funded through advertisers, may purchase a program or commercial time during or between programs; and, the NHK financed through direct charges to the audiences all over the country. NHK sends two types of programs using two channels. One channel, begun in 1953, is for general programs. The other, started in 1959, specializes in education or cultural programs. These two types of programs are now transmitted over a nationwide network system of 5,732 stations. Privately owned commercial television stations are integrated into four major network systems, each operated through its own key station in Tokyo, and covering the entire nation through affiliates. There were 3,486 commercial stations by the end of 1979, including both VHF and UHF. The VHF stations are owned by 48 companies and UHF stations by 45 (Ministry of Posts and Telecommunications, 1980, p. 253).

The Ministry of Posts and Telecommunications, which controls these stations and the NHK, made two fundamental policy decisions in 1957 and in 1969 concerning increases in the number of commercial television stations. As a result, every Prefecture in Japan has come to possess at least one VHF and one UHF station in addition to the two NHK channels. In main urban areas, the Ministry licenses three to five commercial television companies. In the Tokyo Metropolitan Area, for example, viewers can receive seven VHF broadcasts, including the two NHK channels and one or two UHF broadcasts depending on the location.

In 1978, the revenue received by the industry as a whole totaled approximately 165,800 million yen ($598 million). Of this revenue, NHK received 20.1% and all other commercial broadcasting companies shared the remaining 79.9%. About 42,500 workers were employed in the industry as a whole that year. It should be noted that some companies own and operate both television and radio stations and these figures include both media (Yamamoto et al., 1980, pp. 128–129).

Color broadcasting began in 1960, and the gradual decrease in the price of color television sets contributed to the growing popularity of television. By 1965, 90% of all households owned at least a black and white set. During first ten years of color distribution, less than 20 percent of households owned color sets. In the succeeding five years, however, the figure increased to more than 90%, spreading from the cities to rural or less populated areas and from high-income households, through the middle- to low-income households (Uno, 1970). A little more than ten years ago, ownership of either type of set, or both, reached almost 100% of all households. In 1978, the number of television sets totaled 28,050,000 of which 87% were color sets. There were 25 television sets per 100 persons (Ministry of Posts and Telecommunications, 1980, p. 260).

The hours used for daily broadcasting are, in recent years, about the same for NHK and for the commerical stations. At the NHK-Tokyo station, for example, 17.7 hours per day are devoted to general programs and 18 hours to the other educational programs. The commercial stations broadcast an average of 17.4 hours. Along with the rise in the ratio of television owners per household, the average number of hours of television viewing continued to increase through the 1960s and 1970s, at first slowly, and then rapidly. Television viewing averaged only 56 minutes per day in 1960. Five years later it increased to two hours and 52 minutes. In 1970 it went up to three hours and five minutes and, in 1975, it reached three hours and 19 minutes (Yamamoto et al., 1980, p. 112).

As shown in these data, television has been the most successful of the media not only as an industry but also as an influence thoroughly permeating the daily life of Japanese people.

The quarter century of television's development coincided with the period that Japanese society experienced its rapid economic growth and drastic social changes. During this time, the values strongly emphasized and sought in the society were connected to industrialization and modernization. Broadcasting was a powerful agent for these values. Depicting them as positively has functioned to form attitudes or interests and to form adaptive behavior to the ever changing social milieu. Possibly, the medium has acted, directly or indirectly, as a kind of filtering process (Hayakawa, 1978, p. 22). The programs screened have been quite compatible with the survival of the medium and its development as modern business enterprise, and also with the demands of the public as audiences or consumers of the products (Tamura, 1972, pp. 53–54).

As a result, most programs feature emerging cultural forms, with values related to the modernization of society. Examining them in detail, we may be able to find some programs or types of programs which resemble traditional forms and/or values. However, these might be different from the originals, modified to appeal to the new preferences of the mass audiences and to be better suited to the nature of the audiovisual of the medium. The majority of all television programs today, however, are in the former category. We may call these televised cultural forms mass culture (Hayakawa, 1978, p. 20). Other "genuine" forms of traditional cultures still exist, some actively, everywhere in Japan. However, they are preserved by specialized groups. Performances are held only at specific times and places, sometimes with television coverage.

This general state of Japanese culture has been a result of the continuous and cumulative modernization process of the century since the Meiji Restoration, a process furthered by the Japanese defeat in the World War II, and accelerated even more by the advent of television.

By the end of the 1960s, television viewing had become a matter of course and an indispensable part of people's daily life (Sudo, 1980, pp. 37–38). Factors contributing to this growing popularity include better economic conditions, cheaper sets, shortened working hours, the introduction of housekeeping appliances, and, to some extent, a decrease in sleeping hours. Since the early 1970s, however, there have been changes in audience behavior as evidenced by, for example, a decrease in the growth rate of average viewing hours per day, and an increase in the number of people who watch television while doing something else (Matsuzawa, 1979). In addition, there has been a gradual disenchantment, among young people, with television. Dissatisfaction and criticism has taken the form of organized "citizens" movements. One organization, the Association of Television for Children, for example, was critical of the excessive violence and sex in television programs. Others began to ask for "access," meaning participation in the program production processes.

The broadcasters were then obliged to become more conscious of their social responsibilities and make some efforts to improve programming. They began by developing new prime time programs with more substantial content and more variety to replace amusement-centered shows. Both the NHK and other commercial television stations began to develop more local programming. After a twenty-year trial-and-error period, broadcasters noticed that audiences desired programs dealing with local topics close to them or more substantially informative local news and other programs (Uetaki, 1977, pp. 70–81; Telephone Information Study Group, 1980, pp. 66–70). Improvements were made in the station management or operation and broadcast technology (Tadokoro, 1973, p. 25).

After 1970, the number of stations ordering and broadcasting programs from independent production companies have increased. Since 1962, they introduced computer systems for use in managing accounting, personnel, and other departments as well as for controlling program production and the automatic emitting system for videotaped programs (Yamamoto, et al., 1980, p. 138). In 1978 testing the sound multiplexed systems was begun by utilizing the "crevices" of the electric wave. An experimental broadcasting satellite called *Yuri* was under study; it directly transmits programs to homes without the use of a relay system (Ministry of Posts and Telecommunications, 1980, pp. 327, 345–47).

Why were these measures taken? Television as a technology system is a means of mass production. However, products of the former technology are supplied for mass consumption at the mental level. Through this process of consumption, mass culture has become the major cultural form and has overshadowed other sub-categories, such as traditional types of cultural forms in society. Television, a product of industrialization, is a technological device suitable for, and devotedly obedient to, the fundamental principles of industrial society: mass production and mass consumption (Nakano, 1970, pp. 10–12).

Difficulties and problems with television have been caused by changes in its surrounding circumstances. In this context, we may be able to point out at least two fundamental changes important for the medium. One is a change in demand for information. The other is brought about by the advent of new media dependent on technological development in the field of communication and computer devices (Takeshita, 1981, pp. 19–20; Komatsubara, 1980, pp. 35–40). The change in social structure is inherent in the process of change from an industrial society to a post-industrial or information society (Fujitake, 1978, pp. 125–133). The new media were expected to play a central part in communication and in meeting demands for a growing variety of information (Okada, 1978, pp. 153–160).

Television is now trying to improve in order to adapt and to survive under these difficult circumstances. While becoming one of the "older" media, it faces challenges from the newer media. In this sense, television, a means for mass communication and the mass culture produced by it, has begun to turn into a traditional medium and to constitute an environment for the new media which might succeed it. The Hi-OVIS experiment, our example of the new media, owes its existence to the development of television software and hardware. Technologically it is closer to the cable television (CATV) system than to ordinary television as a mass medium. We will briefly review the state of the CATV system which in Japan, occupies a position between television and the Hi-OVIS type of new media.

The first cable system was introduced in 1955, two years after television broadcasting began in Japan. Through the 1960s, it was mainly installed in isolated villages having difficulty receiving signals sent from distant stations. It caught and retransmitted these signals through a master antenna and a cable to the residents (Takahashi, 1970), pp. 10–11). Cable gradually became more common through the 1970s, especially in larger cities and in newly developed housing areas with high-rise buildings which obstructed ordinary reception (Okada, 1972). Since then, the number of the systems and subscribers continues to increase. By the end of 1978, there were 22,369 facilities and 2,314,426 subscribers (Ministry of Posts and Telecommunications, 1980, p. 273).

The Cable Television Broadcasting Law, enacted in 1972, places controls on the owners or operators of these facilities. Those with more than 501 terminals must be licensed by the Ministry of Posts and Telecommunications. Although the facilities having more than 501 subscribers at the end of 1978 totaled 225, only 31 systems originated their own programs. The first telecast of locally produced programs through the cable system was in 1963 in a remote mountainous town, Gujo-Hachiman, Gifu Prefecture, by a television wave receiving cooperative association (Taki, 1981, p. 13). There are now several organizations using private cable systems (Hayashi, 1979, pp. 198–210). As an industry, however, CATV still remains in the subordinate position of supplementing the ordinary broadcasting industry. In addition limitations are placed on the Japanese CATV systems in general (Ministry of Posts and Telecommunications, 1976, pp. 70–73). Most of the systems are relatively small in terms of facilities or number of subscribers, and their operations are limited primarily to the simultaneous retransmission of signals from stations, both in and out of the area. Even when the CATV stations originate their own programs, the hours of daily telecasts and the variety in the contents are limited, compared with ordinary broadcasting, and the techniques for program production and equipment are relatively unsophisticated (Tadokoro, 1972). Revenues from subscriptions and other sources of financing aren't substantial enough to permit full utilization of multi-channels or two-way communication, despite the technological capacity of the cable system itself (Martin, 1980, p. 155).

A new type of cable system, Hi-OVIS evolved in 1978 from this pattern of television broadcasting and CATV operation. Hi-OVIS resembles other CATVsystems in technological devices and in local origination services. However, its differences make it an important development in CATV, and in the use of communication media in Japan.

Outline of the Hi-OVIS System

Other CATV systems developed as "grass roots" stations, and seem to have gone through an almost spontaneous generation process. The operators, too, have groped their way, using trial and error to produce their local programs. However, in the case of Hi-OVIS, the development has been carried out deliberately, from the first stage of planning to actual operation. It is a future-oriented project with some experimental characteristics in its use of technology, its programming and provision of information, and in its sociocommunicative activities. Hi-OVIS is a national project. The Visual Information System Development Association (VISDA), which planned the development of the system, has the status of an extradepartmental body under the guidance of the Ministry of International Trade and Industry.

The original plan to establish Hi-OVIS system came into being in 1972. However, VISDA was combined the following year with the Daily Life Information System Development Association, which had started another experiment, called CCIS project, in Tama New Town, Tokyo the year before. With reorganization, these two associations became two major sections of the Highly Interactive Optical Information Development Association and the Hi-OVIS project came under the control of the new organization's project center. In 1973 a pilot town, Higashi–Ikoma was selected as the experimental site. A reexamination of the planning phase at the end of 1976 resulted in a decision to use optical fiber cables instead of coaxial cable.

Production of programs and other informational services began in 1976. Construction of the central building, including its studio and other facilities, was completed in mid-1978, as well as the cables connecting the center with terminals in the subscribers' homes and in other places. Operation and service began on July 12, 1978 (Visual Information System Development Association, 1979, pp. 14–15).

The major concern of this report is in the sociocommunicative aspects of the project. However, because the differences between Hi-OVIS and ordinary broadcasts and other CATV systems are due to the technology and hardware used, it is necessary to discuss the hardware first, since the system's software and its use, is heavily dependent on the technological system.

The major characteristics of hardware system Hi-OVIS are:

1. Optical fiber cable and other optical communication technologies are used, because they are a broad band transmission line and, thus, are economical. Use of this technology enables the system to supply a large amount of information and to satisfy increasing demands for different kinds of information in the near future.

2. An ordinary television receiver, a keyboard, a TV camera, and other terminal equipment devices are provided to subscribers without charge. Through this home terminal, subscribers can send pictures and sound from their homes to the station where programs, including requests from subscribers, are processed. Thus, the system is operated as an integrated combination of communication and computer technologies, which might be called as "compunication" system (Kawahata, 1980, pp. 116–121).

The fundamental units of the system include the center sub-center, mobile center, and home terminal.

The center building is located in the center of the experimental, geographical area. The building includes a studio equipped with three TV cameras and lighting equipment, a video/audio control room equipped with a video/audio console, a two-way televote display, an auto program transmitter, a set of telecine, telop, and a turntable in addition to other equipment. In addition to office space, there is an equipment room with autocassette changers, a character display generator, and an optical transmitter/receiver. Almost all of these devices are controlled by the computer system. In addition to this function, the computer system controls as line management, visual sources, automatic edition and transmission of characters (and/or voice), the collection of statistical data, and system supervision.

On the top of a mountain near the center and on the center's roof, two antennas are constructed to catch VHF and UHF television waves from stations both inside and outside of the area. The center and the mountaintop antenna, as well as the City Hall, the police station, the fire station, some schools, a university, all other buildings are all connected by two-way optical fiber cables, and are equipped with terminals in order to make communication between them possible. A microbus, with two units of cameras and video cassette recorders, and a light van, with a television camera are used mainly as the mobile-center for gathering materials in the community and for relaying programs through the terminals installed in the area.

Most of the facilities and equipment may not be very different from those used in ordinary broadcasting and in CATV stations, but most important device is an indispensable element of two-way communication; the terminal equipment allocated to each subscriber's home. It consists of a keyboard, a black and white TV camera, a microphone, a 20-inch television receiver, and a terminal controller. The keyboard has 23 function keys and 10 numbered keys. By touching a single key or a combination, the subscribers can select channels or programs, and can also request certain information. When they want to send their own picture, voice, and other signals from their homes to the station, they can use other keys or a switch on the keyboard (Kawahata et al., 1981, pp. 65–69).

The system is set up in an area called Higashi-Ikoma, Ikoma City, Nara Prefecture. Ikoma City adjoins Nara City, the seat of the prefectural government. About 25 kilometers west of Ikoma City, lies Osaka, one of the larger industrial and commercial cities in Japan, with a population of more than two million. Between the two cities, Ikoma City extends about 7 kilometers east and west, and 14 kilometers, north and south. Once an agricultural district, it has developed during the past ten years into small residential towns around Osaka. The population of the city has increased from 48,848 persons in 1975 to 70,456 persons as of 1980 (Statistic Bureau, Prime Minister's Office, 1981, p. 104). Although Mount Ikoma stretches from north to south at the west edge of the Ikoma City and separates Nara and Ikoma from Osaka, the Osaka-Nara line of a private railway (Kintetsu), and a highway, both run conveniently through Ikoma from east to west and link the three cities.

Higashi-Ikoma is a district in the eastern part of Ikoma City. The railroad divides this area, with the Higashi-Ikoma Station in the center. The Hi-OVIS center occupies a part of the ground floor of the station, and the cables extend from there to the homes of the subscribers in Higashi-Ikoma Itchome and in Tsuji-Machi, Kita Garden Heights. Higashi-Ikoma was an ideal site because it was a newly developed community of upper-middle- and middle-class residents who showed an interest in such a communication system and in information and education in general. Furthermore, among the residents of these two housing area, 158 out of 334 homes registered as subscribers to the system in response to the appeal for public subscriptions by VISDA. The experiment began with 156 homes, each provided with a terminal, and another 10 terminals were located in Higashi Ikoma area. These homes with terminals are referred to as the monitor homes, and the approximately 600 individual family members are referred to as the monitors.

How do the monitors have access to and respond to the various messages offered by the medium through two-way communication?

The name of the Hi-OVIS station is HCT (Higashi-Ikoma Cable Television). Twenty-nine channels are used to telecast HCT's services. There are four different services. The first consists of telecasts of programs produced by HCT itself and retelecasts of the HCT programs. The second consists of telecasts of stored video programs sent on the monitors' requests. The third service is stored, still pictures sent on the monitors' requests. The forth consists of simultaneous retransmission of ordinary television broadcasts from stations in and out of the area through the cable.

The fourth service is provided because the Higashi–Ikoma area, at the foot of Mount Ikoma, is in a shadow area for ordinary television waves. Thus like the non-monitor homes without the terminals, those in the monitor homes can also watch programs sent from seven nearby stations in Nara and Osaka and, additionally, two stations outside the area from Kobe and Kyoto. These last two and two local stations are UHF, the other five are received through VHF waves. Almost all the monitor homes also have at least one ordinary television set on which they can watch programs from local stations (Kawahata et al., 1981, p. 65).

For all the programs televised live, two kinds of two-way communication services are available: inquiry and answer through the visual/voice feature and inquiry and answer using the keyboard. The visual/voice feature allows the monitor, operating a keyboard, television camera, and microphone at the home terminal, to send questions and answers to the master of ceremonies or the instructor at the studio. The second permits the monitor to respond, for example, to a televote, used to collect opinions. This is done, following instructions from the studio, by pushing any one of the numbered keys on issues proposed by the studio. In both of these ways, monitors can participate directly in programs telecast live. Retelecasting is usually offered on the same or the next day for the monitors' convenience. Since they have already been videotaped, two-way communication cannot be used. One channel is provided for the live programs and for retelecasting.

The monitors can also use two other forms of two-way communication, requesting videotaped programs (the second service) and requesting other information stored at the station (the third service).

There are three possible ways for the monitor to receive the second service in his/her home. These are called: scheduled service, by-request service, and reservation service. If the desired videotaped programs has been stored and the transmission time is scheduled in advance, the monitors must request the programs at that fixed time only. There are three channels which transmit scheduled videotaped programs, so any of three different programs can be received. However, two homes cannot request the same programs at the same time. If the desired program isn't schedules, the monitors can still select and receive it. Four channels are available to transmit unscheduled programs, so four separate videotaped programs can be received in four different monitor homes. The monitors may reserve programs several days, weeks, or even months in advance, specifying the day and time of the desired transmission. One channel is used for this reservation. For the second service, requests are received on a 24-hour basis.

It is also possible to request information in written form which has been stored in computers at any time. Photographs on microfiche or in slide form are available through the third service, called still-picture service.

Three channels carry news and the Hi-OVIS guides in print form. This type of telecasting is repeated regularly for the convenience of the monitors. These are constantly updated and voice can be added.

Four channels are provided for other written information, to which voice can be added. For these channels, a forward/backward function for the display is available. The monitor at home can change the frames by pushing a keyboard button and thus spend more time with at frames of interest, or go back several frames, or skip quickly forward. This information includes a public transportation timetable, addresses of public facilities and institutions such as hospitals, city hall offices or emergency services, schedules of local events such as art openings, festivals, and ceremonies, or weather forecast and shopping information. These programs can be seen in four monitor homes at the same time.

Photographs on microfiche and slides can also be requested through the still-picture service. One channel is used for this service. It also has a forward/backward function. The viewer can select up to 750 sheets of microfiche, each sheet containing 60 frames, or 80 sheets of slides.

The few remaining channels are used to inform the monitors of the technological state of the system, for example, sending a telop showing a line-busy sign for the monitoring terminal (Visual Information System Development Association, 1980, pp. 70–75).

This type of two-way communication is heavily dependent on optical "compunication" technology. The Hi-OVIS a system uses technologies that have been developed recently, and as such, is an unprecedented field experimentation with unique applications. Since modern technologies depend principally on human rationality, they must be universal and be able to reflect the background of any culture. However, when they have been introduced into a society, they cannot avoid bearing some of the special cultural characteristics of that society. Different societies will react differently on the introduction of new systems and devices, and will reflect their sociocultural contexts in the utilization of these systems (Bidney, 1967, pp. 27–28). This applies to the introduction of Hi-OVIS. We should regard its sociocultural context as the local community in which the system is installed. We thus have to pay attention to the monitors' reaction to the medium.

Since technology introduced into a society is a physical object in the society, we should also include it in our concept of culture as one element at the material level. Our fundamental premise here that culture as a whole constitutes three basic levels: mental, behavioral, and material (Bidney, 1967, p. 130), which, individually or in combination, appear concretely as stratified and hidden value systems in a society. So, technology and systems of technology also must be considered a constituent element of the material level of a culture.

However, communication media as technologies, compared to other sorts of technologies, are special to the extent that they are mainly and directly involved with the mental level of culture and life. Audiovisual media, such as movies and television can reproduce, more easily than other media, any element of these three levels of culture into another element at the mental level. In addition, they are capable of dealing, in principle, with any element or levels, and any combinations of them in any culture. Consequently, the pattern of combination of the programs or information are characteristic of the nature of the messages of the medium as a whole.

It is from these perspectives that we describe in the following section the programs and information telecast by HCT, and the monitor's viewing and reaction to the message, considered as elements within the mental and the behavioral levels of Japanese culture.

Programming Pattern and Utilizing Behavior

The guiding principle for preparing the programs and information in the HCT service were focused primarily on the following four points: (1) aid to the residents in forming a better community; (2) contributions to lifelong education; (3) promotion of healthier and safer lives; (4) aid in the acquisition of information necessary in their daily lives. The emphasis on these points may have stemmed from a recognition of people's growing concern with community life, self-education, social welfare, and the changing role of media and information in the midst of drastic social changes towards an information society (Katou, 1978, 241–243).

The programs and information services of HCT are organized, following these guidelines, into these genres: local events, education and culture, medical care and welfare, local life and security, and leisure and amusement. Since the beginning of the service, live programs have been telecast five days a week, with none on Tuesday or Thursday. The time allotted to each program is usually between 30 and 90 minutes, and one or two programs are telecast each of five days every week. However, the time frame of the live programs is flexible because discussions between the studio and the monitors through the two-way device don't often allow programs to finish within the time allotted. The program content and time-frame of the telecasts and retelecasts are usually re-examined and revised biannually and the opinions of the advisory committee and the monitors are incorporated.

A closer look at the programs may be helpful in an understanding of the programming pattern. For example, during the period between July 1978 (the beginning of the service) and January 1979, seven programs were telecast. The names of these programs and the target audiences among the monitors are *Hi-OVIS Wide Show* (adults, female), *Program for School* (school children), *Hello English* (students and adults), *Program for Nabata Kindergarten* (children), *Local-Oriented Program* (general), *Hi-OVIS Special* (family), and *Young Space 20* (senior high school, university students, and youth in general). Programs such as *Hi-OVIS Wide Show*, *Hi-OVIS Special*, and *Young Space 20*, were retelecast usually at least twice for the convenience of those who had missed the original live telecasts.

Example of the types of programs telecast follow:

The *Hi-OVIS Wide Show* was developed mainly for housewives. Since most of them spend their time at home, they seemed, in the beginning, to be a most suitable audience for the two-way services. The production staff estimated that housewives were relatively free in the late morning to watch and to participate in this program. Thus, the telecast was planned to begin 10:30 in the morning and to last one hour.

From Monday through Friday, the program was divided into three parts: the *News Corner*, the *Shopping Information Corner*, and the *Main Planning Corner*. The first two were provided to give the show continuity. The *News Corner* was directed by reporters hired from the newspaper offices near the experiment area. They included information closely related to the lives of the residents; coverage of, and commentary on, local news, school activities, and local festivities, topics which had rarely been offered on regular television and other media. The *Shopping Information Corner* was planned to provide guidance for daily shopping in the community, and featured goods or dealers. A few housewives in the community were employed as reporters for this corner. They showed, for example, how well the goods tested. At the same time, they attempted, through the two-way device, to elicit the opinion of housewives who used the products. About 20 minutes were used for this corner.

The *Main Planning Corner*, as a main part of this program, was intended to allow variety in the show's content. Each day highlighted a topic closely associated with housewives' daily lives, such as home education, cooking, health care, or hobbies. The length of time allocated to this corner was between 40 minutes and one hour. During one week, the features of this corner were "Hot Line of Intimate Communication" (Monday), "HI-OVIS Cooking" (Tuesday), "Hobby Promenade" (Wednesday), "Health Bulletin" (Thursday), and "Life in Ikoma" (Friday).

"Hi-OVIS Cooking" is a representative example of these programs. Housewives are very interested in cooking, but cooking programs are broadcast by ordinary television stations almost everyday. In addition, there is a large stock of videotaped cooking programs which are available on request. So, the production staff of Hi-OVIS, to make its program more appealing, invited some area residents to participate as instructors in the preparation of local foods or specialty dishes. A question and answer session through two-way communication system was provided (Visual Information System Development Association, 1979, pp. 106–120).

Another example of live programming is *Hello English* which begins at 4:30 p.m., when the target audience is home from school. This program consists of three levels of courses in English conversation: a beginners course on Monday; a children's course on Wednesday; and an intermediate course on Friday. The first course is mainly for housewives and students unfamiliar with English conversation; the second is for children from six to twelve; and the third is for high school, and college students who have had some experience with English conversation.

The instructors, both of whom live in the community, are a housewife who sponsors an English conversation academy and an American who teaches at a university near the experiment site. A few area residents are always invited to participate as guests or students on the live programs. In each course, pronunciation drills and simple conversation exercises are emphasized, because, English classes in the formal school usually stress text readings. Following the direction of the instructor at the studio, the monitors respond through the microphones and the television camera in their homes. After synthesizing their voices and images with the teacher's into one frame, the studio sends the picture to the homes of the monitors who are watching (Visual Information System Development Association, 1979, pp. 125–129).

Other types of two-way service should be mentioned. Videotaped programs are stocked in the center video warehouse to meet the requests from many monitors. These programs are classified into three groups. The first includes programs produced by HCT itself and others which deal mainly with local history or topics of local interest, such as *Cultural Assets in Ikoma*. The second consists of commercial films such as *Aladdin and his Magic Lamp, Japanese Lacquer Craft, Cooking (Omelette and Frying Pan)*, and *Making Beautiful Body Proportion*. The third consists of videotaped programs unavailable on the open market, such as *Central Europe*, distributed by foreign embassies and government offices. The number of stored videotaped programs totaled 966 in 1978. Their contents vary from such subjects as culture and education, medical care and health, English conversation, locality and life, shopping information, sports and hobbies, cooking, entertainment, to programs produced by the monitors themselves (Visual Information System Development Association, 1979, pp. 164–170, 178–181).

The still-picture service is another offering of Hi-OVIS. A still-picture is composed of one or more pictures produced by using characters, illustrations, and/or photographs. This type of frame-by-frame advancement of the picture is very effective when used in the field of education, the pursuit of hobbies or culture, and also for entertainment. Stored at the station, the pictures can be classified into the following groups: local life totalled 640 single frames; education and culture, 2,474 frames; hobbies and entertainment, 1,358 frames; prevention of crimes and disasters, 735 frames; and health, 285 frames. *Kintetsu Railway Time-table for Osaka, Difficult Kanji (Characters), Books, Newly published, Medical Facilities Guide, Concert Information, Measures Against Typhoons,* and *Next Move,* concerning Shogi-chess, are representative titles (Visual Information System Development Association, 1979, pp. 178–181).

We need to survey some trends in the viewing behavior of the monitors regarding the programs and information offered by HCT for the same period.

Hi-OVIS Wide Show: The News Corner because of its unique focus, enjoyed high ratings. Viewers themselves have been known to bring news items to the station. *Hi-OVIS Cooking,* after one month averaged two or three participants for each telecast. However, since October the average has increased to five or six. On October 31, the program had 14 participants. Monitors have begun to react positively to the program production process suggesting the type of cooking featured and the guests. The contents of the program have become a topic of conversation among monitors. Some housewives gather at a monitor's home and try to cook the menu shown in the "Corner." Others hold a small party, with the food prepared according to the show's directions, and communicate their reactions on the next program.

From September to December the viewing rate for *Hi-OVIS Wide Show* was between 20 to 30 terminals. In the last week of November, it exceeded 35 terminals, and on November 30 reached 85, including the retelecasting program (Visual Information System Development Association, 1979, p. 43).

Audience reaction to *Hello English* was also measured. As expected, use of the two-way feature, for example, to show how to form the lips by comparing the teacher's with the student's in one picture, was more effective than the method used in other ordinary television English courses. This sort of picture formation technique seemed to be helpful in removing the distance between studio and home. In the beginning and intermediate course, despite the eagerness in learning, participants in the studio were shy, especially about showing their failures over television. However, the children in the studio as well as at home, were less hesitant. Children whose homes were without terminals participated in the live telecasts by visiting their friends' homes (Visual Information System Development Association, 1979, p. 46).

One to two months after the start of request service, in the stocked videotaped program, the number of requests from monitors, especially for the time-free service, totalled over 4,000 in one week. However, many requests were not registered because the lines were constantly busy, causing monitors to complain. This was due to the many requests for comics for children, and consequently the comics service was stopped. Audience requests have remained at a fairly high and stable level.

The trend was the same for still-picture service. At the initial stage of this service, the number of requests for microfiche was very high, but because the content of information was fixed, the requests rapidly decreased after three months. The character display service, however, has been attracting a comparatively stable audience. This is because of the many requests for the traffic timetables which are constantly updated (Visual Information System Development Association, 1979, p. 55).

In the monitor homes there are at least two television receivers, including the Hi-OVIS terminal and an ordinary television set. A VISDA Survey reports that the monitors watch the Hi-OVIS terminal receiver for two hours and 58 minutes, on the average, each weekday. In addition, they watch the regular television set for an average of another hour and 33 minutes. Combined, their weekday total viewing time amounts to four hours and 31 minutes, or about one hour more than the national average.

The Hi-OVIS viewing averages one hour and 49 minutes to ordinary television broadcasts on HCT retransmission; 37 minutes to locally originated programs of HCT including its retelecasting; and 32 minutes to the videotaped programs and still-picture service (Visual Information System Development Association, 1981, p. 9).

This pattern is, of course, different from that of conventional television audiences outside of the experiment area. A survey reported that the monitors rated the HCT station higher than the other television stations. The rating on HCT programs between 7:30 and 10:30 p.m. was 28.9%, the highest of all the stations, while the rating for broadcasts from other stations retransmitted through the terminal was 5.5%. On the other hand, the rating on the six VHF stations by the audiences living in the Kansai Region ranged between 5 and 15% (Visual Information System Development Association, 1980, pp. 136–139).

Participation of the Monitor

Two-Way Features. A survey conducted by VISDA one day in October 1978, showed that the number of monitors who had, at least, on one occasion utilized the two-way feature while viewing a local program televised live totaled 22 out of 117 monitors who responded to the survey. About one month after this survey, another questionnaire was distributed. This time, the number had increased to 68 monitors or 44.4% of the 153 monitors who filled out the questionnaire. At the end of December 1979, the figure increased to 250 monitors, and the total participation count was 4,000 times. Until the summer of 1979, the number of monitors who joined the user-group as first-time participants constantly increased. However, after the summer, the number became gradually smaller and at the end of the year it was under five monitors per month. Nonetheless, this number of 250 monitors, who have used the two-way feature, constitutes about half of the total number of monitors, excluding children and the very aged (Visual Information System Development Association, 1980, pp. 168–169).

In the survey, 85 nonusers of the two-way feature out of 153 monitors gave reasons for their nonuser status. A typical reason was "because it is shameful and somewhat unendurable that my picture and picture of the interior of my house are sent to others." Another is "because I have no time to watch the local live programs, or during the telecast, I was always away from home." These two reasons, one psychological and the other physical, are consistently given by nonusers who also say they are satisfied "just to watch the program," or that they have no "special interest in this kind of program" (Visual Information System Development Association, 1980, pp. 142–44).

Some local programs occasionally include an experiment devised to elicit answers or opinions from the monitors through the televote function as another feature of the live program. Looking at the period from July to October of 1979, more than 50% of the monitors who watched these programs used this feature. This was especially true of the program *Life Style, Now*. Televote usage amounted to 75% of the monitors who watched the program. Participation through two-way communication with visual/voice feature is possible only when the monitors push the Q/A function key and the studio can pick it up from all of the candidates at the same time. In the case of televote feature, the monitors can participate instantly. This may be the reason why the percentage of televote usage is higher than the rate of participation through visual/voice feature (Visual Information System Development Association, 1980, p. 192).

The participation count in using the request service through stored videotaped programs and still-pictures was 173 by the end of 1979 and the highest user-group was the housewives.

Performance in the Studio. Data from October to December, 1979, showed the proportion of monitors appearing in the programs for the period was 21.5% on the average, of all 335 monitors who answered the survey questions. However, among these participants, a considerable number of monitors had appeared several times on the programs, including those who played the part of the master of ceremony or reporter. During the three months, live programs were telecast for about 70 days, and 700 monitors had participated directly. This number of participants is fairly large, but it is necessary to note that it included about 120 participants who were non-monitor residents in the area. According to the data above, there is a problem with the form of participation in live programs in HCT; participants are drawn to some particular monitors who appeared on the programs relatively often. In addition, most monitors who had participated in the programs said that they were requested to do so by the HCT station, or by friends or neighbors. Therefore, we may be able to infer a passive attitude toward participating in the programs.

We can trace three stages or phases of the experiment thus far. The first is the period of adjustment of the Hi-OVIS staff to various operations of the system, including use of the two-way feature in live programs, and the establishment of the monitors' habit of watching HCT programs and participating through the two-way feature. The second is a period of audience expansion with emphasis on attracting adult males, and developing other ways of encouraging monitors' participation such as programs production by themselves. The third is the adapting to practical or business use, such as pay television and examination of the future diffusion of the system.

In January 1979, the program structure and the programming in general were revised. The purpose was to involve male adults as a new target audience, and to encourage their participation. It also aimed at expanding the time-frame into the evening, when the new target audience is usually at home. Beginning in the summer of 1980, there were new attempts to produce programs for which the monitors could be the subscribers by paying special fees. These kinds of programs, a form of pay television, were a series of lectures on psychology, a typing clss, and a speech class. The first two were under the direction of professors from a nearby university. These programs which usually took advantage of the two-way feature, sometimes gathered the monitors in the studio or the university to have direct communication among them.

The Hi-OVIS experiment was scheduled to continue until the end of June 1982.

Some Implications

There are three levels of social communication: mass communication; direct interpersonal communication; and various types of so-called middle range communications (McQuail, 1979, p. 197). In mass communication in general, the feedback process between sender and receiver is unusual and quite restricted, while in this case two-way communication was common. This was possible because of a special feature in the hardware system and a policy of soliciting audience response and participation. Another reason may be that the installed system had a relatively small range of service area. In other words, this system was developed as a two-way local communication medium. The Hi-OVIS type of new medium has a greater possibility of supplying various messages in addition to the programs and information offered now, which other mass media cannot offer. On the other hand, it seems that, even in this kind of system with only a small number of monitors, it is difficult to satisfactorily meet every individual need, given the present production and storage capacity. With only a single medium, it might be impossible to do so. One possibility would be forming a network of this type of system, covering the country, and exchanging different sorts of messages. On the other hand, there might be other possible application of the Hi-OVIS type of information medium. As far as the Hi-OVIS application is concerned, the target of the experiment was limited to the resident of the Higashi-Ikoma area, and the main puprose was to offer information pertinent to the monitor's daily life in the community. However, we can see other applications, such as in the industry. In Kyoto, the Nishijin-Ori Textile Industry Association, which is an organization of manufacturers, is now planning to introduce a Hi-OVIS type of system by 1985. By connecting optical fiber cables from the association hall to each of 1,500 manufacturers' factory, the system can be used to offer and process various kinds of industrial or managerial information. Furthermore, it will be used with a computer for drawing the *kimono* (traditional silk garments) design and for communication among these manufacturers. The system, in this case, is mainly intended to enhance the cost-efficiency of production, so the objective and function of its operation would be different from that of the Hi-OVIS (Nishijin Fabric Industry Association, 1980, pp. 1–8).

The live and the stocked videotaped programs are not so different in nature from conventional television broadcasts, which constitute the prevailing cultural form in Japan. On the other hand, the monitors are so accustomed to the conventional television viewing that they show some bewilderment in the use of the "new" medium which involves two-way, instead of one-way communication. To the monitors, most participatory elements of the Hi-OVIS programs may still belong to a minor cultural form in Japan. The experiment has, however, brought changes in the elements in the behavior of the monitors.

The pattern of watching HCT programs among monitors has come to be fairly stable, both in viewing hours and program preferences or participation. However, the monitors have spent more time watching television than previously. This increase in viewing time is a result of the introduction of the Hi-OVIS system. Perhaps the monitors are watching television more intently than before because they are watching programs which invite them to give their opinions.

The preference for program content, is changing from mere entertainment to more useful information, as is demonstrated by the audience rating of the Hi-OVIS. Through their experience with the two-way features or participation in the program production, the monitors seem to have changed their attitudes toward television viewing and television in general (Hayakawa, 1976, pp. 16–19). They have begun to consider the television receiver as a terminal for their own active use, different from passively watching conventional television. Also, through participating in the programs or helping with production, they became familiar with the status as "sender" which is rare for the "recipient" of ordinary mass media, especially conventional television. The monitors seem to have found, in short, that they can easily play both roles by using the new medium, and they sometimes feel that their home can become a studio.

We can see some changes in community life brought about by the introduction and operation of the system. The effect of introducing this medium into a community is two-fold; life in the community improves because the subscribers are better-informed about the community, and solidarity is enhanced through active participation (Satou, 1974, pp. 81–87).

According to the results of a survey conducted in the autumn of 1979, 43% of the 335 monitors answered that, through watching the HCT programs and information service, their understanding of the area in which they live has been largely enhanced. More than 25% said that they think more often about issues or problems concerning the community, and 23.9% answered that the number of people with whom they had become acquainted had increased (Visual Information System Development Association, 1980, p. 292).

Participants have formed clubs and circles around hobbies or sports. Through one program, they began to discuss local problems and issues through use of the two-way feature. They began to greet each other in railway stations, for example, upon recognizing one another after an appearance as a guest on a program or as a person who asked question through the two-way service. Through the efforts of monitors living in the northern housing complex, they were able to organize a self-governing association for the residents, including non-monitors. In the southern housing complex such an association existed prior to the beginning of this experiment.

However, in spite of these rather positive findings, the experiment had some negative aspects. One is that some stored programs or information are popular and frequently requested, but others are not. And for certain topics, the monitors often utilize other information sources such as circular notices from the local government or the local community papers rather than the stored information service. Furthermore, it has recently become apparent that there are three behavioral groups. One is active in participation via the two-way service or in the studio; another watches the HCT programs, but their participation is not so active; and the last is a group which watches but is indifferent to the HCT programs (Visual Information System Development Association, 1981, p. 23).

Although the number of monitors utilizing the two-way service is usually larger than that of monitors participating in live programs in the studio, in each case, the monitors say that they find the experience pleasant once they have participated in the programs. As a whole, participants slightly outnumber non-participants. Non-participants often refer to their reticence as a reason for not participating.

The reason for non-participation may be cultural. In Japan, the norm usually emphasizes inconspicuousness; in other cultures, different behavior might be acceptable and encouraged. A well-known Japanese proverb says that a nail higher than others is hammered down to a level equal to others. Thus, an individual in Japan conforms to the behavior of the group. Participants often stated they experienced a sense of shame, sometime mentioned as a Japanese characteristic, when they felt they were behaving differently from others (Lebra, 1976, p. 28).

The number of participants is gradually increasing and non-participants are induced by their monitor friends to participate in the programs as performers. The fact that there exist both active participants and non-participants shows their reaction to the new medium is not only influenced by culture, but also by other factors such as personal interest, age, and socioeconomic status.

It is clear that the new medium has initiated changes in communication. There is a possibility that, when this type of information access is introduced into society at large, social life will be profoundly influenced. Because, unlike other technologies, it works directly upon our mental level of culture and our mental life.

About ten years ago Williams (1974) considered the appearance of television a new technological device for mass communication. At present, the rapid development of new technologies is bringing new possibilities to our communication field. Television as a mass medium has been for passive viewing, but it seems that the character of television is going to change. We may be able to say that the nature of televsion audiences is in transition and that they will move from "passive viewers" to "active users," depending on the "compunication" technologies. Thus television "for active use" is about to become an "information machine." Hi-OVIS is an example. In this sense, it is surely a medium of the sort described as "de-massified" by Toffler (1980). Although, we may need considerable time before this type of television will be managed fully and easily, we should begin to inquire into its introduction into our society (Gotou, 1981, pp. 63–68).

In spite of our present one-way communication model, we need a two-way communication model to understand people's active information seeking behavior and its use through the new communication media (Nakano, 1980, pp. 216–230).

REFERENCES

Bidney, David. (1967). *Theoretical Anthropology* (2nd Ed.) New York: Schocken.
CATV Study Group (CSG). (1978). "The Coming of the 'Future-Oriented Me-

dia': The Studies." *Sougou Jānalizumu Kenykyu* (No. 86), 108–126. (in Japanese).
Fujitake, Akira. (1978). "The Development of an Information Society in Japan." In Edelstein, Alex, et al. (Eds.), *Information Societies: Comparing the Japanese and American Experiences*. Seattle: International Communication Center.
Gotou, Kazuhiko. (1981). "Examination of Broadcasting Systems in the Light of Emerging New Media." *Housougaku Kekyu* (No. 33), 63–94. (in Japanese).
Hayakawa, Kouichi. (1976). "Mass Communication and Daily Life." *Shakaigaku Ronsou*, (No. 66), 13–22. (in Japanese).
Hayakawa, Kouichi. (1978). "Structure and Contradiction in Mass Mediated Culture." *Shakaigaku Ronsou* (No. 72), 14–23. (in Japanese).
Hayashi, Shigeki. (1979). "Development of CATV." *Tokyo Daigaku Shinbun Kenkyusho Kiyou* (No. 27), 196–201. (in Japanese).
Inoue, Hiroshi. (1980). "Two-Way Information System and Resident's Participation: The Hi-OVIS Experiment at Higashi-Ikoma." *Kansai Daigaku Shakaigakubu Kiyou* 12(1), 143–169. (in Japanese).
Katou, Harueki. (1978). "Communication and Community: CATV in Japanese New Towns." In Edelstein, Alex S. et al., (ed.), *Information Societies: Comparing the Japanese and American Experiences*. Seattle: International Communication Center.
Kawahata, Masahiro. (1980). "Hi-OVIS Project: Towards Future Optical Information Society." *Studies of Broadcasting* (No. 16), 115–158.
Kawahata, Masahiro et al. (1981). "Two-Way Visual Information System—Hi-OVIS: Report on Operational Experiment at Higashi-Ikoma." *Housou Gijutsu*, July, 64–72. (in Japanese).
Komatsubara, Hisao. (1980). "Japanese Newspapers Look at New Media Technologies." *Studies of Broadcasting* (No. 17), 35–48.
Lebra, Takie Sugiyama. (1976). *Japanese Patterns of Behavior*. Honolulu: University of Hawaii Press.
Martin, James. (1978). *The Wired Society*. New York: Prentice-Hall. Transl. by Kazuhiko Gotou. (1980). *Tele Komu*. Tokyo: Nihon Buritanika, (in Japanese).
Matsuzawa, Masaru. (1979). "Daily Life Information and Media." *Kokumin Seikatsu Kenkyu* 19(2), 62–73. (in Japanese).
McQuail, Dennis. (1975). *Communication*. New York: Longman Group. Transl. by Masatsune Yamanaka et al. (1979). *Komyunikeishon no Shakaigaku*. Tokyo: Kawashima Shoten. (in Japanese).
The Ministry of Posts and Telecommunications (MPTC) (1976). (Ed.), *Trends in Mailgram, Broadcasting and CATV in the U.S.A. and Canada*. Tokyo: Printing Bureau, The Ministry of Finance, (in Japanese).
The Ministry of Posts and Telecommunications (MPTC). (1980). *White Paper on Communications*. Tokyo: Printing Bureau, The Ministry of Finance, (in Japanese).
Nakano, Osamu. (1970). "Economic System and Social Function of Broadcasting." *Sougou Jānalizumu Kenkyu* 15(1), 7–15. (in Japanese).
Nakano, Osamu. (1980). *People's Information Seeking Behavior*. Tokyo: Nihon Housou Shuppan Kyoukai, (in Japanese).
Nishijin Fabric Industry Association (NFIA). (1980). *Research Report on Utilization of Nishijin Fabric Industry Optical Visual Information System*. Kyoto: Economic Bureau, Kyoto Municipal Office, (in Japanese).
Okada, Naoyuki. (1972). "CATV Development and Its Background in Japan." *Masukomi Bunka* (Sept.) 54–57. (in Japanese).

Okada, Naoyuki. (1978). "Some Aspects of Japan as An Information Society." In Edelstein, Alex S. et al., (ed.), *Information Societies: Comparing the Japanese and American Experiences.* Seattle: International Communication Center.

Satou, Tamoo. (1974). "News Demand and Information Media in Community." *Housougaku Kenkyu* (No. 26), 69–100. (in Japanese).

Statistic Bureau, Prime Minister's Office (SBPMO). (1981). *Population Census of Japan: 1980.* Tokyo: Nihon Toukei Kyoukai, (in Japanese).

Sudo, Harou. (1980). "Commerical Broadcasting System and Its Social Function: As 'Local' and Advertisement Media." *Shakai Roudou Kenkyu* 26(3 and 4), 31–53. (in Japanese).

Tadokoro, Izumi. (1972). "Circumstances in CATV Industry." (*Housou Bunka*) Sept. 26–29. (in Japanese).

Tadokoro, Izumi. (1973). "Television Industry." *Shinbungaku Hyouron* (No. 22), 20–26. (in Japanese).

Takahashi, Shinzo. (1970). *The Third Television: CATV.* Tokyo: Sougou Jān-alizumu Shuppankai. (in Japanese).

Takeshita, Kyouichi. (1981). "Advent of New Media and Broadcasting Technology." *Studies in Broadcasting* (No. 33), 9–61.

Taki, Kouji. (1981). "Problems in the Use of CATV." *Ningen Kagaku, Kansai Daigaku* (No. 17), pp. 3–27. (in Japanese).

Tamura, Jousei. (1972). "Television, Mass Media, and Daily Life: Reexamination of Concept of Audience." *Housou Bunka* (Jan.) 52–57. (in Japanese).

Tanaka, Kikujirou. (1980). "On the New Media." *Toyou Daigaku Shakaigaku Kiyou* (No. 17), 79–98. (in Japanese).

Television Information Study Group (ISG). (1980). *Television News Studies.* Nihon Housou Shuppan Kyoukai. (in Japanese).

Toffler, Alvin. (1980). *The Third Wave.* New York: W. Morrow.

Uetaki, Tetsuya. (1977). "Local Community and Television Journalism." *Nihon Daigaku Geijutsugakubu Kioyu* (No. 7), pp. 65–81. (in Japanese).

Uno, Yoshiyasu. (1970). "Pattern of the Spreads of Television Sets among Japanese Families." *Tegsugaku* (No. 55), 97–142. (in Japanese).

Visual Information System Development Association. (VISDA). (1979a). *Hi-OVIS Project: Interim Report,* Tokyo: Diamond Service.

Visual Information System Development Association. (1979b). *Daily-Life Visual Information System Experiment: Its Operation and Evaluation Report.* Tokyo: VISDA (in Japanese).

Visual Information System Development Association. (1980). *Daily-Life Visual Information System Experiment: Its Operation and Evaluation Report.* Tokyo: VISDA, (in Japanese).

Visual Information System Development Association. (1981). *Research Report on Monitor's Change in Orientation and Reaction Through the Hi-OVIS Experiment.* Tokyo: VISDA, (in Japanese).

Williams, Raymond. (1974). *Television: Technology & Cultural Form.* Fontana: Collins Sons & Co.

Yamamoto, Akira et al. (Eds.), (1980). *Mass Communication in Japan: with Illustrations.* Tokyo: Nihon Housou Kyoukai. (in Japanese).

13

Chivalric Stories in Hong Kong Media

Kenneth Ka-fat Pang

Kung Fu became a household word around the world with the advent of Bruce Lee movies a few years ago. Today, through television reruns and locally produced series, even more people have become acquainted with the underlying philosophy and other concepts represented by the term.

Kung Fu stories, or more precisely, chivalric stories,[1] are a special genre of popular literature which dates back thousands of years in China. Although most of the stories originated in imagination, with a few historical facts blended in, they are engrained in Chinese culture, live with it, and change with it. Chivalric stories as they appear in the Hong Kong media constitute an interesting case for study, not just because of their attraction, popularity, and, sometimes, virtual dominance of the media, but also because, like news reports, they too reflect and influence society with the unique message they transmit.

The purpose of this chapter is to examine this specific feature, the chivalric story as depicted in the mass media of Hong Kong, its historical development, change, popularity, and social function.

Historical Development of Chivalric Tales

In 1952, after the Chinese civil war had ceased, there was an unarmed combat between two famous Hong Kong martial artists, of different styles, in Macao. The exaggerated reports of this encounter aroused interest in Chinese chivalric stories among newspaper readers. The first

[1]The Chinese term "Hsia" has various translations including "martial hero," "knight-errant," "gallantry," or "chivalry," while "Kung Fu" refers to martial art which rules out the use of weaponry. It should be noted that the term "Hsia" does not have any religious connotation, which distinguishes it from medieval European knights.

new style chivalric novel[2] was published in the same year, and, ever since, these tales have been featured in novels, newspapers, periodicals, comics, films, radio, and television programs, and are included in the repertory of street storytellers.

Wei, in his book, *Liang Yu-Sheng and His Chivalric Novels* (1980), points out that the Chinese chivalric tales have attained this popularity in Hong Kong for several reasons. First, chivalric novels provide distraction and thus are read as a form of relaxation. Because the heroes and heroines are of all ages and professions, they appeal to a wide audience. Furthermore, these tales contain references to famous resorts in China, folk customs, and to traditional poetry, which makes them appealing to the overseas Chinese who want to stay in touch with Chinese culture. In a highly competitive and highly commercialized society like Hong Kong, men are used to pursuing excitement. The super martial heroes in the novels usually have their way by using force; this reflects reality. It is said that the more severe the fighting is, the more readers enjoy it, and their frustration can promptly be balanced off. Finally, these tales of physical struggle and winning through the use of force parallel the economic competition of a highly commercialized society, such as Hong Kong.

A quick review of the development of Chinese chivalric tales reveals that some of the above reasons were also applicable in the past. The origin of chivalric literature in China dates back to the essay, "On the Sword," in *Chuang Tse* during the Spring and Autumn Annals Era (770–476 B.C.) (Liu, 1981). Swordsmen in this short novel are described as having "bristling hair on their temples, dangling hats tightly tied with plain streamers, and gowns that are short at the back. Anger shows in their eyes, and they dislike conversation." This fearsome image is typical of the martial hero in many modern chivalric novels and films.

Prose romances, known as "chuangi," emerged in the middle of the Tang Dynasty (780), after the insurrection of the feudal lords. Authors wove martial arts with tales of miracles and parables into complex plots. *The Hermit Lady Nie* is an example. In this novel, the Lady is arrogant but magnanimous. She is taught by her martial art master that "a professional killer is to be cold-blooded when he executes orders, and divination is essential for a skilled martial hero." This Satanic voice symbolizing an iconoclastic attitude towards traditional values has been adopted in many later Hong Kong chivalric tales.

Prompt books used by story-tellers in the Song Dynasty (960–1277), known as *Huaben*, also contributed to the early stage of Chivalric literature. The story of "The Eleventh Heroine" in a popular fiction, *Pai An Jin Chi*, portrays the archetypal Chinese knight-errant as a Taoist who chooses his disciples with discrimination, does not kill without reason or seek fame or gratitude, and never helps the evil (Ma, 1980).

---

[2]"New style" is a term relative to the "chapter stories" as well as the romantic melodrama before the 1950s. It is characterized mainly by its brevity and simple plots.

Detective stories of the Ching Dynasty (1644–1911), known as "Gong An," combine the features of the Ming Dynasty (1368–1644) mysteries, prose romances from the Tang Dynasty, and prompt books in the Song Dynasty. The romantic tragic heroes are usually endowed with human characteristics. For instance, Bai Yu Tang is an arrogant, aggressive, and rash character who died a violent death in the book, *The Three Knights-Errant and the Five Altruists*. The tragic ending is an innovation in the traditional knight-errant novels. Unfortunately, the casual attitude of the knights-errant toward the government in the novels greatly conflicted with the Ching Court's tight control on the Chinese people; hence, an order to ban the novels was effected in 1710. Yet the popularity was rapidly regained when the book, *A Tale of Heroic Lovers*, was published in 1878. Steeped in Confucian and Buddhist ethics, the romantic story-line of the book centers on a mysterious heroine who always delivers goods to the poor and needy by robbing corrupt officials. The slogan in this novel is that God always keeps an eye on a good man, and the evil one will get what he deserves sooner or later.

The May Fourth Movement of 1919 in China called for counter-Confucianism and a break with tradition. This was reiterated in some of the chivalric novels published during that era. The *Legend of the Strange Hero* (1928) by Siang Kai-ran, for example, depicts a couple fleeing from the clutches of their family in pursuit of personal freedom. This was interpreted as a revolutionary way of thinking, and marked conflict between generations. However, in the first half of this century the writing styles of the Chinese chivalric novelists were at variance with each other because of regional differences. Writers in Peking, the old northern capital for many dynasties, borrowed and embellished stories from the traditional novels and prompt books. They wrote in classic Chinese prose, and their tales were based on historical characters and events which had contributed to the perpetuation of traditional values.[3]

The southern Shanghai writers were more adventurous. Their highly romantic and stylized writings used Western devices, such as an indefinite ending to a story. The heroes in most of these works are mainly "agents" able to perform special feats. Conflicts sometimes exist between these heroes and the ruling authorities.

Chivalric novels of Canton, which is further south, all share a common regional quality. The tradition of clancentrism had been the cause of conflicting territorial interests, which usually continued over generations in rural Cantonese society. The Cantonese writers emphasize this as well as the traditional themes of loyalty, filial piety, chastity, and altruism.

The proliferation of small newspapers in Hong Kong after the Second World War led to the rise of sensationalism among competitors, in order to capture a wider readership. Chivalric stories became popular

---

[3]The Ching Dynasty was overthrown in 1911 but its legendary heroes and gallant swordsmen continued to provide abundant material for writers.

with audiences because of fancy flying-swordsmen possessing super-natural combat skills. Many of these stories included love and sex, all avoided in traditional Chinese chivalric literature.

Some background information is necessary to help the reader situate the Chinese knights-errant in the indigenous Chinese communication tradition.

The Philosophical Background of Chivalric Tales

The popularity of Chivalric literature among the general public can be ascribed to its combination of philosophical and cultural concepts. Chivalric fiction found inspiration in three sources: Confucianism, Taoism, and Buddhism.

Confucianism. The book, *The Analects,* is the formulation of Chinese ethics. The author expounds upon ideas of Heaven, Earth, Rulers, Parent, Teacher—five characters which represented a hierarchy of obligations in the olden days in China. Heaven and Earth belonged to the metaphysical realm but their authority and power were vested in the Son of Heaven, the emperor, who ruled because of the mandate from Heaven. Society was based on deeply-ingrained moral principles. Absolute loyalty to the Emperor was demanded, as well as unquestioning filial piety and unconditional servitude to one's Teacher. In the *Book of Rites,* it is written that "one will not live under the sky with the murderer(s) of his father," meaning that a dutiful son shall not rest until he has avenged his father's death. It further propounds that, "Every Wrong must be Avenged." Thus, most chivalric stories center on avenging the death of a father or martial teacher. Subjugation to the higher interests of the family or clan is applauded in the Confucian philosophy. In the social hierarchy of chivalric stories is a gerontocracy governed by the principle of loyalty. The social hierarchy is absolute; the relation between father and son, or between master, symbolized as surrogate father or godfather, and disciple, is highly formalistic. Unfortunately, such a rigid moral code and hierarchy often go beyond the dictates of law and reason, and become a narrow system of sects and secret societies, which might even allow a member to commit a crime with an easy conscience provided it is within the rules. The Confucian spirit manifested in the chivalric stories, therefore, appears unbalanced.

Taoism and Buddhism. Taoism appreciates the natural and looks down upon the artificial. In general, it sides with the weak. What appears as a disability on the surface, might be, in fact, a mask hiding some unusual and strong qualities. Reading the book *Chuang Tse* carefully, one might discover that the protagonists are all eccentrics who are "abnormal among men, but akin to nature." Most of these eccentrics are either disfigured, disabled, or from the socially disadvantaged. But their virtue is always far greater than that of hypocrites held in high social esteem. This concept is consonant with the fictitious martial arts world, in which cripples, beggars, thieves, women, children, and scholars may appear weak, but are often martial art experts with great inner strength and superhuman capabilities.

Buddhism preaches that man must do good deeds, cultivate good relationships, and achieve both compassion and wisdom in order to become Buddha. It focuses on the attempts to transcend the negative aspects as sin, guilt, and the transient nature of life. The view of a knight-errant as a savior is based on this.

Confucianism, Taoism, and Buddhism have been instrumental in shaping the world view of the Chinese. In his monograph, *A Study of Huan Chu Lou Chu* (Master of the Huan Chu House), Hsu describes the characters in Huan Chu Lou Chu's novels:

> They are people imbued with the spirit of Taoism (propensity for freedom and frugal simplicity). They have the eyes of Sakyamuni (exercising compassion even in a fight), but behave like the disciples of Confucius and Meng Tse (insisting on filial piety, brotherly love, loyalty and trustworthiness) (Koo, 1981, p. 25).

The knights-errant thus balance the philosophies of Confucianism, Taoism, and Buddhism in their virtue.

The change in a knight-errant's supernatural powers in the post-war martial arts films in Hong Kong can be divided into two phases. In the early 1950s magical feats were included in the storyline. Because of the negative influence of these films on teenagers, who sometimes ran away from home in search of magic power, the Nationalist Government had banned their showing two decades earlier, but after World War II they re-emerged in Hong Kong. The second phase is marked by the secularization of the knight-errant, beginning in the late 1970s, and in which excellence in martial skills is always the highest ideal pursued by a knight-errant. Strict discipline and grueling training symbolize a humanistic and realistic attitude toward life.

Since historical, political, and cultural changes all leave their mark on literary forms, the evolving concept of the knight-errant contains seeming contradictions. Liu's (1967, pp. 4-6) definition is a good summary of the traditions embodied. He describes the knight-errant in the Chinese culture as a composite of the following ideals: altruism, justice, individualism, personal loyalty, moral and physical courage, truthfulness and mutual faith, honor and fame, generosity, and contempt for wealth.

Martial Art (Wu) and the Legends of Shaolin Monasteries. When referring to the Chinese word, *Wu*, one must recognize that most of the traditional Chinese theories of natural science and religious philosophy, as well as legends, customs, and graphic symbols all have made a contribution to martial art. Therefore, Chinese martial art does not merely serve as a means of fighting or self-defense. It is, first, a form of knowledge related to human physiology. At a higher level, martial art is also an "inner force" designed to expand the power of human ability; it is a process of self-discipline.

The use of martial art in military strategy and as a scholarly subject dates back to at least as far a period known as the War States (approximately 400 B.C.). Yet in the field of Chinese martial art, there is a popular saying that claims, "Shaolin is the origin of all martial art." That is, all the many varieties and schools of Chinese martial art ultimately derived from the techniques originated in the Shaolin Monasteries.

According to legends, there were two Shaolin monasteries, but both were destroyed by the Ching Court, in 1736 and 1768 respectively, due to their anti-Ching activities. Shaolin disciples thus wandered around the country and formed the *Huangmen* secret society in order to continue their anti-Ching resistance. As time passed by, these knights-errant became fictionalized and ever since chivalric tales were told about the Shaolin monasteries.

It is said that the more chaotic the era, the greater the demand for the legendary knight-errant stories. The popularity of the martial art novels in the late Ching Dynasty, for example, could probably be attributed to the intense longing for superhuman heroes strong enough to resist foreign aggression and the repressive Manchu government. For the same reason, the popularity of the Shaolin legendary novels in Hong Kong after the 1950s could be viewed as an outlet for discontent with colonial rule, as well as with the Communist takeover of mainland China where the population contained a large percentage of Chinese refugees (Ng, 1981).

Popularity of Chivalric Stories in Hong Kong Media

As mentioned earlier, chivalric tales have almost become a fixture in Hong Kong mass media. Except for a few specialized publications, such as magazines on real estate or automobiles, chivalric stories can be read in every form of mass media. Their popularity is evidenced by the number of writers and the quality of the books they produce. It is estimated that during the 1960s, there were three hundred chivalric novel writers in Hong Kong and Taiwan (Liu, 1981). In the early 1980s, more than two hundred chivalric novelettes could be found in most of the book stores. The Hong Kong 1981 Telephone Directory lists 48 chivalric novel rental stores, allowing people the pleasure of reading chivalric novels without paying the full price of a book. Weekend magazines, such as the *New Knowledge*, devote at least a whole page to chivalric serials in order to satisfy readers. A quick survey of the market shows that currently there are two kinds of magazines featuring chivalric stories: regular and cartoon. Most of these magazines are of tabloid size, and appear either weekly or monthly. There are also magazines which specifically report local martial art activities and discuss the theories and practices of various schools of Kung Fu.

Just as there are people who buy newspapers only for the advertisements, there are also those who buy newspapers just to read and follow the chivalric stories. A survey of the 10 most popular newspapers in Hong Kong showed that chivalric tales accounted for no less than 12%, but no more than 30% of the literary page, an important part of Chinese newspapers. It usually features novels, fiction, essay, and other genre and covers from one-half to two pages of newsprint (Newspaper Literary Page Content Study, 1981). All of the newspapers included chivalric tales, and many newspaper owners deem chivalric stories as the major attraction to readers, especially for the four-to-eight page newspapers (Liu, 1981). *Hung Lok Daily,* a four-page "pillow and fist" newspaper, for example, devotes 40% of its literary page to chivalric tales. Radio stations also have chivalric tale programs, as does, for example Station One of the Hong Kong Commercial Broadcasting.

The popularity of televised chivalric stories is even more noticeable. The Hong Kong television program schedule of 1981 contained an almost nonstop showing of chivalric series from January to December, with only a brief "intermission" of no more than two weeks. Often the audience is bombarded with chivalric television series which are shown by both Chinese language stations at the same time, usually in prime time. In addition, there are chivalric movie reruns in the afternoon. In general, this wasn't resented by the viewers. As a television audience survey undertaken in 1981 indicated, over half of the 250 respondents interviewed felt that the number of chivalric television programs was adequate while 15% wanted the programs increased. Thirty-one percent complained that there were too many programs on the air (Small et al., 1981). One reason there were so many was, of course, because this kind of TV series received top ratings.

None of the chivalric tales attracted as much attention as the Kung Fu films did. Statistics show that there are some 800 Mandarin and Cantonese *Wu Hsia* (knight-errant) movies, as compared to about 200 Kung Fu films produced in Hong Kong over the last 30 years. Usually, most of the chivalric tales shown on theatre, TV, or broadcast on radio are based on paperback, best-seller novels. *The Story of the Book,* for example, was adapted from the most popular chivalric novel by Jing Yong, a prominent Hong Kong chivalric novelist. Although, to many non-native moviegoers, Kung Fu and Wu Hsia films may look alike, there are important differences which have become accentuated over the past few decades.

The Chinese film industry was founded soon after the turn of the century, at a time when China was plagued with domestic turmoil and external pressures. Traditional Chinese values underwent drastic adjustment. In particular, after the failure of the Boxer Rebellion (I-He-Chuan, in 1900), the whole nation recognized that spears and swords, not to mention martial art, were inadequate against the foreign guns.

Hence, the Chinese martial art films in the twenties tended to assert the power of the supernatural to imbue audiences with a strong sense of patriotism. During the 1920s and 1940s, the years of World War II and the Civil War, the production of martial art films was extremely limited. The authentic Chinese martial art films flourished again in the late 1950s, the 1960s and 1970s in Hong Kong.

The Huang Fei-hong Films of the 1950s

Hong Kong is a British Crown Colony, greatly marked by Western influence, yet the ideology, values, and emotional responses of the Hong Kong people remain very Chinese. Most of the martial art films produced in the 1950s were used to promote the orthodox Confucian code. Martial art heroes were uncompromising champions of the weak and the dispossessed, on whose behalf they performed brave and righteous deeds. Plots invariably centered on filial piety as well as on the master-disciple relationship, which, when destroyed, led to violence, glorified and justified as revenge.

The martial art films of this period could be broken down into three thematic groups: the romantic type which features superhuman heroes; the residual fantastic martial arts films; and the realistic chivalric films which emphasize both chivalry and folk culture.

The most striking example in the last category was the familiar Cantonese Huang Fei-hong martial art series, the production of which peaked in the mid-1950s. More than 85 films and 13 TV series were presented over a span of 30 years (1949-1980) (Yu, 1981). These series still maintain their appeal for the audience.

Characteristics of Films on Huang

Huang Fei-hong was a Cantonese, born in 1847 and died in 1924 at the age of 77. He excelled in martial skills and was respected by most of his contemporaries.

The story in the Huang series center on the main character and reflect the folk culture and dialect of Canton from where the majority of Hong Kong residents come. Tales are always set in Cantonese towns and define their characters' existence in specifically Cantonese ways. They feature, for example, the tea-house, fondness for pet birds, cricket and cock fights, Dragon-Boat races, and contests for the luck ball-flower. Similarly, the music is rooted in the traditional Cantonese opera. Dragon-Boat songs, street-ballad singing, drumming techniques, and dragon, lion, unicorn and centipede dancing are always demonstrated. In fact, when the theme song of the series, the Cantonese melody, "Under the General's Order," is heard, almost everyone knows there is a Huang film on the air. Furthermore, certain Southern-style martial art forms are demonstrated in the series.

Genuine Knight-Errant Films

As mentioned above, according to the traditional concept of martial virtue, a true martial artist practices the art only as a form of self-discipline and self-defense; he is a protector of the weak and the oppressed and an uncompromising champion of truth and justice. Generally a martial artist is a man of peace; he declines violence unless he is forced to use it. Huang's manner in the series exemplifies this spirit. He consistently subordinates his personal grievances to the public good, and, when he confronts the villain, he first tries verbal persuasion, using combat only as a last resort. The Confucian virtues, such as Propriety, meaning humility and courtesy; Righteousness; Charitable Love, meaning veneration for the old and compassion for the poor; and Peace, or the non-violent resolution of disputes, are central themes to a majority of the productions in this category. Huang also fully incarnates the image of a strict Chinese martial teacher, passionately concerned with the moral well-being of others but prepared to be firm when necessary. Many of the youngsters interpret this as a reinforcement of parental supervision.

However, in terms of the ideology of the series, Huang's films began to appear outmoded in the 1960s, and in the 1970s characteristics and merits portrayed were lost on the audience.

The Diversification of the 1960s

By the 1960s more northern Chinese entered Hong Kong from mainland China, and after a period of adjustment, Hong Kong society was ready to develop into a hybrid of old and new ideologies, as well as Eastern and Western cultures. Filmgoers began to demand more romantic approaches, newer styles and subjects. Mandarin films which have a greater feeling of nationalistic identity began to flourish. At the same time, chivalric novels published in Hong Kong were unbelievably popular, inspiring a new surge of interest in martial art.

A number of chivalric films in the 1960s were adapted from the martial art novels of the time. Those by the prominent chivalric novelist, Jin Yong, are typical examples, they have been regularly adapted for the screen since 1959, e.g., *The Brave Archer* (1958), the *Flying Fox of the Snowy Mountain* (1964).

Most of Jin's novels centered on the maturation of a martial art hero in a more realistic setting. The distinction between good and evil is blurred; the heroes exhibit a more eclectic style of martial skills learned from several masters, and usually loyalty to any particular school is downplayed. The heroes have romantic relationships. Overall, the hero is focused upon as an individual, and the group is relegated to the background.

In the transition period during the 1960s many chivalric films still employed the basic theme of struggle between good and evil. The protagonist of the film was usually the leader of the virtuous side and engaged in combat with his evil counterpart. While film producers may agree that competition for the top position in the world of martial art might not necessarily be a good course to pursue, such a struggle is justified if the position symbolized good, threatened by evil forces.

It is worth noting that the rise in the popularity of martial art films coincided with the outbreak of the "Cultural Revolution" in mainland China. Hong Kong was affected by the outbreak of riots in 1967. Fighting was as rife in the streets as on the screen. Even Huang's film, after a period of inactivity, returned to join the struggle, in protection of "the moral and the orthodox." Martial arts and Western fighting styles were featured with Chinese forms of combat on the screen. Huang's series, in a sense, actually anticipated the Kung Fu films of the 1970s, although their techniques and ethic were much more conservative.

To a certain degree, martial art films play a role in the cultural exchange. The story of *The Dragon and the Tiger Hunchback Hero* (1962) alludes, to *The Hunchback of Notre Dame*, while *The Swordswoman and the Seven Friends* (1963) exploits the popularity of *Snow White and the Seven Dwarfs*.

Japanese samurai films and television series are, however, the most striking examples here. In one of the series, Zatoichi is made popular as a skilled, but blind swordsman who brought the prowess of fantasy into the real world. Kung Fu films such as *Magnificent Trio* (1967), *Downhill They Ride* (1967), and *Flying Hero Little White Dragon* (1968) clearly are influenced by the Japanese samurai movies.

The Revived Old Tradition But New Style Form of the 1970s

Beginning in the 1970s, mainstream chivalric films changed their emphasis from swordplay in an ancient setting to unarmed combat in the modern world as Kung Fu fighting films. The genre of the Kung Fu film is thought of as closer to the audience in time and in spirit.

In these films, the superiority of traditional Chinese Kung Fu over the Japanese Judo and Karate, Thai Boxing, Korean Taekwondo, and Western boxing is reaffirmed. The stories are often set against the background struggle of overseas Chinese in different countries and nationalism is strongly depicted. This theme had wide appeal. Kung Fu cinema began to enjoy international popularity with the advent of Bruce Lee, who was seen as an individual who excelled in martial art, and as a Chinese proud of his ethnic background.

After Lee's death in 1973, the scramble for new ideas to fill the void gave rise to several new developments. One was the adaptation of chivalric novels by Koo Long, currently one of the most prominent writers. He created a new formula for mysterious, fantastic films, which placed greater emphasis on plot and character relationships. The martial art hero became a lone fighter instead of a virtuous and moralistic knight-errant. He showed a disdain for worldly pleasure, although he indulged in alcohol and appreciated wealth. He often possessed a suicidal streak. Another development was the exploration of traditional Chinese martial techniques. Films began to draw again on the Shaolin monasteries and on the heroes of Canton. They conveyed the message—all those who practice martial art are members of a family, presided over by the paternal masters.

A few Kung Fu comedies, however, neglected the rituals and the respect owed by disciple to master. The underlying idea of honoring the master only holds true if the master can be exploited thereby. This idea reflects a modern competitive society in which only the fittest survive, and these are usually the young.

Conclusion: Tradition Versus Change

Folktales have provided a rich source of material for ethnographic research into Chinese society. At a theoretical level, they can be approached as expressions of the experience and fantasy of an ethnic group. The very fact that some tales have survived through generations attests to the value and significance they have for the ethnic group.

One example is the residual Shamanism influence of the White Lotus Secret Society in the Ching Dynasty. Its superstitious beliefs in Spiritual Boxing (*Shen Da*) have inspired some martial art novels and many other Kung Fu films such as *Burning the Red Lotus Monastery* (1963), the *Spiritual Boxer* (1975). The influence of such beliefs propagated by the movies can be found in the developing New Territories side of Hong Kong. In this area, youths are eager to learn Spiritual Boxing to acquire its mystical prowess[4] without being required to undergo long-term intensive physical training.

Recently, the knight-errant has emerged in the Hong Kong chivalric stories as self-centered and materialistic. Whereas the traditional knight-errant devotes his life to upholding justice or defending the reputation of his school, he is now depicted as someone motivated by monetary gains, fame, which comes from the title of Supreme Swordsmanship, personal power, acquired through possession of secret combat manuals or priceless blades.

---

[4]It is believed by the followers that supernatural ability can be acquired by calling the spirit of martial gods. Charmed potions and prayers are the major spirit-invoking methods.

Mass media have contributed to the popularity of the knight-errant as a sort of role model for youth, to the concern of many adults. A sample survey was conducted by the Hong Kong Discharged Prisoners' Aid Society in January 1981. A total of 613,100 primary and secondary school students, from grades 5 to 12, responded (*Sing Tao Evening News*, Sept. 23, 1981, p. 19). Among them, 5.59% said that they admired their school mates and friends who belonged to some kind of underground society; 5.46% of the respondents acknowledged that they would like to join the gangs. A majority of respondents (78.3%) understood gang jargon, which students learned mainly from television programs, movies, newspapers, magazines, or from their schoolmates and friends.

According to the survey, the various reasons why these young students respected the gang members were complicated, but the following seemed to predominate. Gang members were seen as trustworthy, capable, and able to protect the weak and the needy; they were considered charming heroes; and their lives were seen as colorful.

The report denounces the contribution of mass media towards creating a heroic image of gangs, particularly through their portrayal in films and on television. Chivalric tales, in a way, have also helped in formulating the romantic image of a hero who is not concerned with respect for the law.

From the perspective of the early 1980s, future changes in social values might be expected to become more pronounced. Will the image of a Chinese knight-errant eventually fade as an anachronism in an ever more industrialized and commercial Hong Kong? Time alone will bring us the answer.

REFERENCES

Koo, Siu-fing. (1981). "Philosophy and Tradition in the Swordplay Film." In Shiug-Hon Liu (ed.), *A Study of the Hong Kong Swordplay Film* (1945–1980). Hong Kong: Urban Council.

Liu, Da-mu. (1981). "From Chivalric Fiction to Martial Art Films." In Shing-hon Liu (ed.), *A Study of the Hong Kong Swordplay Film* (1945–1980). Hong Kong: Urban Council, 47–62.

Liu, James. (1967). *The Chinese Knight-Errant*. London: Routledge and Kegan Paul.

Ma, You-yuang. (1980). "Knight Errantry in Prompt Books." In *Collectanea on the History of Chinese Novels*. Taiwan: China Times Publisher, 105–145. (In Chinese).

"Newspaper Literary Page Content Study." (1981). *Chu Hai Journal* (April 15), 4. (In Chinese).

Ng, Ho. (1981). "When the Legends Die—a Survey of the Tradition of the Southern Shaolin Monastery." In Shing-hon Liu (Ed.), *A Study of the Hong Kong Swordplay Film*. Hong Kong: Urban Council, 56–70.

Small, Frank, et al. (1981). "An Audience Survey." *Ming Pao Monthly*, (Sept. 23), p. 2. (In Chinese).

Wei, Ching (ed.). (1980). *Liang Yu-sheng and his Chivalric Novels*. Hong Kong: Wai Ching Book. (In Chinese).

Yu, Mo-wang. (1981). "The Prodigious Cinema of Huang Fei-hong: an Introduction." In Shing-hon Liu (ed.), *A Study of the Hong Kong Martial Art Film*. Hong Kong: Urban Council, 81–82.

14

Village Meetings in Korea: Yesterday and Today

Kyung J. Lee

The role of development communication has become an important area of inquiry in communication research, and may be the single most studied area in the entire field (Lerner, 1958; Lerner and Schramm, 1967; Pye, 1963; Schramm, 1964; Rogers, 1976a).

Tradition vs. Modern: A Questionable Conceptualization

In recent years however, after nearly three decades of research on the topic, there has been a "deepening sense of disappointment, doubt and disenchantment" among development communication researchers (Yu, 1976, p. 227). Such frustration grew out of field experiences in developing countries of Asia and Latin America (Rogers, 1976a).

Some of the sources of frustration and disappointment are found in the ideologies and assumptions behind the "classical" paradigm of development and development communication which guided most development plans and development communication research in the earlier years.

The tradition-modernity dichotomy is the predominant ideology behind the classical paradigms of development and development communication. Under this concept, development was associated with "tradition." It assumed that underdevelopment was attributable to traditional values and that development was the transformation of such traditional modes of thinking and behavior into "modern" values and styles, often meaning those of the well-to-do Western nations. Development was viewed as a "catching up" effort by the underdeveloped nations trying to adopt Western values and systems. Tradition was considered an impediment to the change and, therefore, an obstacle to development.

There was great faith in the ability of modern communication technology to bring the desired change. Mass media had been considered as playing a direct and powerful role in transforming tradition into modernity. In the earlier days of development communication research, many researchers believed that the power of mass communication would bring about the downfall of traditional society and consequently that traditional communication institutions would be replaced by mass communication (Pye, 1963; Lerner, 1958; Schramm, 1964).

Many development plans, and much development communication, in various parts of the world were guided by "classical" concepts of development and communication effects. Before long, at least some developing countries were recognized as experiencing political and social frustration, disorganization, and instability, as a result of modernization efforts. Iran and several Asian and Latin American nations are examples. In addition, experts conceded that in countries, such as England and Japan, social change had occurred without displacing traditional elements: tradition and modernity continue to exist in harmony (Eisenstadt, 1966; Ward and Rustow, 1963).

One assumption inherent in the classical paradigm of development is that people in the underdeveloped countries want changes, and will, therefore, change in the manner the change agents desire. This is now considered to be questionable. Nisbet (1972, p. 6) argues that our common "refusal to recognize the sheer power of conservatism in social life: the power of custom, tradition, habit, and mere inertia" is the greatest barrier to our understanding of change. Yu supports Nisbet's theory of the conservative nature of mankind. He (1976, p. 234) maintains that the history of China up to the nineteenth century demonstrates that "continuity and conservatism rather than change have been the aspiration or desire of mankind."

Thus the classical paradigm of development has been attacked because it ignores human nature and the relationships between the traditional and modern elements in the process of change. Experts in the field have begun to search for new perspectives.

New meanings of development are constantly sought, and emphasis has shifted from economics to human values. The definition given by the Working Committee on Communication in Support of Development of the International Broadcast Institute in 1975 clearly demonstrates this shift. They defined development as "the improvement of the well-being of the individual and the betterment of the quality of his or her life" (Yu, 1977, p. 171).

Relationships between traditional and modern institutions in the process of change came to be viewed in a different light. The dichotomy was replaced by a scheme of "manifold variations" in the relationship between the two (Gusfield, 1967). The idea of alien superiority and traditional inferiority, implicit in the classical paradigm, has been abandoned. The relationship between the traditional and the modern is no longer viewed as antagonistic or adversarial. Rather, development is thought to be the "syncretism of old and new ideas" through the integration of traditional with modern institutions (Rogers, 1976b).

There have been significant revisions in our attempts to explain and to understand development. In view of these new perspectives, a reappraisal of the role of traditional institutions and their relation to modern elements in shaping the direction of social change becomes inevitable.

This chapter attempts to shed some light on the relationships between "tradition" and "modernity" in the process of change.

How do indigenous culture and modern elements interact in the process of national development? Have indigenous cultural institutions been destroyed in the wake of social change? Or have they survived? If so, how? These are the kinds of questions this chapter seeks to answer. To do so, an example of an indigenous cultural institution, the informal village gathering, the *Sarangbang*, is used.

There has been little research on the status of indigenous communication institutions and their relationships to mass communication in Korean rural communities. This exploratory study is based on field observations, and personal interviews with folklorists, anthropologists, and colleagues in communication research.

Sarangbang as an Indigenous Communication Institution

Wang and Dissanayake define indigenous communication as a communication system "embedded in the culture which existed before the arrival of mass media and still exists . . . with a certain degree of continuity, despite changes, as a vital mode of communication" (Wang and Dissanayake, 1982, p. 3). The Sarangbang conforms to this. It served Korean society as an important communication institution long before the arrival of mass media, and is very much alive today despite significant changes in its form and functions.

The Sarangbang has two significant aspects in communication: (1) the Sarangbang as a place of gathering, and (2) the functions it plays.

The word *Sarang* was formerly associated with men. In a traditional Korean house, the men's quarters, or the *Sarangche*, were detached from the main body of the house. Literally, Sarangbang means the drawing room where men receive and entertain their guests.

In traditional Korean society there were two distinct social classes: *Yangban*, meaning the gentry, and *Sangmin*, meaning the commoner. The gentry controlled all important resources, both material and intellectual; commoners were only there to serve the gentry. The receiving and entertaining of the guests was largely the occupation of the gentry.

In a well-to-do gentry home there were three kinds of Sarangbang, each distinguished by the age and social status of those present; the *Sarang*, where the head of the household resided and entertained his guests; the *Jung Sarang*, where the younger men of the house received and entertained their guests; and the *Chodangbang* where the servants and commoners gathered. In traditional Korean society, social status, age, and sex were determinative factors. The gentry did not mingle with the commoners. The old and the young did not socialize with each other, nor did men and women. Men of the same social status and age group gathered together at Sarangbang to socialize and exchange ideas and information on personal as well as community affairs. Thus, in traditional society the Sarangbang was the communication and cultural center of the community. The fact that the Sarangbang was the gathering place of people with similar social background and interests, is significant.

The Sarangbang has always been a forum for discussing common interests and opinions on various matters and where solutions to the problems were sought. In a way, the Sarangbang has always been a "marketplace of ideas." The public opinion of the community was formed there.

It was largely well-to-do gentry who had the means to facilitate the gatherings, and thus the well-to-do were important in the formation of public opinion in traditional Korean society.

Confucian philosophy was at the core of the ancient Korean traditions, and still is today, although to a much lesser extent. Confucianism values status, age, and knowledge, all of which traditionally legitimized authority. The old and learned gentry, therefore, exerted control over many aspects of village life. The elders among them made all key decisions, set rules and regulations, and saw to their observance by the younger, the less learned, and the consumers.

The elderly gentry of each community gathered at the Sarangbang functioned as a type of governing body. The younger people and the commoners got together and expressed their opinions and ideas among themselves, but the decisions were made by the elderly. If their decisions and rules were not observed, which, according to one informant of the village of Yangdong,[1] would not be likely, the villager who flouted the rules and regulations "would not be treated as a decent human being by the village people." In other words, recalcitrants were ostracized.

Sarangbang in the Midst of Social Change

Rapid and drastic changes have occurred in practically every aspect of the Korean society over the past 30 years, and the physical setting and the functions of Sarangbang have changed accordingly. Every social phenomenon is too complex to be explained by a single factor, and many factors have contributed to the changes in Sarangbang. In this

---

[1]Yangdong is located in *Kyungsang Bukdo*, in the southern part of Korea. It is known for its preservation of traditional life styles, customs, and rituals.

paper, however, only two factors will be considered: the Korean war and the arrival of mass media, each a major influence on Sarangbang.

The Korean war contributed significantly to rushing Korean society into the modern age. It was instrumental in bringing about the downfall of the *Yangban-Sangmin* status system. The war, lasting about three years, literally destroyed everything, and after the war everyone had to start from scratch, regardless of prior social status. In this context, the gentry had little to offer to the commoners, economically.

In addition, the entire population was reshuffled during and after the war. Traditionally, people had lived on the same land generation after generation, making a person's status easily recognizable. However, the large scale migration during and after the war allowed one to conceal one's status. In fact, after the war, two types of migration were noticeable. Upper class people who were no longer able to keep up appearances moved to an area where their old status would not be known and they lived there as commoners. Commoners who wanted to escape their own relationship with the gentry migrated.

In traditional Korean society, formal education consisted of tutoring. A modern school system had been introduced in Korea in 1895, but education remained the privilege of the few, who consequently exerted social influence because they were literate and learned. Primary school education became compulsory in 1949, a year before the war, marking the beginning of mass education in Korea. After the war, educational opportunities were available to everyone regardless of background or status. The educational gap between the gentry and the commoner narrowed significantly. Literacy and learning were no longer the province of the few. Mass education opened new doors for the commoner.

As the position of the gentry in Korean society weakened, so did their role in the Sarangbang. Logistically, they no longer had exclusive control of the gathering, and, functionally, they no longer had the kind of control over the commoners that they had had in the past.

New communication technology also affected the indigenous communication system. We have noted that before the arrival of mass media, the Sarangbang was the communication and entertainment center of the town. It was where people saw each other, talked, and heard about what was going on in and out of the village. It was where they entertained themselves. When radio and television were introduced to rural areas, villagers gathered around the radios and television sets, and the houses with radio and television sets became the new communication centers of the town.

The villagers[1] enthusiasm for new communication technology when it first arrived in the rural areas was vividly illustrated to a folklore scholar.[2] On a field trip to Yangdungdo, one of the isolated islands in Chunrabukdo in 1970, he was told that the island was very conservative

---

[2]The story was told to the author by Mr. Suk Jay Yim, a retired professor from Seoul National University, Korea.

and "traditional," and that he might have difficulty interviewing women. According to Confucian teachings, men and women should not sit together after the age of seven, and this was strictly observed in traditional society. However, when the folklorist reached the island, a group of island women gathered around him. Soon he realized that they were attracted by his tape recorder. Everyone was so anxious to tape record his or her voice and hear it on the machine that he had to record voices and play them back until three o'clock in the morning.

Perhaps the curiosity and enthusiasm of the village people contributed to the acceleration and penetration of mass media into Korean rural areas.[3] There is now an average of one television set per 2.4 households in the villages. Each family's living room is an information and entertainment center, thus reducing the frequency with which the villagers go out for information and entertainment.

Dr. Janelli, a professor of folklore at Dongkuk University in Seoul, confirms these changes in Korean life style after the arrival of television in the villages. For more than 10 years she studied ancestor worship in a traditional village in Kyungkido, in the central part of Korea, where she observed that as television saturated the village, the villagers' evening get-together became more infrequent, and, eventually, if they got together at all, it was around a television set.

Thus, the arrival of new communication media affected the indigenous communication institution. The appearance of mass media, especially electronic media, has changed the physical setting of the Sarangbang from the gentry's drawing room to the area around anyone's television set. The function of the Sarangbang has also changed.

As mentioned earlier, social status, age, and knowledge were the bases of one's social influence and power in traditional Korean culture. Knowledge was acquired through disciplined individual study or tutoring. The most important area of study was the past—the classics and the teachings of the ancestors. Knowledge of the past was valued very highly in traditional culture because the past was considered the "proper guide" for the present. In this cultural context, gentry elders who had knowledge of the past exercised influence over a wide spectrum of community affairs, formally and informally. Through the authority and influence of such old men, the community achieved and maintained consensus and harmony.

In a changing society, however, knowledge of the past is an insufficient, if not irrelevant, source of social influence. A command of up-to-date technical knowledge and information is more relevant, and this is provided by schools and mass media. The content of mass media and the content of formal education have displaced old men's wisdom and

---

[3] In 1976, government figures (Handbook of Korea, 1978) indicated that while 46.2% of the total newspaper circulation was concentrated in Seoul and Pusan, radio distribution averaged one set for every 3.5 Korean, city dwellers and villagers alike. Additionally, radio loudspeaker systems have been widely adopted in rural areas.

knowledge. Younger people with modern education and access to media have become influential in the community.

Sarangbang—Its Revised Forms and Functions

Pye argues that "the process of development is going to change the basis of power among different groups. It will favor one, and hurt another, and there will be more tensions" (Yu, 1976, p. 235). The changes in the Sarangbang illustrate Pye's point. The basis of power now favors the educated young and not the old *Yangban*. Tension between the two appears inevitable.

The antagonism between those who are favored and those who are hurt in the process of change was observed in Yangdong village, where the gentry elders are much more attached to the past than to the present. An elderly man, interviewed by the author, appeared proud of his ancestors and was happy to demonstrate his knowledge of the past— observation of rituals, traditions, and customs. The old man did not hesitate to express his frustration with younger people, because "they simply don't know the right way for a man to live." He meant that young people don't want to live according to old traditions, and he blamed mass media. He also expressed his nostalgia for the old Sarangbang and the power and influence the gentry elders exerted on the village. He complained that today young people do not seek advice from the old people often enough. When asked why, his answer was "because they don't even know what to ask."[4]

If we accept that development means a change in society towards a better appreciation of human values, as recently suggested by many development researchers (Schramm and Lerner, 1976), change which only increases social antagonism is not development. If social antagonism is created in the process of development, it should be eliminated, or the society, as a system, will eventually break down.

China appears to be a good example of a society coping with tension created in the process of change. According to Yu, China was confronted with the problem of the past and present in the process of change. The issue was whether there should have been a "preference for the past over the present or for the present over the past." Yu (1976, p. 234) maintains that the correct answer to the problem is "to make the past serve the present," and that was exactly what the Chinese did.

The creative and skillful use of the past to serve development has great strategic value because it is a viable means of maintaining continuity with the past in the development process, through which the tension between tradition and modernity can be resolved. Perhaps this is the very heart of the whole issue of reconceptualization of develop-

---

[4]The interview was conducted in September, 1981, in *Yangdong*.

ment and development communication, and is the reason for the importance of indigenous culture in the process of development.

The Sarangbang has undergone serious alterations in the process of social change. For a while, it seemed that it might disappear, but attempts were made to revive the physical setting, and today the Sarangbang exists in a different form.

The Korean government launched a nationwide rural area development program in the 1970s. During the course of the program, the government promoted *Kyungrodang*, which literally translates as "a house built in respect for the elderly," in rural areas.

The *Kyungrodang* became a new gathering place for the elderly, regardless of sex. The old men and women of the village gather at Kyungrodang to meet socially, to play cards or chess, or just to chat. The new village leaders and local government officials often visit and entertain the elderly with food and drinks. They also listen to the problems and opinions of the elderly at Kyungrodang.

In the process of modernization, the elderly become the most frustrated sector of society. Their role has been usurped by the younger people, and there is little left for them to do. Naturally there is antagonism between the old and the young, and such antagonism must be eliminated. Kyungrodang appears to work as a means for dealing with such antagonism. Communication efforts made by local government officials and younger village leaders at Kyungrodang assure the elderly, especially the males, that they are still very much a part of the system, by giving them a sense that they are recognized, their voices are heard, and they are consulted by the younger people.

Despite significant cultural and social changes, the Confucian ideal of respect toward the elderly is still deeply rooted in the minds of people, and it affects social behavior directly or indirectly. In Korea, it is not uncommon to find elderly people on the advisory boards of various social organizations and institutions. Often the old-timer's function in the organizations is cultural and symbolic, rather than functional.

Efforts by local government officials and young village leaders to visit the elderly, to entertain them, and to communicate with them at the Kyungrodang can be viewed as additional evidence of a cultural expectation: the expectation to respect the elderly.

The entertainment function of Sarangbang has been revived in today's Kyungrodang. The old men of the village gathered at the Kyungrodang to entertain themselves. However, today the function of Kyungrodang is no longer that of decision-making or rule-making and enforcement. Another genre of village meeting—*Ban-Sang Hui* has assumed the major decision-making function in the community.

Ban-Sang Hui was also instituted by the Korean government during the New Village Movement in the early 1970s. Like Kyungrodang, it exists in almost every village and town in Korea. The head of Ban-Sang Hui is not the most senior member in a community, but a government-appointed officer, who, assisted by young aides, regularly meets and works with community members on important local projects such as road building or family planning.[5]

In contrast to the Sarangbang, there is no discrimination against women or the young in the Ban-Sang Hui meetings. It is simply stipulated that each household should be represented by one family member. The better-educated, middle-aged community leaders, therefore, often become the core of the organization. Attendance, throughout the nation, is reportedly high since it is directly related to the chances of acquiring government subsidies for local projects.

A third difference between the Ban-Sang Hui and the Sarangbang is in the process of decision making. While in the Sarangbang meetings, older males took care of community affairs in an authoritarian fashion, the Ban-Sang Hui encourages open discussion among members before a decision is reached. The decisions are then communicated to the public through the well-established, radio-loudspeaker system.

If the elderly in today's Kyungrodang do have a role in decision making, it is to approve or to confirm the decisions made by young village leaders or government officials in the Ban-Sang Hui. The function of the Kyungrodang, in terms of the decision-making process is more of an ex post facto approval or confirmation. This ex post facto approval or confirmation has a cultural and symbolic significance for government officials and village leaders. It is a symbolic attempt to maintain cultural continuity in the decision-making process. It is also an attempt to achieve consensus through harmonious relationships between the old and young, thus minimizing possible tension between the past and the present.

Conclusion

Human nature is very complicated and often times self-contradictory. People desire change and stability at the same time. They are attracted by the new and yet nostalgic for the old. Development involves people, and, in thinking of development, one should consider the balance between the desire for change and stability and between attraction to the new and nostalgia for the old. This is what makes development a more difficult and complicated process than many planners and researchers once thought. The realization that human nature is complicated requires that researchers examine the indigenous culture in the context of development.

This article has explored the status of an indigenous communication institution in rural Korea in the context of social change. Has this institution, the Sarangbang, perished in the midst of social change? Or

---

[5]While decision making in *Sarangbang* is often limited to the social aspect, e.g., funerals and weddings, *Ban-Sang Hui* is much better organized and has a distinct goal: the improvement of community life.

has it survived in a somewhat different capacity? There is no doubt that it has gone through serious changes in the development process, with the arrival of modern communication technology accounts for the changes. Nevertheless, contrary to the predictions of earlier development communication researchers, the indigenous communication institution is seldom completely replaced by mass communication, nor is it destroyed in the process of development.

What we have witnessed in the case of Sarangbang, is continuity of the form—the village meeting—and of the functions—entertainment and decision-making. However, many changes did take place. The entertainment function of the traditional village meetings is now carried out mainly by the Kyungrodang, with its participants expanded to include both sexes. However, the decision-making function has been transferred to the younger, better educated members of the Ban-Sang Hui. The Sarangbang in its original form failed to survive. However, its underlying base, the cultural tradition of promoting community ties through village meetings accounts for the achievements of development programs. The key to success therefore, is not destroying, but adapting and utilizing cultural heritage to meet current needs.

REFERENCES

Eisenstadt, Shmuel N. (1966). *Modernization: Protest and Change.* Englewood Cliffs: Prentice Hall.

Gusfield, Joseph R. (1967). "Tradition and Modernity: Misplaced Polarities in the Study of Social Change." *American Journal of Sociology* 72(4), 351–362.

A Handbook of Korea. (1978). Seoul: Korean Overseas Information Service.

Lerner, Daniel. (1958). *The Passing of Traditional Society: Modernizing in the Middle East.* Glenco: Free Press.

Lerner, Daniel and Wilbur Schramm (eds.). (1967). *Communication and Change in the Developing Countries.* Honolulu: East-West Center Press.

Nisbet, R. (ed.), (1972). *Social Change.* New York: Harper Torchbooks.

Pye, Lucian W. (ed.), (1963). *Communication and Political Development.* Princeton: Princeton University Press.

Rogers, Everett M. (ed.), (1976a). *Communication and Development: Critical Perspectives.* Beverly Hills: Sage.

Rogers, Everett, M. (1976b). "Communication and Development: The Passing of the Dominant Paradigm." In E. M. Rogers (ed.), *Communication and Development: Critical Perspectives.* Beverly Hills: Sage.

Schramm, Wilbur. (1964). *Mass Media and National Development: The Role of Information in the Developing Countries.* Stanford: Stanford University Press.

Schramm, Wilbur and David Lerner. (1976). *Communication and Change: The Last Ten Years and the Next.* Honolulu: University of Hawaii Press.

Wang, Georgette and Wimal Dissanayake. (1982). "The Study of Indigenous Communication Systems in the Development: Phased Out or Phasing In?" *Media Asia* 9(1), 3–8.

Ward, R. and D. A. Rustow (eds.), (1963). *Studies in Political Development.* Princeton: Princeton University Press.

the past behavioral codes. General behavior patterns and interpersonal relations, however, have persisted in two different ways. First, kinship networks may still be important in political and economic activities. Javillonar (1978), pointed out that extended families in the Philippines exert an ubiquitous influence on all other social organizations: political, social, economic, educational, and religious. Second, people may not be loyal and feel obligated to the members of a kinship system as they used to, but these obligations of loyalty and duty have been carried over to other organizations. Bennett, for example, found various forms of *oyabun-kobun*, a paternalistic organizational style existing in Japan. Individuals in such an organization act as if they were members of one extended family (Bennett and Ichiro, 1963, p. 40):

> Persons of authority assume obligations and manifest attitudes toward their subordinates much as if they were foster parents, and conversely the subordinates behave dutifully and hold feelings of great personal loyalty toward their superior.

Bennett pointed out that this organizational style can be found in labor unions, between landowner and tenant farmer, in corporations, and, perhaps least surprisingly, in criminal organizations and syndicates. Similar patterns undoubtedly exist in other Asian cultures.

Organizational Communication in Paternalistic Corporations

Corporate styles in ASEAN nations reflect the persistence of paternalism. The series of case studies on ASEAN corporations, from which this paper draws its data, reveal several characteristics typical to corporate paternalism: the emphasis on loyalty and obligations; the concept of organization as one family; a concentration of decision-making at the top and weak middle management. Our discussion focuses on these characteristics and how they help to pattern the communication and information flow within organizations.

Loyalty is highly valued by people in the region. The spokesman for a Malaysian conglomerate said that "one hundred percent loyalty" is demanded, and that it is considered before either talent or ability. As one would expect in a paternalistic system, authoritarianism often comes with loyalty, but loyalty also entails mutual obligation—the obligation of the employer to take care of the employee, and the obligation of the employee to serve the employer to his/her best ability. Therefore in an ASEAN corporation, an employee who has proved loyal to the employer is almost guaranteed a position; if one position is abolished or the person is found to be incapable of handling the job, reassignment instead of termination is likely to take place.

The obligation to take care of employees is not limited to the scope of that employee's job; it encompasses every aspect of the employee's life. The kinds of services and welfare (e.g., personal loans, mortgages, medical care, and education for the employee's children) usually provided by social institutions in many other nations, are provided by the employer. In Indonesia, for example, the housing of employees becomes the responsibility of the manager-owner of the firm. The employees in ASEAN firms usually know the owner of the firm; some have even enjoyed social contact with the family; he or she would "lose face" if they let the benefactor down in a moment of need.

The employer's obligation is, of course, reciprocated. The rules governing loyalty are often unwritten, but are commonly understood. It is not unusual to find employees turning down attractive opportunities elsewhere because of the personal bonds they feel towards the employer. A case study revealed that the chief engineer of a large commercial fishing company in the Philippines was offered a better paying job on a German ocean liner through the company's local agents. The offer was politely refused because the engineer was content with his job and with the benevolence of the company president. The principle holds particularly when the employer encounters difficult times. During periods of financial distress, it is not uncommon for an employer to expect moral support from the employees, and he also expects them, if necessary, to understand and tolerate problems such as late salary payments, cut-backs in fringe benefits, or vacation cancellations.

The emphasis of obligation and loyalty in the employer-employee relationship is a communication pattern unique in its own way, depending on the direction, for upward and downward communication have distinctly different styles. In most instances, when communication moves downward, it does so in a highly authoritarian manner. Acting like the *datu* or grandfather in an extended family, the ASEAN leader seldom explains his action or policy to subordinates; nor does he expect straightforward criticism from them. The manager occupies a position of authority and his words are almost automatically obeyed.

On the other hand, since employees' loyalty and obedience are rewarded by care for their personal well-being on the part of the employer, upward communication is found to be particularly open when concerned with personal problems and troubles. Workers at all levels are usually provided with a direct line of communication to the chief executive officer.

Such channels, of course, aren't necessarily suitable for any kind of message, e.g., criticisms of company policies. Because of the authority associated with a paternalistic leader and the general lack of formal channels, such as reports and internal publications, upward communication beyond personal matters is very limited in a paternalistic organization. However, there is a need for the employer to know what is happening at the lower levels, and upward communication is at times maintained by a manager unofficially appointing a few trusted people to serve as his eyes and ears. These selected individuals find out what the opinions and feelings of the staff are, and pass them on to their boss. If a lower-level staff member wishes to have something revealed to the boss, he/she confides in one of the boss's men or women who feels freer in reporting to the head man. The employee however, must be wary about whom he/she confides in when he/she does not want certain information passed upwards.

The General Manager of a Philippine bus company explained his information network as follows:

> In our setup, there is, of course, the danger of collusion because of friendships. I try to control this by employing some *"secret agents"* who report to me periodically but who are not known to the others. This is for the freight lines. For the buses, we have what are known as "riders," passengers under the employ of the company. We make the drivers know there are agents—make them think there are many, by saying for instance: . . . "according to my agent number 207 . . ." when we actually have only a few. It's really psychological warfare.

Closely associated with the concepts of loyalty and obligation is the perception of the organization as one extended family. Under an employer who is perceived as a "grandfather" figure, the employees see themselves as members of one big family, and behave accordingly. The "personal touch" in a paternalistic organization is often visible, as is communication within such organizations. For example, Western executives tend to rely on formal communication channels; routinely communicating orders and decisions through a secretary or department heads, telephone calls, written memos, and formal meetings. The ASEAN managers, in contrast, often deliver instructions and orders verbally, in person.

An upper-level manager in charge of administrative matters in a logging camp in the southern Philippines summarized this communication style:

> When I have something to do, I do it myself; I don't phone the department head to do it. I go to the man himself and personally request it. That way, my instructions carry more weight. I also get faster results.

Similarly, upward communication carries a personal touch. Employees who wish to communicate their personal problems to the employer seldom do it through formal channels. Personal visits are usually considered as a sincere gesture. Similar style is followed with the "hidden agents," who collect information for the top management.

The "personal factor," whether inside or outside of an organization, is a potent force in achieving managerial information. The ASEAN manager builds up his network over a period of time. Starting with his family, the circle expands to include relatives, friends from school and from the same home town, relatives of friends, and friends of friends. If he has developed his social skills well, by the time he reaches a managerial position, he has a well-developed informal human resource group that he can tap for information as the need arises. As he progresses upwards in his job and in his organization, he joins various professional and civic associations, and meets more and more people in the business community and his network becomes more extensive. He then reaches a level of visibility in the community allowing him to exercise influence.

Western managers traditionally tend to be forward-looking. They look ahead, using statistical data to predict economic conditions and to make market forecasts. Their planning is based on sophisticated documentation to help them anticipate coming events and take the necessary steps to direct their organizations away from losses and towards opportunities.

In contrast, the ASEAN manager has traditionally relied on a network of relatives and personal and professional friends, built up over the years to feed him privileged information on critical events and happenings in the marketplace. This personal information network is usually more sensitive to the present or the immediate future than to the next 5 to 10 years. The ASEAN executive's preference for current information instead of long range statistical forecasting is understandable given the more volatile and constantly shifting economic and political environment of Southeast Asia.

Decision making concentrated in the upper echelon is another distinguishing feature of paternalistic organizations. Since family organizations are prevalent in ASEAN nations, top-level personnel are often related by blood or related by marriage. There are many examples of this. In a Malaysian conglomerate, the owner's son and son-in-law were both members of the management committee, and the Chinese owner of a corn-milling company in the southern part of the Philippines hired his nephew as the office manager. Decision making in these organizations often follows a pattern: almost all of the decisions are made at the top by the family members with the most authority and who have access to information withheld from those at lower levels. Little authority is delegated to middle-level management. Decisions tend to be more subjective than objective, based on intuition and informal communication and information networks. They also tend to be spontaneous and made by an experienced top manager who is highly respected and almost revered, by subordinates. Because of his influence in the community, his decisions may ignore the established organization rules in order to accommodate the current situation. This flexibility is thought to be necessary in an ever-changing environment.

Decision making at the top is typical of smaller organizations. Thus, when an organization begins to expand beyond the proportions which one person or a few family members can control, there is a tendency for new ventures to spin off under the guidance of a trusted member of top management. Diversified products are produced in different firms, under the centralized control of a holding company whose board is composed of executives who concurrently are the decision makers in those firms.

These executives are usually versatile because of their many responsibilities. Because of this exposure to different phases of business, they must be highly capable and adept at their jobs. At the same time, those at the mid- or lower levels are put in a disadvantageous position, and are unable to participate in many decisions. The information flow generally stops at the inner circle constituted by top management. On the other hand, authoritarian downward communication and "mediated" upward communication assumes the ignorance of the mid-level management. The information disseminated downward is usually not enough to solve problems at the lower levels. The existence of a few "hidden agents" who may confide everything to the employer compounds the operation. The lack of systematic and open channels of communication leads to the development of rumors through grapevine-like informal channels and networks which may be detrimental to an organization.

The culture rewards loyalty to, and encourages reliance on, the boss. If the mid-level manager takes on more responsibility than is expected, this may be perceived as usurping authority or as "showing-off." In either case, the mid-level manager may encounter the ridicule or hostility of colleagues. He/she thus plays it safe by obeying the orders of superiors, with, however, authority suffering.

As ASEAN family organizations expand, the decision making and the corresponding information flow are forced to the lower levels of the organizations, and there is corresponding professional growth. However unpalatable as this may be to top management, it is necessary in order for an organization to remain viable in a competitive regional or international market. The chairman of a Malaysian conglomerate put it this way:

> I do not expect to keep management (of the company) just between me and my sons. I have to give power to the best man and the best teams.

Should this path to benevolent paternalistic leadership be revised so that as young managers get older, they gradually delegate and relinquish authority and decision-making to their junior staff? Should the size of the organization dictate style? These questions have yet to be answered.

As pointed out earlier, the ASEAN business environment is changing. Local organizations face the need to grow or then will perish in a more competitive regional and international marketplace. Conceivably, the style of conducting organizational communication will change accordingly. As the example of Japan demonstrates, however, it is possible for an organization to expand with a paternalistic infrastructure. Evidence shows that mutual obligations and loyalty often contribute to the rapid growth of the corporation as a whole. With employees dedicated to the future of the organization, its success is predictable. There is no need, however, to view differences in ASEAN and management styles of other nations as absolute and irreconcilable opposites. Sometimes the differences are more a matter of degree. The key is not to abandon one type and embrace the other, but to understand and employ the best of both within a given social and cultural framework.

The study of organizational communication in ASEAN countries demonstrates at least one important fact: the need to rid our minds of the overly simplistic notion that tradition and modernity are polar opposites. As we see how organizational communication takes place in the ASEAN countries, tradition and modernity are mutually reinforcing entities and interaction between the two is fruitful. Hence the need to examine continuity and change in Asian communication systems undergoing the process of social environment.

REFERENCES

Baird, John E. (1977). *The Dynamics of Organizational Communication*. New York: Harper & Row.

Bennett, John W. and Iwao Ichiro. (1963). *Paternalism on the Japanese Economy*. Minneapolis: University of Minnesota Press.

Conboy, William A. (1976). *Working Together*. Columbus, Ohio: C. E. Merrill.

Downs, Cal W., David M. Berg, and Wil A. Linkugel. (1977). *The Organizational Communicator*. New York: Harper & Row.

Javillonar, Gloria V. (1978). "The Filipino Family." In Man Singh Das and Panos D. Bardis (eds.), *The Family in Asia*. New Delhi: Vikas Publishing House.

Katz, D. and R. Kahn. (1966). *The Social Psychology of Organizations*. New York: Wiley.

Krech, D. and R. Crutchfield. (1948). *Theory and Problems of Social Psychology*. New York: McGraw-Hill.

16

The Information Economy and Indigenous Communications

Meheroo Jussawalla and Debra Lynn Hughes

> Where is the life we have lost in living?
> Where is the wisdom we have lost in knowledge?
> Where is the knowledge we have lost in information—?

T. S. Eliot in *"Two Choruses from the Rock"*

The concept of an information economy is still vague, even though research on the subject is burgeoning in industrialized countries. The fact remains that as the communication revolution speeds its way through the rich countries of the North, more activities are generated in producing, processing, and distributing information. Such activities have become part and parcel of modern society, and participants within that society do not stop to consider their magnitude or their impact. The acceptance and widespread use of constantly changing communication technology has resulted in social acceptance of the concept of an information society. When these information activities generate income and employment and are priced in the market, the information economy becomes a spin off from the information society. Countries that inherited the Industrial Revolution have transformed the theory of communication technology into common practice within a decade. The explosion of instant communication and the research and development that makes it possible have accelerated development and productivity in major industrialized countries like the U.S., Japan, France, West Germany, and the U.K. However, the countries that did not inherit the Industrial Revolution and have not participated in its progress are conscious of the prospects for development through transfer of communication technology. They are averse to letting this new information revolution pass them by. They want to participate in its benefits without permitting themselves to be colonized once again by technology. There-fore, the newly industrializing countries have staked a considerable part of their investment resources on making communication technology work for the betterment of their society. The less developed countries are also looking for affordable technologies that can help their processes of development without enslaving their economies with unbearable debt. What are the options open for the low-income countries to enter the information age without losing their cultural identities, their socio-cultural mores, and their political sovereignty? Can they avail them-selves of low-cost technology transfer appropriate to their basic human needs? With controversy raging about cultural imperialism, is it possible to stop the wave of the microelectronics revolution from sweeping all cultures old and new? Do traditional media have a chance for survival? These are issues that need to be addressed when we speak of the role of indigenous communication in a New World Information Order and within the framework of a global information society.

The concept of indigenous communication is equally vague. Where does indigenous communication end and imported technology begin? Why is it that when we think of indigenous communication we usually refer to the low-income countries? Is it because industrialized countries have so merged their old and new systems that what was indigenous a century ago is transformed to universal application now? Why is it that it is primarily the LDCs that are pressured to utilize their indigenous forms of folk dances, puppet shows, and ballad singers for carrying communication messages? Do European, American, and Japanese so-cieties that are in control of the information revolution look on such media as outmoded or antiquated? If technology transfer is preferred by low-income countries, does it pose a threat to traditional media? Is it all that bad for developing countries to merge their traditional media into the new electronics age? These issues which confront policy makers in developed and developing countries require careful handling. On the one hand, new technologies may induce consumerism in the periphery, which LDCs cannot afford. On the other hand, rigid adherence to tradi-tional media may deprive people of the right to speedy and accurate channels for communication. The international demonstration effect is bound to penetrate all societies as global interdependence grows. A strictly isolated country like the Peoples Republic of China now finds that with an open door policy it cannot stem the tide of modernization or hold back the new technologies of television and computers from its people. It is up to the policy makers to devise a media policy which will not bring the economy of the developing country to the brink of bank-ruptcy and, at the same time, will foster productivity and increase out-put of goods and services.

What are the Implications of the Information Society for LDCs?

At a conference held at Ditchley Park in Oxfordshire, England in June 1979, delegates from six industrialized countries (U.K., Canada, West

Germany, Japan, the Netherlands, and the U.S.A.) met to discuss the impact of the silicon chip on societies across continents. Microelectronics does not cause pollution, uses minimal energy, and has infinite capacity for serving mankind in day-to-day living. The silicon chip or micro-processor is a low-cost information handling device. In its applications, it can program "washing machines, control the flow of oil through refin-eries, play chess, feed gasoline to motor car engines, book airline flights, educate children and adults, diagnose illness, give legal advice . . . you name it" (Sieghart, 1981, p. 2). It appears then, that the impact of the microprocessor lies in the power of its applications—not so much on the hardware and software, but on the "peopleware." However, even in-dustrialized countries are concerned about the impact of such technol-ogy on unemployment. Economists call it frictional unemployment, re-quiring large programs for retooling of personnel. Can LDCs, already burdened with disguised unemployment, afford to invest in micro-electronics that is both cheap and benign? Will it add to their existing staggering problems of migration from rural to urban areas, or can the technology shift the base of operations to remote areas? These questions remain largely unanswered. Experiments with greater use of micro-electronics, like digital telephone exchanges, have only now begun in a few LDCs. The results will determine future use, which is being pro-jected at exponential growth rates.

The advent of an information society heralds instant information flow without prescribing the direction of the flow. For LDCs the flow is likely to be one-way; from the center to the periphery. There is no technical barrier to changing this to interactive two-way communication. But computer networks and media systems have to be fed with informa-tion. While low cost systems can simplify access to information, infor-mation input is not as easy. How many people in the periphery will use the information that is readily accessible to them and use it to their advantage? Does an information society presuppose a certain minimum level of literacy and an ability to use information? If so, those who do have the skills to turn information into knowledge will acquire power and control, resulting in a new information elite and new forms of inequality.

There are no easy and sure answers. The market system ignores those who do not command purchasing power, and low-income coun-tries fear that market forces have already given monopoly power to the corporations in industrialized countries in generating, processing, and distributing data and information. If information technology is trans-ferred, there will have to be an international guarantee that information and knowledge flows facilitated by such transfers are not hampered by tariff and non-tariff trade barriers and that they reach the periphery and do not strengthen elite enclaves that already exist. An information soci-ety should cater to all income groups within that society or lose its *raison d'etre*. In practical terms, such an assurance will not be forthcoming for a long time. Developing countries remain uncertain about the allocation of common property resources, such as the magnetic frequency spectrum and the allocation of orbital space. While these discussion proceed at international fora, technology continues to change and develop. As it does so, it poses new challenges to traditional media.

When Fritz Machlup first published his estimates of the American information society scholars were skeptical of his results. Machlup (1962) estimated that the ratio of workers in the labor force engaged in knowledge production in 1959 was 31.6%. Fortune Magazine (Burck, 1964) estimated that from 1958 to 1963 knowledge had been the biggest growth industry, having grown at 43% during that period. Jacob Marschak (1968) estimated that the knowledge industry's share of U.S. GNP was 40%. In his book *The Age of Discontinuity*, Peter Drucker (1968) wrote that the knowledge economy contributed one-third of the GNP in 1965. Marc Porat (1977), in his breakdown of a primary and a secondary information sector for the U.S. economy, brings his estimate to 46.2% for the same year (1967). The Organization for Economic Cooperation and Development (1981) has confirmed similar trends in other First World countries. The Nora and Minc Report (1980) for France is a reflection of the information society in France "as it confronts a major technological-sociological change." Daniel Bell (1979) believes that the post-industrial society is an information society which is becoming increasingly information oriented under the influence of rapidly changing computer and satellite technology. Herbert Dordick et al. (1981) have researched the growing impact of network information services and their potential for handling large numbers of remote users in a conversational mode and to adapt to a wide range of information products.

In a development context, while information leads to productivity gains, it also may result in unemployment. Anthony Smith (1980) believes that this has not happened in the past. Printing presses did not lead to loss of jobs, because new skills were needed and the demand for the printed word increased. It is problematic for LDCs to keep their economies geared to capital-intensive, technological changes when they are faced with surplus labor. Retooling and transforming skills also calls for investment. Information technology creates the same problems for employment as industrial technology has done in the past. Developing countries have grappled with these problems in civilian and military production in order to modernize and provide higher real, per capita incomes for their people, and have achieved a fair measure of success. They have found that adhering to old technology and traditional labor-intensive forms of production resulted in diminishing returns. The same trend will probably hold good for information goods and services. The cost effectiveness of traditional media will have to be weighed against the cost effectiveness of new forms of information technology.

The issue to be considered in this context is one of the efficacy of traditional media to reach the largest number of people and to induce a response from them. By keeping the technology simple are we sure that people will respond with greater enthusiasm? Is labor-intensive communication technology superior as a delivery system to telecommunications? What is the cost of selecting one or the other? The answers to these issues will depend on a country's development goals. The goals, being location specific, will induce strategies that are best aligned to development programs. If television programs routed via low-cost satellite earth stations carry development messages as effectively as village level workers, then the costs and benefits of either need to be assessed in the context of optimal social welfare. However, many social costs and benefits defy quantification and cannot be computed for an information economy. For example, when the ATS 6 was loaned by NASA, as the SITE program it was employed in India's agricultural extension and teacher's training programs with considerable success. The experience led India, with a per capita income of less than $300 a year, to initiate a huge satellite program involving the launching of the APPLE satellite in 1981 and the INSAT in 1982. The country has not scrapped its folk media. It continues to utilize traditional forms for communicating messages and it plans to expand the possibilities for its use by merging it with more sophisticated technology.

The Historical Development and Role of Indigenous Communications in LDCs

In the face of technological advancement and its potential for the expansion of the information society throughout the Third World, one wonders whether the traditional communication channels will be obviated and replaced by modern information technology, or whether the indigenous systems can coexist and serve as an integral component of an information society. If, in the final cost benefit analysis, optimal societal welfare is a heavily weighted factor, then both the implicit and explicit contributions of indigenous communication systems to society must be noted. By examining the role of indigenous communication systems as components of a New World Information Order, it is possible to more closely analyze the potential role and function of these channels within an information society.

The phrase "indigenous communication systems" includes the social and cultural channels of communication which form an integral part of the heritage of a people and which usually pre-date modern mass-media methods. These systems are embedded within the traditional mores of the people and contribute significantly to their history and culture. Included within this category are folk media (story-telling, puppetry, folk drama, folk songs, folk art, shadow plays, praise poetry, etc.) and traditional communication networks (traditional midwives, shamans and healers, market and gathering places, ceremonies and celebrations, traditional leaders, etc.).

For our purposes, indigenous communication systems are defined as those systems of communication which have relied historically on informal channels to convey information and which obtain their authority from the cultural mores, traditions, and customs of the people they serve. The strength of these systems lies in their community orientation (UNESCO/IPPF, 1972). Because they are local traditional forms of communication and often serve as primary sources of information, indigenous channels enjoy a high degree of credibility and acceptance by the people (Adhikarya, 1974; 1975; Ranganath, 1975). This is particularly true of rural populations.

Traditional media do not compete in an open market. They are part of the public domain and, unlike many of the modern information systems, do not face issues of privacy proprietorship (Jussawalla, 1980). They are insular and inward looking. Indigenous channels protect special cultures and special historical antecedents.

Traditionally, indigenous communication systems have been an essential part of the maintenance mechanism for a given society (Evans, 1976). Coseteng points out that folk media serve as "a means of establishing unity and conformity . . . they give a social system cohesion, stability, and a sense of direction" (Coseteng and Nemenzo, pg. 3, 1975). Rogers notes the importance of traditional networks as "communication channels for the kinds of [information] content that usually flow in neighborhoods, like news and gossip, cultural information reinforcing traditional values, and price information on local goods" (Rogers, in McAnany, 1978, p. 86).

The indigenous channels provide an interesting, if not unique, example of a symbiotic interaction between traditional antecedents and modern society. For example, tradition dictates the format and content of folk drama performances within given parameters passed from generation to generation. The stories are drawn from religious epics, mythology, legends, romance, and history with the specific function of transmitting and reinforcing cultural beliefs, customs and values. The works mix tragedy and comedy, pathos and ethos, romance and devotion, the sacred and profane (Gunawardana, 1974). Although the subject matter is determined by tradition, the precise content can be modified by the performer to fit the needs of the audience, often introducing local issues or topical events into the classical frame of the medium (Adhikarya, 1974). In other cases, the altered content may revolve around the express objective of socializing community members into abiding by dominant cultural norms (Evans, 1976). As Brandon states, the folk performers have "considerable latitude with regard to content. They don't choose the subject matter . . . but they have the freedom to rearrange scenes, improvise the plot and ad lib. There are many occasions on which they do use the opportunity to propagate particular messages" (Brandon, 1967).

Indigenous communication networks can also be viewed as culturally based systems for education and training (Interim Report, 1979). They facilitate the dissemination of information in an informal manner and in contexts in which the learning process is not separate from the social experience of the people they serve (Nketia, 1970). This function has been recognized and utilized by development planners. Several nations have acknowledged the potential contribution of indigenous channels in the education of rural populations. The Home Science Association of India has used puppetry, folk songs, folk drama, and dances to teach nutrition concepts to the country's predominantly illiterate rural population (Devadas et al., 1965). In Malaysia, religious gatherings have been used as a channel for the dissemination of agricultural information. During the late 1970s, approximately 185 mosques were furnished with texts developed by the Muda Agriculture Development Authority. These texts combined specific agricultural messages with religious sermons (Mohamed, 1980). In such examples, the process provided a linkage between ideas and information new to the population and the teachings and knowledge of the past.

Within the last 30 years, indigenous communication systems have come under considerable scrutiny by practitioners and scholars of development communication. The dominant focus of this examination was the potential use of indigenous channels for effective and efficient communicating of development messages to a largely illiterate rural audience in the Third World. Theories of social change emphasize the need for basing such communication efforts upon the values and beliefs of communities and peoples, as well as upon existing, trusted, and respected communication channels. Indeed, India has a particularly long history of utilizing indigenous communication systems as instruments for directed change. In the 15th century, the Emperor Akbar experimented with employing indigenous media to spread the tenets of a nondenominational church called *Deen–e–Ilahi* (Word of God). This is considered to be the first attempt at national religious integration in India. In the last half of the nineteenth century, *Tamasha*, a folk drama from Maharastra state was used to awaken the Indian people to the need for social change by the Satya Shodhak Samaj, a social reform movement. Throughout the 20th century, *Tamasha*, continued to be engaged as a means of dealing with such issues as illiteracy and the oppression of women (Abrams, 1975).

Researchers and scholars have advanced several arguments for the use of indigenous communication systems in development communication strategies. Parmar argued that a communication system unfamiliar to the masses and which did not function close to their cultural predispositions and institutional values would have little impact (Parmar, 1973). In order to convey a message with effect, Lent felt that the communication attempt must utilize the language, symbols, and styles familiar to the intended receivers (Lent, 1978). This is of particular importance with messages containing information perceived as new by receivers. Family planning research in several LDCs revealed that fertility and birth control concepts were more comprehensible to the public when couched in the same terminology as that used for discussing fertility in agriculture (Adhikarya, 1974). Wang et al. (1980) suggest that a peoples' culture acts as a mediating force in the process of development and change; that "changes do not occur in a vacuum, they must be mediated by the culture throughout the whole process." Thus, culture provides the basis for people to form attitudes about information, in general, and information perceived as new, in particular. These attitudes determine how people interpret the information and what action might be taken regarding the information.

Indigenous networks were promoted as a more persuasive means than modern mass media for putting across development messages because of their specific cultural relevance and function. Research established that behavioral change directly attributable to mass media varied from 10 to 15% and that the percentage rose to 54% when mass media and interpersonal communication were integrated (Information, Education, Communication in Population, 1975). UNESCO experts projected that the added use of traditional channels, specifically folk media, in such efforts would increase the rate even further (Information, Education, Communication in Population, 1975). The indigenous networks were viewed as conducive to the transmission of development information because of their traditional authority and extensive credibility with the general population. Rogers reported that traditional midwives in Indonesia, Malaysia, the Philippines, Thailand, and Mexico have high credibility in matters related to health because of their perceived "safety," due to their similarity to the populace in socioeconomic status and life-style, and their perceived "competence" as a function of their advanced age, religiousness, special knowledge, and skills (Rogers, 1975). This source credibility is a key factor in any communication process concerned with the introduction of information.

Policy makers and planners were increasingly hopeful that indigenous communication systems would provide a means for processing and transmitting information regarding development and modernization. As a result, many LDCs increased their promotion of traditional channels as part of their development strategies. Indonesia's national information policy was amended to incorporate indigenous communication networks into its communication strategies (Dahlan, 1981). India initiated several projects through the national Ministry of Health and Family Planning employing indigenous medical practitioners in assisting government health programs (Neumann and Bhakia, 1973). Folk media performances became an operational part of many extension programs, and sponsorship of performing troupes was undertaken by development planning agencies throughout the Third World. For example, the *Wayang* puppet shows of Java (Adhikarya, 1974) and the *Baltesung*, a musical comedy of the Philippines were among the many folk forms used for the dissemination of family planning information.

In general, it appeared that indigenous channels could provide a built in information system capable of interpreting, processing, and disseminating development information. If traditional media proved to be cost-effective, employment-intensive, and high-impact generating, they would serve public service organizations as effective delivery systems for development programs.

Prospective Role of Indigenous Communications in a New World Information Order

Daniel Bell postulates that the coming century will see the emergence of a new social structure which will determine largely the way "economic and social exchanges are conducted, the way knowledge is created and retrieved and the character of the occupations and works in which men are engaged" (Bell, 1979). The primary characteristics of this new age include: (1) a change from a society based upon the production of goods to a service-oriented society; (2) the creation of a new "intellectual technology," and, (3) the centrality of theoretical knowledge and its role as the director of social change.

The critical variables in this post-industrial society, according to Bell, are information and knowledge. Information refers, in this context, to "the storage, retrieval and processing of data" (p. 166). Knowledge refers to an "organized set of statement of fact or ideas presenting a reasoned judgement or an experimental result, which is transmitted to others through some communication medium in some systematic form" (Bell, 1979, p. 166). Put another way, "information is a pattern or design that rearranges data for instrumental purposes, while knowledge is the set of reasoned judgements that evaluates the adequacy of the pattern for purposes for which the information is designed" (Bell, 1979, p. 171).

Bell's basic premise is that knowledge and information are the strategic resources and transforming agents of an information or post-industrial society. Information is power. To the extent that knowledge is involved in some way with the application and transformation of information as a resource, then knowledge can be regarded as a primary source of value. In Bell's post-industrial information society, knowledge provides a framework for the coding, translation, and interpretation of information for subsequent usage. The role of indigenous communication systems has traditionally paralleled that which Bell envisions for "knowledge." That is to say, historically the indigenous communication systems have provided the mechanism by which information has been codified and processed according to specific cultural mandates and traditions. While transmission is an integral component of any information system, coding determines outcome and utilization of content. Messages must pass through channels, and frequently they encounter some sort of resistance and/or are distorted. The indigenous communication channels encode a message so that it may be transmitted with as much integrity as possible while being integrated into the cultural framework of the receiver. Thus, information, which may be outside the frame of reference for a given society or community, is coded and transmitted via the traditional networks in the manner which least distorts the message, yet is compatible with the culture or particular value system involved.

The indigenous communication systems performs functions which compliment the modern information and knowledge systems, foreseen as being an integral part of the post-industrial society. They set up a reciprocal relationship between culture and knowledge and provide a linkage between the culture and information. The relative importance of this function is difficult to assess, particularly in terms of quantifiable measures which may be used to compare the costs and benefits of indigenous communication systems against other communication technology. In light of the concern expressed on the part of many LDCs regarding the potential for cultural domination through the transfer of technology, it is a factor which must be given careful consideration.

The relationship of any communication system to a society is not only economic, but also political. To an extent, it is determined by the power relations which exist within a society and by value judgements regarding the shape of the society, the direction of its development, and the utilization of resources to achieve that end. Indonesia's recent decision to eliminate all commercials from television broadcasting reflects a value judgement on "consumerism." This decision has implications, not only for that particular communication technology, but for all of the country's communication systems and for the society. As Schiller (1976) states, "communication includes much more than messages and the recognizable circuits through which the messages flow. It defines social reality. . . " Thus, the value attached to a communication system which provides a culture-based infrastructure for the transmission and processing of information, as the indigenous communication systems do, is a function of the extent to which a nation is committed to the retention of its unique sociocultural mores and cultural identity.

It must also be recognized that communication is no longer merely a support function but can be, in its own right, a catalyst for development and change. The real utility of information networks here is determined by the capacity to which they are user-oriented; that is, the extent to which they are relevant to user requirements and needs and the extent to which access is obtainable. Most information structures are designed for uni-directional communication flow; from the top to the bottom of society, or from the center to the periphery. There is little participation of the message recipients in the communication process and little, if any, opportunity for receivers to send messages back through the system. With modern communication technology, the issue is not the capability of the system to accommodate a two-way information flow, but rather the ability of all users to gain access to a system, impart information, and transmit messages. Modern communication channels generally represent vested economic interests. It is not usual for an individual, group, or conglomerate to own a major channel for information. When proprietary concerns dominate utilization patterns of communication systems, issues of equity and access inevitably arise.

Situations will exist where, for economic or political reasons, access to modern communication channels is either difficult to gain or is unobtainable. Under such conditions, the potential role of indigenous communications in affecting an information flow from the bottom to the top of society must be examined. As public media and as communication networks which historically have served the people, the indigenous communication systems are a means for originating messages at the periphery and transmitting them back to the center of society. A recent example of this can be gleaned from U.S. history. During the late 1960s and early 1970s, folk music served as a primary vehicle of the populace for expressing their dissatisfaction with government handling of the Vietnam War. The anti-war message, transmitted via the traditional channel of *folk* music, originated with the people and was directed to those in power, although it must be admitted that folk media was but one part of the people's attempt. Nonetheless, it was a significant and powerful mode of communication and served in its role as a catalyst for change.

The Challenge of the Future

The communication-information industry is a mature industry. Indigenous communication systems, in their role of providing a cultural infrastructure for the coordination and processing of contemporary information, are very much a part of that industry. They may be viewed as part of what Porat terms the primary information sector, or "that group of industries which produce, process or transmit knowledge, communication and information goods or services" (Porat, 1977). Folk performers and other traditional leaders who are charged with the responsibility of interpreting, processing, and disseminating information in this way may be viewed as information workers. Information workers consist of those "individuals holding a job where the production, processing and distribution of symbols (information) is the main activity" (Porat, 1977).

As an industry, information systems are subject to the economic imperatives of the market. Information workers relay only those values and messages which the market will support. Policy makers need to identify their values, the goals of their nation, and the contributions which information can make toward achieving that end. For example, if a nation is oriented toward information as a consciousness-shaping mechanism, then information systems should be constructed toward that end. Policy makers need to ask what functions various kinds of communication systems perform and in what contexts. They must examine their options in terms of political, economic, and social costs and benefits. They need to assess which communication system or combination of systems best suits their purposes, while contributing to overall societal welfare.

If indigenous communication systems are to meet the challenge of a technological age, they must retain the capability for flexibility and responsiveness to society that they have demonstrated in the past. Policy makers and members of indigenous networks need to ask whether the content and form of a traditional medium are important or whether the cultural mediating and interpreting function of indigenous communication systems make them special and unique. As long as that function is retained, can not the form of traditional media evolve and merge with modern communication technology? If it retains its cultural integrity and community/public orientation, can indigenous communication systems take advantage of innovative technology to promote and strengthen their special appeal?

It would appear that the successful integration of traditional and modern communication systems in an information society has some foundation for support. The American example of the role of folk music during the Vietnam War era is evidence. Initially, folk music was used in its traditional format to broadcast the message of the people. Music expressing the protest was heard most commonly at coffee houses, political rallies, concerts, etc. Eventually, performers took increasing advantage of communication technology to relay their message. The integration of folk music with radio, film, and recording increased audience size for the communication process and strengthened the impact of the message on receivers by increasing frequency and distribution. This merger of "old" and "new" communication channels did not detract from the special characteristics of either system, but served as a foil for the attributes of each.

The marriage of traditional forms and modern technology has also been harnessed for development communication purposes in the U.S. The evolution of traditional tales of heros and heroics into modern comic book/cartoon versions of the traditional stories was a result of the coalition of storytelling with mass media. The format is heavily influenced by contemporary U.S. society, yet reflects the cultural values and mores which have been a mainstay of the traditional tales. Much like the folk performers who adapted content toward specific ends within the traditional structure, today's "super-heroes" deal with such issues as drug addiction, education, and racism within the cultural framework passed on from prior generations.

Another example of this evolutionary process is apparent in the development of puppetry in the U.S. Puppets have long been a favorite medium for societal values and mores. From Punch and Judy to the Muppets, puppetry has been used in education and development. Miss Piggy and Kermit are the evolutionary products of the interaction of puppetry and modern communication systems. They have grown, progressed, and adapted to modern technological requirements, evolving into a new and valuable communication medium.

As Third World nations hasten their involvement in the information age and use increasingly sophisticated technology to meet their communication requirements, the indigenous communication systems of these countries will face tremendous challenges. Some of the traditional forms will be incapable of adjusting to the demands of modern technology and will be unable to keep pace with a society undergoing change at an exponential rate. The ensuing loss of their unique ability to reflect and reinforce the past within a contemporary context will result in the death of some forms.

Others will be able to merge quite naturally with modern technological systems. The marriage of traditional media and electronic media can serve to extend the capability of the channels to reach large numbers of people and to elicit a response from them. However, such an interaction may result in changes in composition and structure such that the forms no longer can be said to be a medium which emanates from the people. Central production by media specialists in contexts removed from community orientation will result, in some cases with the loss of direct interaction between performer and populace. Historically, the delicate relationship of audience and performer has served as a check-and-balance system; a means of insuring that the forms retained their cultural integrity and honored tradition while simultaneously meeting and reflecting the needs of the people. Taken out of this framework, the merger of indigenous channels with modern technology may be accompanied by a shift from the values and norms of the people served to those reflective of central decision makers and media and information specialists. This evolution of folk media is neither inherently bad nor harmful. Rather, the utilization of such forms ultimately determines their value. Under thoughtful and considered guidance, these channels can become a powerful medium for the promotion of change. The *Muppets* and *Sesame Street* characters represent contemporary products of the interaction between puppetry and television. Both are exciting examples of how this form can be used to educate and enhance development in a manner compatible with societal expectations and requirements.

There are also those indigenous forms that will not only be able to make an easy transition into the technological age, but will be able to retain those special and unique characteristics which have allowed them to function and serve the people across time. These forms will serve as media for exchange and communication between all levels of society. They will link culture, information, and knowledge, and mediate change and growth framed by terms of tradition and culture. These forms represent the cumulative experiences, values, and customs of people. They possess the special attributes of flexibility and responsiveness to society allowing for the successful integration of traditional and modern communication systems in an orientation directed toward the people they serve. In the U.S., cartoons and comics are utilized not only for purposive development communication but they also enjoy common use by the general population as a means of voicing their opinions, beliefs, and attitudes. These popular and local versions of the media are found in school and community newspapers, business and organizational newsletters, graffiti, billboards, etc. While they lack the sophistication of their more technological cousins, they nonetheless are a variation of the same form and serve to reflect community value and belief structures.

In the planned formation of a New World Information Order, it behooves policy makers and planners to re-examine the inherent qualities and functions of indigenous communication systems and take the necessary steps to develop those systems to their fullest potential.

We believe that indigenous communication systems have a role in the information society. How fully they will be allowed to fulfill that role will depend upon a great many factors. It must be emphasized though, that few, if any, information systems are qualified as the indigenous media to preserve a people's culture and traditions. It will be up to the policy makers to find the path by which traditional media can best serve the people and strengthen their heritage in the forthcoming technological age, without putting the clock back. To cite T. S. Eliot:

> "The endless cycle of ideas and action
> Endless invention, endless experiment
> Brings knowledge of motion but not of stillness
> Knowledge of speech, but not of silence
> Knowledge of words and ignorance of the word."

REFERENCES

Abrams, Tevia. (1975). "Folk Theater in Maharashtrian Social Development Programmes." *Educational Theatre Review* 27 (3), 395–407.

Adhikarya, Ronny. (1974). "Communication Support for Family Planning Programs: The Potentialities for Folk Media in Indonesia and the Problems Involved in Pre-testing and Evaluation." Paper prepared for the UN Economic Commission for Asia and the Far East (ESCAFE) meeting on Evaluation of Educational Materials used in Family Planning Programmes, Bangkok, Thailand.

Adhikarya, Ronny. (1975). "The Use of Traditional Communication Networks for Development Programmes." Paper prepared for a workshop on Communication as a Development Strategy, Penang, Ministry of Information and the Universiti Sains Malaysia.

Bell, Daniel. (1979). "The Social Framework of the Information Society." In Michael Dertouzos and Jorl Moses (ed.), *The Computer Age.* MIT Press, 163–211.

Brandon, James. (1982). *Theater in Southeast Asia.* Cambridge: Harvard University Press.

Burck, Gilbert. (1964). "Knowledge: The Biggest Growth Industry." *Fortune* (November), 90–101.

Coseteng, Alice M. L. and Nemenzo, Gemma. (1975). "Folk Media in the Philippines." UN Family Planning Association, Commission on Population. (Monograph Series No. 6.) UNESCO.

Dahlan, Alwi. (1975). "Indonesian Experience in Satellite Communication." Paper prepared for the International Seminar on Communication Policy for Rural Development, East-West Communication Institute, East-West Center, Honolulu, Hawaii.

Devadas, Rajammal et al. (1965). "Diet and Nutrition Survey of a Village Community in South India." *Journal of Nutrition Dietetics* 2 (2), 83–87.

Dordick, Herbert, Bradley, H., and Nanus, B. (1981). *The Emerging Network Market-place.* Norwood: Ablex Publishing Corporation.

Drucker, Peter. (1968). *The Age of Discontinuity.* New York: Harper and Row.

Evans, David R. (1976). "Technology in Nonformal Education: A Critical Appraisal." Center for International Education, University of Massachusetts.

Gunawardana, Trelicia. (1974). "Folk Theater in Family Planning Communication." Paper prepared for the Inter-regional seminar on the Integrated Use of Folk Media and Mass Media in Family Planning Communication Programmes, New Delhi, India.

Information, Education, Communication in Population. (1975). *IEC Newsletter,* No. 20, East-West Center Communication Institute, Honolulu.

Interim Report on Communication Problems in Modern Society, submitted to UNESCO by the International Commission for the Study of Communication Problems. "The Established Structure: From Traditional Communication to Communication on a Planetary Scale." *Indian Journal of Communication Arts,* May 1979.

Jussawalla, Meheroo. (1980). "Communication Technology Transfer." In Proceedings of *2nd Pacific Telecommunication Conference, Honolulu,* Jan.

Lent, John A. (1978). "Mass Media, Folk Media and Rural Masses of the Third World." Paper prepared for the Role of Mass Media in the Development of Non-Western Societies panel, International Studies Association, Washington, D.C., Feb.

Machlup, Fritz. (1962). *The Production and Distribution of Knowledge in the United States.* Princeton: Princeton University Press.

Marschak, Jacob. (1968). "Economics of Inquiring, Communicating, Deciding." *American Economic Review* 58 (2), 1–18.

Mohamed, Ramli. (1980). *Communication Planning Processes in the Muda Agricultural Development Authority* (MADA). East-West Communication Institute, East-West Center, Honolulu.

Neumann, Alfred K., and Bhakia, J. C. (1973). "Family Planning and Indigenous Medicine Practitioners." *Social Science and Medicine 7,* 507–516.

Nketia, J. H. Kwakena. (1970). "Use of Traditional Media in Social and Health Education." Paper presented at the Family Planning in Education in Africa Workshop, Accra, Ghana.

Nora, Simon, and Alain Minc. (1980). *The Computerization of Society: A Report to the President of France.* Cambridge: MIT Press.

Organization for Economic Cooperation and Development. "Economic Analysis of Information Activities and the Role of Electronics and Telecommunications Technology." Cited in *Telecommunications Policy,* Dec. 1981, p. 244.

Parker, Edwin B. (1981). "Information Services and Economic Growth." *Information Society 1* (1), 71–78.

Parmae, Shyam. (1973). "Coalition of Traditional and Electronic Media," *Communicator,* November 49.

Porat, Marc Uri. (1977). *The Information Economy.* Washington, D.C.: U.S. Department of Commerce, Office of Telecommunication.

Ranganath, Hassan K. (1975). "Traditional Media." Paper prepared for the Seminar on Traditional Media, East-West Communication Institute, East West Center, Honolulu.

Rogers, Everett M. (1972). "Communication Strategies for Agricultural Development." Report prepared for the Agency for International Development.

Rogers, Everett M. (1975). "Traditional Midwives in the Developing Nations." Unpublished manuscript.

Schiller, Herbert. (1976). *Communication and Cultural Domination.* White Plains: Arts and Sciences Press.

Sieghart, Paul. (1981). "The International Implications of the Development of Microelectronics." *The Information Society 1* (1), 1–15.

Smith, Anthony. (1980). *Goodbye Gutenberg.* New York: Oxford University Press.

UNESCO/IPPF Experts Group Meeting to study the Integrated Use of Folk Media and Mass Media in Family Planning Communication Programmes, London, 1972, *Report* UNESCO and IPPF, Paris and London.

Wang, Georgette, et al. (1980). A Cultural Mediation Approach to Development and Change." Unpublished manuscript.

Yount, Barbara. (1975). "Using Folk Media and Mass Media to Expand Communication." *Information, Education, & Communication in Population* (IEC Newsletter) (No. 20), 1–16.

Yount, Barbara. (1976). "Use of Folk Media in Developing Countries for Motivational Purposes." East-West Center.

Yount, Barbara (Ed.). (1977). "Blackboard Newspapers Communicate News in the Philippines." *Information, Education, Communication in Population,* (IEC Newsletter) (No. 25/26).

Yu, F. T. C. (1976). "Research Priorities in Development Communication." In W. Schramm and D. Lerner (eds.)., *Communication and Change: The Last Ten Years and the Next.* Honolulu: University Press of Hawaii.

Yu, F. T. C. (1976). "Communication Policy and Planning for Development: Some Notes on Research." In D. Lerner and L. M. Nelson (eds.), *Communication Research—a Half-Century Appraisal.* Honolulu: University Press of Hawaii.

Yu, Mo-wang. (1980). "The Prodigious Cinema of Huang Fei-hong: an Introduction." In Shing-hon Liu (ed.), *A Study of the Hong Kong Martial Art Film.* Hong Kong: The Urban Council, 81–82.

Author Index

Subject Index